Critical Concepts™ Series . . .

Catfish
Location

Finding Catfish In Lakes, Rivers, & Reservoirs

Critical Concepts™ Series . . .

Catfish Location

Finding Catfish In Lakes, Rivers, & Reservoirs

Expert Advice from North America's
Leading Authority on Freshwater Fishing

THE IN-FISHERMAN STAFF

In·Fisherman®

Critical Concepts™ Series . . .
Catfish Location—Finding Catfish In Lakes, Rivers, & Reservoirs

Publisher *Mike Carney*
Editor In Chief *Doug Stange*
Managing Editor *Steve Hoffman*
Editors *Dave Csanda, Steve Quinn, Matt Straw, Jeff Simpson*
Publisher Emeritus *Stu Legaard*
Copy Editor *Joann Phipps*
Art Director *Jan Finger*
Cover *Amy Jackson*

Acknowledgments

Dan Anderson: *Solving the Mystery of the Disappearing Catfish,* Chapter 3;
    Exploring Farm Ponds, Chapter 8
Soc Clay: photos, Chapter 8
Larry Cofer: *Tracking Reservoir Blue Cats,* Chapter 4; *Finding Reservoir
    Flatheads,* Chapter 4
Ron Finger: illustration, Chapter 6
Bryan Hendricks: *What Makes a Great Catfish River?,* Chapter 5
Michelle Holbrook: lead photo, Chapter 4
Ned Kehde: *Fall Movements in Reservoirs,* Chapter 4; *Finding and Catching
    Cats During Summer,* Chapter 7
Peter Kholsaat: cartoons, Chapter 8
Chester Moore: *Brackish Water Blue Cats,* Chapter 5
James Patterson: photo, Chapter 4
Jeff Samsel: *Rendezvous With Reservoir Cats,* Chapter 7
Larry Tople: cartoons, Foreword, Chapter 7
Don Wirth: *Fall Movements in Rivers,* Chapter 3; *Pay Lakes Pay,* Chapter 8

Catfish Location—Finding Catfish In Lakes, Rivers, & Reservoirs

Copyright © 2004 by In-Fisherman, A PRIMEDIA Company.
All rights reserved. Printed in the United States of America. No part of this
book may be used or reproduced in any manner without written permission
except in the case of brief quotations embodied in critical articles and reviews.
For information write Editor In Chief, In-Fisherman, In-Fisherman Drive,
Brainerd, MN 56425-8098.

First Edition

Library of Congress Cataloging-in-Publication Data
ISBN: 1-892947-47-1

Dedication

To the hardcore catmen across the country and around the world who have sacrificed sleep and comfort in their search for catfish.

Contents

COFFEES ON THIS GUY

Mischief Afoot with Toadmonster And Flathead Catfish Before The Crowd

A word from In-Fisherman Editor In Chief Doug Stange.

An icy north wind swept through the oaks on the ridge above the reservoir, down a limestone bluff along our bank, whipping our little fire and sending a shower of sparks over the water. It was midnight damp and April cold and lonely along a remote portion of reservoir in a far corner of Missouri. Tomorrow we'd hike a hill and call and kill a turkey on that ridge above us. In the meantime, we were hoping for a flathead catfish—and I was hoping I wouldn't freeze.

"Can see the headlines now," I mumbled to Toad Smith as I shuffled my sleeping bag closer to the fire. "FAMOUS FISHERMAN FREEZES TO DEATH IN WILDERNESS. WORLD MOURNS HIS PASSING." I pulled my camo stocking cap down, hunched up the collar on my coat, and dug my body so deep into my down bag that only the four square inches of skin surrounding my eyes were exposed to the elements.

"I work hard for 20 years," I continued in mock despair, muffled by the bag. "I become the editor of a big-time fishing magazine. I have a budget for a nice warm motel room—a steak even after a hard day of fishing. I could be fishing anywhere in the world, probably at no cost, probably some place warm, and here I am freezing to death in the backwoods, about to share a magnum can of beans with someone who looks like an escapee from a penal colony."

"Lucky man," Toad growled. "Keeps you in touch with the real world."

"Now don't do that," I pleaded as he reached for the beans. "At least use a stick."

But he did, that is stir the beans with his index finger. In the flickering firelight, a bean balanced on his finger before he popped it into his mouth and then slurped the syrup from his hand.

"Gacckk," I choked.

"Nummy," he said, through a syrupy grin, and . . . "So what is it you wanna be, the editor of one of those fancy-pants outdoor magazines in the big city, wear a tie to work, write bogus articles about bears eating people, and drink strawberry margaritas after work? Got news for you, too. Famous fisherman? Nobody'd even know you were gone. Now me they'd miss."

"Right," I said. "There but for campfires like this one and a companion like you go I, led astray by the big city and the gleam of writing bull about bears and beautiful babes in bikinis fishing for bonefish on the flats."

"There you have it," Toad said. "Watch yourself. Next thing you'll be following tournament fishermen around, hoping they'll throw you a bone and thinking it means something. Oh, pwees pwees pwees Mr. Fwamous Toyneyment Fwishermun," he said, paws bent like a puppy dog on his haunches begging for a bone, "tell dis poor witto outdoor whiter how you cwaughts all dose 12-inch bass, woo, woo, woo, woo."

"Think they'll bite?" I asked, peeking out of my down bag toward our rods set along the bank.

"What, the flatheads? Naw, too early. In a month. And then maybe only during daytime."

"Then why are we doing this?"

"Well you never know, you know. They might bite. But I doubt it. Besides, we're camping out, having fun."

I shook my head. Typical trip with the Toadmonster. I'd be at my desk and Toad would call. "Meet me at such and such," he'd say.

I learned not to ask why or what, much less details such as line test or how much food or how much money. "Enough," he'd always say. So I took fishing tackle, enough to cover the bases from cats to crappies. In hunting season, I took fishing tackle plus camo gear and my bow—and bread, lots of bread, whole wheat of course, and onions, bacon, margarine, beans, assorted fresh veggies, and black pepper, lots and lots of black pepper, fresh cracked, of course, and a frying pan.

I am a fair cook, mind you. I can do fancy cuisine. But I've learned my lesson. That flies only so far in the woods, particularly with Toad, who would just as soon do a bacon and bean sandwich. Besides, a man can live for weeks, albeit quite rankly, on bread and onions and beans and whatever decides to sacrifice itself to hunting and fishing skills. No packing, of course, just stuff things in the back of the truck and go, a fresh Van Halen tape pulsing West Coast decadence through my midwestern veins.

And I would get to somewhere—wherever—and Toad would be standing beside his 3/4-ton red Chevy Suburban, a stripped-down barebones job, the better to carry deer and bear and turkeys and catfish, grinning that big tooth-gapped grin of his

"So what is it you wanna be, the editor of one of those fancy-pants outdoor magazines in the big city, wear a tie to work, write bogus articles about bears eating people, and drink strawberry margaritas after work? Got news for you, too. Famous fisherman? Nobody'd even know you were gone. Now me they'd miss."

through a burly beard. Toad was a big man. "Not bad for a fat boy," he was fond of saying after one of his spectacular feats. "Not bad for a fat boy," I'd say. And there he'd stand by his truck, looking like a chubby cherub, a fat Friar Tuck, mischief dancing in his eyes and in that smile. And I'd look at him and just have to smile.

The ritual was that I would walk up and put my hand in that big paw of his and he would try to crush it. Haw, haw. "Good to see you again—missed you," we'd both say without saying it. And I always knew we were going to have a good time, although a good time at what was hard to say and sometimes I'm not sure we figured it out ourselves by the end of the trip. But we were always prepared by not being too prepared, except to hang loose.

One time in fall we were floating a river catching catfish when we happened upon what Toad referred to as the mother of all squirrel kingdoms—hundreds of big fat fox squirrels running up and down the bank and around in trees and so on. "That's really something," Toad usually would say in a situation like that. "Sure is," I'd usually answer.

So we parked the boat and wandered around pursuing squirrels for the day. That was always one of the things I liked best about Toad, the squirrel thing—not squirrels really, but the fact that it was OK with Toad—perfectly natural—to spend an entire day after something like squirrels—two 40-year-old men who have been around the block a time or two both in and out of the woods, out in the woods trying to outsmart a bunch of furry damn rodents, when both of us had the connections to be in Alaska hunting moose or in Montana hunting elk. So there we'd be, totally absorbed, totally oblivious to the rest of the "really important" things in the world, sneaking around trees, crawling around trees, to get a clean shot. "Office sissy," he'd say to me when we spooked one. "No woods sense anymore." "Maybe saw your big butt," I'd say matter of factly. "Humph!" he'd grunt indignantly. And then we'd go after another squirrel.

Yes, the squirrel thing. Squirrels aren't exactly big game, but neither are bullheads or carp or green sunfish or stonecats. And, yes, we once spent a day fishing for stonecats below the dam in Crookston, Minnesota. The channel cats just weren't going and I happened to catch a stonecat. And somehow instead of frantically running up or downriver forcing the channel cat issue, we just sort of drifted into trying to catch stonecats. And before we knew it the sun was setting and we'd been fishing all day for a little tiny catfish that rarely grows to 10 inches. Near as I can recollect, Toad caught 4 and I caught 2. And if I were to tell you more about it you would realize that it was one of the best days I have ever spent fishing—the wonder of it all, one of those "first time" things, finding the best spots for stonecats and what they would bite on best.

I would walk up and put my hand in that big paw of his and he would try to crush it. Haw, haw. "Good to see you again—missed you," we'd both say without saying it.

But as I was saying, there we were, wandering the hills in this mother kingdom of squirrels. We didn't have to be anywhere in the world in particular, doing anything in particular, so late in the afternoon I walked back to the boat for the sleeping bags and a frying pan, and we camped on a hill somewhere near the river and ate catfish and squirrel and wild onions—at least we thought they were wild onions. The next day we were sure they were wild onions. Funny how your intestines can verify what you can't find in a field guide. And Toad's intestines were better at such verification than almost anyone I've ever met—Chief Wildflower, the Brule Indians called him, with a good bit of straight-faced sarcasm on one of his trips out West to hunt and fish on reservation land.

The next morning we wandered down to this old farm place to borrow some coffee for breakfast. "Hell, no," this old farmer said, we couldn't have any coffee but we could sure as hell come in and fix ourselves and him some breakfast. And so there I stood cooking pancakes and bacon on an old kerosene stove and drinking boiled coffee, stuff with a razor edge on it, chasing cats off the counter and listening to this salty old rooster who hadn't been to town in a year and who probably hadn't had a visitor in months talk about "those old times," "Hellava cook," they both chortled as I set down plates of cakes. "You'd make someone a good wife," Haw, haw.

Pretty soon Toad and the old farmer were busy poking around what was left of the farm, the old farmer hobbling on a cane and Toad trying to keep up, the farmer talking nonstop about farming with mules and this old tractor and that old pile of assorted junk that lay rusting in the open. Made Toad's day.

People like old farmers could tell that Toad was in no hurry, that he really cared and would gladly stay a week if they needed help, particularly if the hunting and fishing were good.

Next to hunting and fishing and picking wild things like asparagus and onions, Toad liked poking through old junk. Junk. Not antiques or artifacts. It was junk and Toad knew it, just like he knew that he liked it, that it made him think about those old times.

Made me smile. We'd be walking a river bank, catching cats from brushpiles as we went. And Toad would find a bone sticking up from a gravel bar. "Buff (buffalo)," he'd grunt two octaves below middle C, and his eyes would glaze over, his nose would naturally shift into the wind, and he'd stand there like some aborigine envisioning an unending parade of buffalo steaks moving over the next ridge. Toad wanted desperately to be there, you see, for those more than these would have been his times.

It was something we'd talk about around a campfire—those times. "Should have been there," he'd say. "Would have been a bad deal for buff," I'd say. And I suppose I could take a moment to explain. Toad's catfishing prowess is well-known. He was that good with stick, string, and arrow, too. If he could have been there, the Indian tribe that adopted him would have had meat for winter and spring beyond. I do not believe, however, that he would have been popular around the council fire in an enclosed teepee—Chief Wildflower.

People like old farmers could tell that Toad was in no hurry, that he really cared and would gladly stay a week if they needed help, particularly if the hunting and fishing were good. People like insurance salesmen, on the other hand, always sensed that they should be in a real hurry if they happened to strike a Dale Carnegie chord, wasting even a moment of Toad's hunting and fishing time. Toad was going to live forever . . . or at least long enough. And beyond that, what the heck.

We spent two days in those parts, poking around with that old farmer, some 20 miles short of the destination on our float, as near as I could tell. "Could of sworn we were going to float for catfish," I said back at our trucks, as each of us was about to head for our separate worlds.

"You mean we didn't?" he asked, and shrugged.

Typical. And so there we sat on another hot spot. Another adventure, heaven help us.

"Gotta tell you something," Toad said as he passed a plate of beans, "we're after flathead catfish, right?"

"That is correct," I said. "And turkeys."

"Well, we will kill a turkey tomorrow, but tonight, well, about the catfishing. As far as I know, there's never been a flathead catfish caught in this reservoir."

I didn't answer at first. Ah, I thought to myself. Now this is beginning to make sense. I have driven 8 hours to a destination I know nothing about without asking any questions. And now I am someplace in the wilderness in the middle of the night, freezing to death, fishing for flathead catfish a month before they should bite in a reservoir where they don't exist and sharing a plate of beans with a backwoods philosopher whose logic would have stumped Plato.

"But you never know, you know," he said. "They just might bite. And besides, we are having fun camping out."

"Yes," I answered, adopting his logic as best I could. "We are having fun . . . and they just might bite . . . assuming, of course, that we aren't a month early, which we are, and further assuming that they should be here, even if they aren't, because this spot is so good that they should, like their cousins the walking catfish, have hiked from the nearest river so they could be here, so we won't catch them tonight because we're a month early."

"There you have it," he said. "You are a smart man for an editor."

So far I realize that this probably seems to have little to do with catching catfish. But not so fast. Catching flathead catfish—any catfish, really, but particularly flatheads—can be taught via formula other than the typical how-to formula you might find in say a bass article. Bass fishing has become a complicated and in many cases quite a frenzied and serious affair. Toad would have verified that. "Very serious business," he would have said, trying to keep a straight face. Fishing for flatheads is, or I'm suggesting should be, the antithesis thereof.

This flathead deal really isn't complicated, you see, and I have no reason to try to make it so, much less try to get you to hurry to make it so. Trust me, you will catch flatheads if you want to. The process is easy, and I will show you how. Trust this, too, though, it takes time— there aren't many big flatheads. And I am suggesting that because it's easy but takes time,

I am suggesting that capturing the spirit of this catfishing affair is as important as the final act of catching the fish

and because catfishing generally hasn't been the type of high-profile sport that bassing has been—thank God!—that capturing the spirit of this flathead affair is as important as the final act of catching the fish.

I am saying, I guess, that catfishing is a matter of pace and attitude, things that become part of a lifestyle, something you settle easily into as you learn about life and begin to live it and love it, even the bumpy parts, even the big bumps like the passing of a close friend, a Toad. And I guess I'm wondering in print if the spirit of the thing can't best be felt by looking at someone who did it right. Toad did it right a lot of the time, and I'm thankful I was along for some of the ride.

But about catching big flatheads. About being a flathead catfisherman. About flathead catfishing being a lifestyle as much as something you occasionally do. About any of this having anything to do with catching flathead catfish early in the season.

It has occurred to me that all the great catmen I have known are, like Toad, men of a certain distinction. They certainly aren't the only people of distinction

I am saying, I guess, that catfishing is a matter of pace and attitude . . .

Toad did it right a lot of the time, and I'm thankful I was along for some of the ride.

in the fishing world, but they are distinctively different.

Al Lindner, whom I dearly love and respect, is a fisherman of distinction. But although we have taken Al catfishing, and he is quite good at it, he is not and I suspect never will be a catman. "Go there. Do this. Try that. You mean I just let the bait sit there?" Al's life has a certain rush that doesn't quite fit catfishing. It's like trying to dress Pierre Cardin (don't worry—Toad wouldn't have known who he was either) in a flannel shirt. Even when Al's catching catfish, he's really catching bass or walleyes, and that will never change.

That doesn't mean that Al doesn't enjoy an occasional bout with cats. But what Al does even when he's catfishing is not catfishing—just as the man who catches a 35-pound flathead on a crankbait while casting for bass has not really caught a flathead. I know the fish looks like a flathead, but the fish is not a flathead, only a small token of desperate good fortune—outright luck, nothing more. There is nothing desperate about becoming consistently good at catching flatheads. If it's difficult, that's only because it's time consuming and you end up having to fish at night, which disrupts the rhythm of most lives. But that's another story.

Fishermen with their underwear snugged up too tight, those fishermen who seek no more than one of these desperate acts—one or two old flatheads for no more than the thrill or the fame of it—won't understand. Indeed, the preceding pages may even be seen as a desperate and singular waste of time. Get to it, they will insist. Tell us where, when, and how. Forget campfires and old farmers and fishing for fish where they don't exist. These men and women should take up tournament bass fishing—or bowling—the sooner the better.

If, however, you really are interested in flatheads, I understand the rush to catch that first big one. But along the way, as you're working on number 5 or 50, consider that the rush isn't the thing. Consider, too, that even if you go on with the rush and become singularly successful, even if you eventually pose with tons of catfish hanging crucified on fence posts, a sacrifice to something—ego perhaps—that for what it's worth, from where Toad and I used to sit together on the bank, you are not a flathead catfisherman and you have not really been catfishing, and you've wasted part of your life only on a scale different than men like The Donald (as in) Trump may be wasting theirs, gathering trophies, accomplishing many singularly outstanding (but desperate?) acts, being noticed by many, but still somehow missing the point.

And the point is? Well, it feels right to say that if you don't understand by now, you've missed it. But that's not true, because the truth is, I don't know exactly what the point is either. Maybe that's the point. All I want to do now is to get back to showing you how easy it is to catch a big flathead.

So far, you have learned that you probably should fish in waters where flathead catfish exist. And that April is too early almost everywhere, even throughout most of the South. May's the month—sometime in May. And you best be home by the fire with a bowl of popcorn reading this, dreaming, and getting ready for May.

Maybe you are learning trust, too. I'm telling you about craziness because we have been there. We have fished for flatheads. And we have fished for them too early. Call it research. You never know, you know. If they would have bitten in April, we would be here telling you about it. As it is, I can tell you, that you will catch them in May or June if the water's right and you're in the right place at the right time fishing with the right bait. Because we have done that too. Of course, you must fish with the right tackle if you expect to land fish.

April's the time to be out there just poking around. Time to drive to one of those reservoirs where you think the big guys live to get the feel of the place. Check the best places to fish from shore. Stop for a cup of coffee at one of those little old coffee shops off the beaten trail. "Coffee's on this guy," Toad used to announce, pointing to me when we'd walk for the first time into a little place. Of course, every head would turn. "Geez," they must have thought, "would you look at those two." The bait set, we'd sit there drinking coffee and munching a major order of fries, not saying a word, while the locals eyed us curiously. Finally, one of them would have to walk over and say something, if nothing more than "You really buying the coffee?" And before long, Toad would have invitations to birthday parties and chicken dinners and church socials—and catfishing spots no man had ever fished before.

Oh heck no, it doesn't hurt to wet a line way too early—in April. Toad would, even when it was beyond hope, even if no catfish were present. "Good practice," he'd have maintained, because you won't be catching much and that gives you plenty of time to think and to dream and to figure out what the point is. And if you figure it out, well, good.

I know part of the point for Toad and me was friendship shared during what suddenly became, "those times." And I guess that, more than anything, is what this is about. This, you see, was my first article about cats since Toad's death. And it has not been easy because I didn't know exactly where I was going until just now.

Addendum: In the years since Toad Smith's death, hundreds of you have written to express your sympathy. Toad was a regular feature with me on TV and magazine articles. Through those adventures, many of you knew Toad as family.

In 1984 at age 43, Toad suffered a massive heart attack. Heart surgery left him with a lot less heart. Doctors didn't give him much chance of hunting and fishing again, much less crawling up into bow stands or walking along river banks looking for channel cats.

The next 7 years were a story of courage and determination to live right— lots of hunting and fishing and a good bit of writing and talking about it—telling others the fine points of being successful outdoors so they could have fun. I don't believe Toad envisioned becoming a celebrity recognized by fishermen from coast to coast. That part of the deal made him smile. And besides, he liked talking with people, telling stories.

Toad was a world-class bow hunter besides being a great fisherman. On the first weekend in November, a huge snowstorm hit northern Iowa—no hunting. Locked up that weekend, he had a chance to call almost everyone who meant a lot to him. I talked with him the night before he died. I was to meet him to hunt later in the week.

Monday dawned bright and clear. Toad headed for his deer camp in the hills bordering South Dakota. Just short of camp he saw three pheasants. "Camp meat," I know he said to himself. He shot all three birds and retrieved them through deep snow. The heart attack took him quickly as he reached the side of the road.

And he would have said about that, "There! Ha! Do I know how to die, or what!"

From the Editors— A Word about This Book

O ne of the easiest ways to improve your fishing success is to be open enough to new ideas to at least think about applying them on the waters you fish. We're convinced that there's something for everyone in this book, even though you might insist that much of the material has nothing to do with you, "Because I don't fish reservoirs." Or, "Because I don't fish for flathead catfish."

The best anglers take information about fishing and transfer some of it to the situations they face. The same techniques used to find channel cats in a small river can be used to find flatheads in reservoir creek arms. Understanding how blue cats relate to heavy current also can help you find other species in slacker water.

Same deal for bodies of water. Fishing a plateau reservoir like Francis Case in South Dakota isn't that much different from fishing other plateau reservoirs across the West. For that matter, many of the ideas also apply to other reservoir types. Channel cats like running water at the head ends of feeder creeks during spring; doesn't make much difference if the reservoir type is plateau, hill-land, lowland, or highland.

Too many anglers search books and magazines for information that specifically talks about the catfish on their body of water, during a specific yearly period. About once a decade, they may find such an article. Better hope conditions don't change before they have a chance to go fishing.

The best fishermen can go to any body of water and feel at home in a short time. These fishermen almost always work out the puzzle and catch some fish. They've found that fishing knowledge is fishing knowledge, and it often can be applied across the board, or at least modified to fit the situation.

Sure, even a blind hog finds an acorn once in a while. But you can do better than that. Successful catfishing can be learned. The basic process is quantifiable and predictable—even relatively simple, although it takes time to learn. We're here to help shorten and simplify the learning process. You just need to be open to the process and willing to modify and manipulate the ideas to fit the situations you face.

Seasonal Periods of Catfish Response

UNDERSTANDING SEASONAL MOVEMENTS

Ten million or so anglers seeking catfish. And while even the best anglers puzzle over exactly how to catch catfish some days, many of the best anglers are steps ahead of the masses who wish to become the type of anglers who usually—not just occasionally—have an honest shot at catching catfish.

Such a paragraph strikes at the heart of why we do what we do, which is why *In-Fisherman, Catfish In-Sider Guide,* and In-Fisherman books always draw the most ardent audience in fishing. You are here in no small part because you want to catch catfish. Makes no difference if by most standards you already do better than most; that's not really as good as you'd like to be. You want to see and understand that which others cannot see and don't understand when it comes to catching cats.

All of the process that is catching catfish probably can't be taught. At least some of the best anglers must bear a gift as Richard Petty bears his gift to drive a race car at impossible speeds around an impossible track. What he does isn't exactly human, but almost superhuman, a gift enhanced by calculated practice. Almost all of us, though, can be taught to drive, and most of us can be taught to drive better, even to drive exceptionally, should we so wish.

The need to learn to understand that catfish pass through different periods of response as the year progresses often strikes novice catfish anglers as, at best, an odd part of the fishing process. Boring. Perhaps even silly. They want to talk secret baits, secret riggings, secret this, and secret that. But only a few real overriding secrets to catching cats exist, and one is found in the seemingly mundane subject before you here.

The In-Fisherman Calendar includes 10 periods in an annual cycle. Dividing the annual continuum into 10 periods is arbitrary; indeed, the periods

The Ten In-Fisherman Calendar Periods

In-Fisherman divides the fishing year into 10 basic Calendar Periods of fish response. A general characterization of each period includes:

Winter: Coldest water of the year. Frozen water occurs in northern regions. River catfish reside in deep holes away from heavy current.

Coldwater: Occurs during late fall and early spring. Fish are grouped in or near winter holding areas.

Prespawn: Fish are on the way to or in the vicinity of spawning areas, often feeding and grouping heavily. Fishing can be good.

Spawn: A brief, variable period linked to the range of preferred spawning temperatures for each fish species. Feeding activity usually slows when fish are spawning, although fish of the same species don't always spawn at the same time.

Postspawn: A brief transition period with length depending on water and weather conditions. Fish begin feeding strategies and move toward areas they use for much of the rest of the year.

Presummer: A continuing transition period. Fish search for areas to spend the summer and begin to establish summer patterns.

Summer Peak: Fish establish a pattern in a habitat that can sustain them for summer. The sudden presence of other fish usually spurs competitive feeding and good fishing.

Summer: Usually a long period when fish remain in habitat areas established during the Summer Peak. Fish activity and location are predictable.

1 Prespawn	2 Spawn	3 Postspawn	4 Presummer	5 Summer Peak

sometimes overlap—and we have further regrouped the 10 periods into 7 slightly broader categories that fit catfish.

Catfishing begins after waters stabilize during spring, as catfish move into a long Prespawn Period. After spawning, they settle into holding areas for summer. At some point during fall, cool water and rain move cats downriver to large deep holes where they spend winter. Catfish in lakes and reservoirs often move deep by late fall. Winter, which may include ice cover, reduces the activity level of most catfish species, except during extended periods of warm weather.

Understanding calendar periods is one basis for learning the patterns of catfish and developing the skill to find them. The calendar periods serve as a reference and thus a means of communicating. Understanding that fish progress through distinct periods of activity that vary only in their length from year to year, based on changes in weather and water conditions, allows anglers to note similarities and difference in fish behavior from one activity period to the next.

One overriding factor in discussion among anglers, therefore, is the calendar period under (or surrounding) which the discussion takes place. It does little good, for example, for catfishermen to discuss the productivity of certain baits—say dipbaits—without also noting the calendar period in question. Dipbaits, they might note, are a classic bait for channel catfish beginning in late spring and peaking during summer. Often, though, they don't perform so well as natural baits during colder-water periods.

Postsummer: Cooler weather lowers water temperatures, and fish move toward areas where they'll spend winter. Cooler water often spurs feeding.

Fall Turnover: Occurs in lakes, ponds, and reservoirs that stratify into three distinct water-temperature layers during summer. As fall progresses, colder weather lowers surface water temperatures, the colder water sinks, and stratification breaks down, allowing fish to use the entire column of water. Usually a time of poor fishing. Rarely affects rivers—Postsummer Period slides into the fall Coldwater Period, then the Winter Period.

Calendar Periods are at the mercy of Mother Nature. They don't last a certain number of days, nor do they occur on specific dates each year. Their length varies yearly, depending on weather trends and water conditions. Calendar periods that last a few days one year may last several weeks the next year.

Of course, the annual rhythm of rivers differs from the rhythm of lakes, and the rhythm of annual channel catfish activity differs from other species. For example, the growth and death of a yearly crop of aquatic vegetation is a major influence in lakes. Weeds don't have this impact on catfish in rivers. Rivers, on the other hand, go through turbulent runoff periods; most lakes don't. Most importantly, though, catfish spawn much later than most other North American fish species. A long Prespawn Period produces an extended period of good fishing.

6 Summer	7 Postsummer	8 Turnover	9 Coldwater	10 Winter

So astute anglers don't just sing praises of their favorite dipbait without defining the Calendar Period (or periods) in question. Occasionally, anglers need to get more definitive in order to be accurately understood. A particular sour cheese dip, an angler might note, is the best dip option during prespawn, while a blood dip or a combination of cheese and blood is better than sour cheese during the Postsummer Period. So such qualifications do more than just spice up conversations among catfishermen. They're absolutely vital to being accurately understood.

YEAR OF THE CHANNEL CATFISH

Channel cats remain the most widely studied catfish species, though when compared to bass, trout, and walleyes, biologists have paid the popular channel cat relatively little attention. Most of our knowledge of the seasonal movements and behavior of catfish is based on several rivers, lakes, and reservoirs that we've observed closely. Fortunately, blue cats and flatheads in many waters seem to follow similar seasonal patterns.

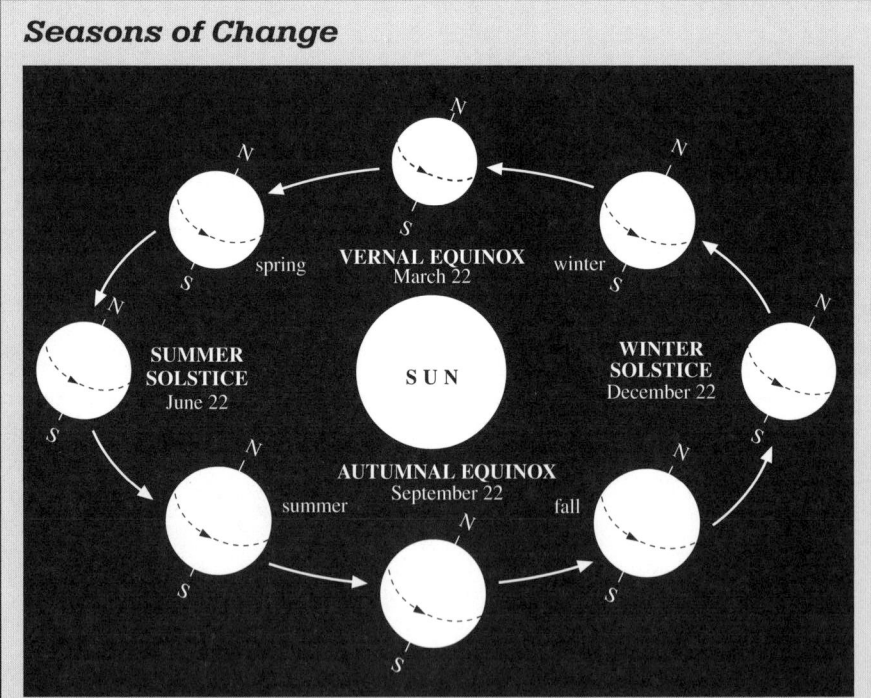

Seasons of Change

Spring, summer, fall, winter. The pendulum swings between seasons, bringing evident changes on land, but more difficult-to-define changes underwater. Studies show that photoperiod (length of daylight) influences the tempo of the environment, from microorganisms to top-of-the-line predators. The intensity and duration of light in a yearly cycle influences migrations, spawning, and feeding.

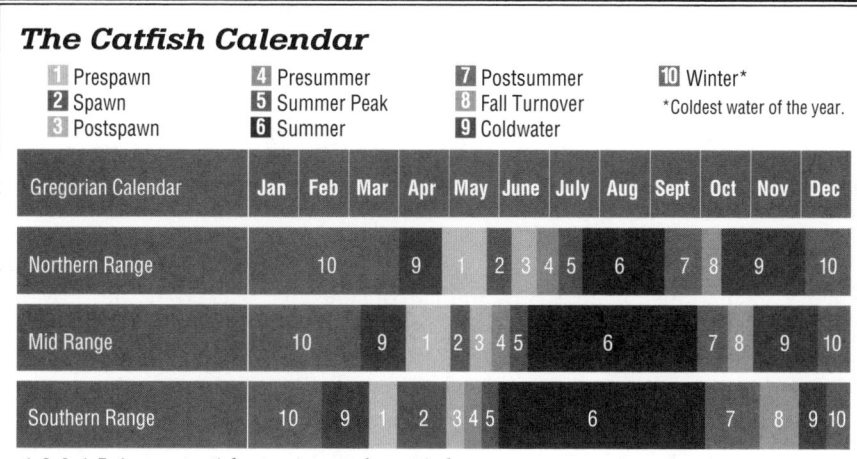

The Catfish Calendar

1 Prespawn	**4** Presummer	**7** Postsummer	**10** Winter*
2 Spawn	**5** Summer Peak	**8** Fall Turnover	*Coldest water of the year.
3 Postspawn	**6** Summer	**9** Coldwater	

Gregorian Calendar	Jan	Feb	Mar	Apr	May	June	July	Aug	Sept	Oct	Nov	Dec
Northern Range	10		9	1	2 3 4 5		6		7 8	9		10
Mid Range	10		9	1	2 3 4 5		6			7 8	9	10
Southern Range	10	9	1	2	3 4 5		6			7	8	9 10

1, 2, 3, 4, 5, 6 are potential extensive overlap periods

The 10 In-Fisherman Calendar Periods of fish response vary in length from year to year. Unusually warm or cool weather affects the length of the periods that can vary as much as four weeks from year to year. The periods aren't based on the Gregorian calendar, so they don't occur on specific dates each year. Instead, calendar periods are based on nature's clock.

In addition, calendar periods vary by regions. Rivers of the South experience an extended Summer Period and a brief Winter Period. In contrast, rivers along the United States-Canada border have extended Coldwater and Winter Periods. Channel cats in Florida or Texas often are in the Spawning Period while those in northern Minnesota are still in the Winter Period.

Unusual about the catfish calendar is the long period during which individual cats within a catfish population may be in one of six different periods. In most situations, this allows for consistent catfish location and fishing patterns.

WINTER OR FROZEN WATER PERIOD

Water Temperature: *Coldest Water for an Extended Period*
General Fish Mood: *Negative*

This extended period can't be defined by precise environmental markers since channel catfish are found in a variety of geographic areas. The Winter Period includes two In-Fisherman Calendar Periods: Coldwater and Frozen Water or Winter. In the southern half of the catfish range, ice-up doesn't occur.

The Winter Period is characterized by almost constant cold temperatures. How cold depends on geographic location and the severity of the winter. In Minnesota and Manitoba, water on lakes and parts of most rivers is under 3 feet of ice. Water temperatures in winter range from about 32°F to 39°F. In southern states, water temperatures usually are in the 40°F range, 50°F in Florida and southern California.

We define this period by catfish activity, which is basically the same no matter the location. In winter, catfish face a long period of temperatures much colder than during the rest of the year. They often continue to feed though not so actively as they do in warmer water. Fish in rivers tend to hold in deep holes or pockets away from the main current flow. In small rivers, a holding hole might be 6 feet deep or less. In bigger rivers, holes may be 20 to 40 feet deep. Lake and reservoir fish hold in deep water, too.

In rivers, scuba divers report seeing catfish behind boulders that break current. Where enough boulders aren't available, catfish appear to snug behind anything that reduces current. To reduce water resistance, other catfish then line up behind the first one, nose to tail in a chainlike formation.

In the middle and southern regions of the country, catfish don't completely stop moving and feeding during winter. A radio tagging study on the Missouri River showed catfish almost completely dormant during a bitterly cold winter. But during a mild winter, they moved short distances. An extended period of warm weather in January or February may stimulate catfish activity near deeper river holes that are easy to locate because the water's usually low. Since fish are highly concentrated in predictable locations, good catches are possible.

During midwinter when cats mostly are inactive, it's often possible to catch them by vertical jigging. It's also easy to snag them, though, which is illegal in most areas.

SPRING COLDWATER PERIOD

Water Temperature: Rising
General Fish Mood: Neutral to Positive

When ice leaves or early spring weather arrives, walleyes, pike, and sauger move quickly through the Prespawn Period and into the Spawn Period. It's a time of rapid transition. Not so with channel catfish that probably won't spawn for months, even in far northern waters where the prespawn-spawn transition is compressed.

In rivers, early spring usually means continued cold and turbid water. Northern areas experience snow melt and cold spring rains. Southern areas receive cold spring rains. As the water begins to warm gradually, catfish activity increases.

In early spring, catfish might still spend most of their time in deep holes. Eventually, rising water temperatures stimulate catfish metabolism. No distinct temperature marks this point. In southern regions, where water temperatures have been in the 50s, catfish might start feeding when water temperatures reach the low 60°F range. In northern regions, 45°F usually means cats will prowl, but temperatures in the upper 50°F range are better.

Mostly, we sense when the first good run of cats will begin aggressively feeding. Spring weather will have whipsawed from nasty to nice, when suddenly the weather's nice for several days in a row. A spring thundershower scents the air, and as you walk across

The Coldwater Period offers some of the finest fishing of the season for blue cats.

your lawn, it bounces with a give in the soil. The ground is about to come alive at night with the first nightcrawlers. Trees are budding; frogs are beginning their evening chorus; and ducks, geese, grouse, and most of the rest of the animal world are active.

Catfish are moving, but still avoiding direct current. And current is stronger now than during any other time of year. Fish are concentrated in areas of reduced current—the core of holes and shoreline holding areas.

This is the season for livebaits or sourbaits. Cats can find plenty of fish that have died over winter and are beginning to decompose as water temperatures rise.

PRESPAWN PERIOD

Water Conditions: Rising Temperatures and Stabilizing River Flows
General Fish Mood: Positive

What river walleyes do in fall, channel catfish do in spring. They move, usually upstream, sometimes into smaller feeder rivers, searching first for food and second for spawning habitat.

No sharp demarcation is present between the preceding period and this one. They blend naturally as water temperatures continue to rise into the 60°F range and river flows stabilize. The main difference is catfish behavior. Their metabolic rate is much higher, so they need more food and are better able to search for it. Higher water also offers a variety of areas.

The earliest upriver movements are motivated more by the need to feed than by a spawning urge. Because more areas are available than earlier in the year, cats no longer accept the limited forage in holes where they spent the winter.

Barriers such as dams temporarily concentrate cats. This period compares somewhat to the prespawn movement of steelhead in rivers, with fish constantly moving, stopping to hold in spots offering food and protection from current, then moving again to better feeding opportunities.

The Prespawn Period offers anglers the finest catfishing of the year.

The Prespawn Period offers the year's best fishing. Fish are moving—searching and actively feeding.

Catch a fish or two from a small spot and return in a day or two and catch three more. The spot is restocked by the restless movement of the fish.

In high water without impassable barriers, catfish may move 75 miles or more—channel cats have moved as far as 111 miles in 36 days. So long as the water's high and fish are finding food, they keep moving. At times, however, they move only a few miles.

The area where catfish spawn is determined by their location when spawning time nears. Apparently, cats don't always return to the same spawning locations, although this hasn't been verified. They do return to general areas, however. Many catfish in the lower portion of the Red River in Manitoba, for example, return to the same slough off the main river each year, despite varying water levels. Catfish move upstream, looking for food and future spawning sites.

Prespawn movement often continues until cats reach an impassable barrier like a dam. They search the area for possible spawning locations like holes in riprap or rocky outcroppings near the dam. If the area below the dam is too silty, they drift downstream to look for spawning sites. Spawners may spread over a long stretch of river.

The Prespawn Period offers potential for the year's best fishing. Fish are moving—searching and actively feeding.

Calendar Period Regional Timetable

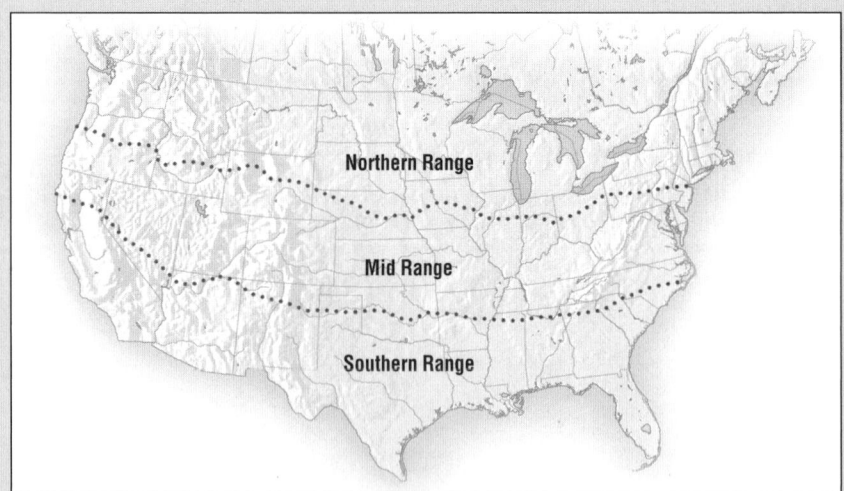

Northern Range

Mid Range

Southern Range

The timing of the channel catfish Spawn Period illustrates the region-by-region progression of the calendar periods. Region (latitude), water temperature, weather trends, length of daylight, and competition for habitat are just a few of the factors influencing the exact timing of the spawn. Remember, not all channel cats spawn at the same time even in the same body of water. While the bulk of the adult fish on a given river may spawn during a few days of ideal conditions, some spawn early and some late. Regionally, the onset of channel catfish spawning may begin in early May in the South and as late as August in southern Canada.

SPAWN PERIOD

Water Temperatures: 75°F or Higher

General Fish Mood: Positive-Negative

Catfish spawning may span a month or more, so the spawn doesn't negatively affect angling as it would if all cats spawned at the same time. Also, channel cats bite almost anything near a spawning hole, so find a spawning area and you may find good fishing.

Typical Spawning Months	
Area	**Months**
Florida	April-early June
Alabama-Georgia	May-June
Texas-Oklahoma	May-June
Kentucky-Tennessee	June-July
Missouri-Illinois-Iowa	June-July
Ohio	June-early August
Minnesota-Wisconsin	June-early August
Manitoba	July-August

The spawn is triggered by the length of daylight (photoperiod), which cats sense in the brain, probably in the pineal gland. Linking spawning in part to length of daylight is one guarantee against eggs hatching too early or too late, which could happen if spawning time were based solely on water temperature. In addition, an internal biological clock causes eggs to mature even with external stimuli absent.

Catfish are motivated to spawn by water temperatures of 75°F or above. According to some studies, temperatures approaching 80°F are ideal. Catfish kept in water too cool for spawning will spawn when water temperatures quickly rise to 75°F, if time of year is appropriate. Spawning, then, is regulated by the interplay of an internal clock, length of daylight, and water temperature.

Spawning can take place as early as April in the South and as late as August in the North. In Missouri, dates range from late May to early July. The most common spawning month across the channel cat's geographic range is June.

To begin the spawn, a male channel cat seeks a hole or pocket in a bank. Catfish in ponds with no suitable spawning locations don't spawn. If artificial spawning structures are added, they may spawn.

The spawning hole should be secure, preferably with only one entrance big enough to admit the male and female. A small entrance not much larger than a fish's body is ideal. Big fish spawn in big holes, small fish in small holes. If the hole's entrance isn't much bigger than the male, he lies with his head toward the entrance, nearly filling it, to effectively guard eggs and fry.

In small rivers, crevices near rocky riffles offer possible spots for spawning holes. Undercut banks, muskrat holes, and objects in the water—hollow logs, car bodies, tires, buckets—are possible spawning sites.

First, the male sweeps the hole to clean and enlarge it. Eventually he lures a female into the hole. The female ejects a gelatinous clump of from 2,000 to over 70,000 eggs, depending on the size of the fish, and the male fertilizes them. Then the female leaves or is driven from the hole by the male. She produces one clutch of eggs a year. Males, however, may spawn more than once if the spawning season is extended. The supply of available males often exceeds the number of sexually mature females.

The male is a good guardian. As mentioned, his massive head usually fills the entrance to the nest. He's aggressive in defense of the eggs. Anything brought near him will be hit or bit. Holes with two or more entrances probably suffer egg loss because the male can't guard them as well. The male also aerates and keeps silt off the eggs by fanning them with his fins.

Little is known about what happens next in the wild, because observations are based on catfish in clear hatchery ponds where they may behave differently. But we do know that eggs hatch in about a week. Then fry spend about a week in the nest being protected by the male before they enter the river to begin life among predators.

Some observers say the young slip into the river and are immediately on their own. Others, who observed cats in small ponds, report that males protect fry for several days after they leave the nest. Survival of the young is probably better in turbid water than in clear water, because reduced visibility in turbid water conceals the young from many predators.

Spring and fall may afford flat-head anglers their best chance for a giant, but summer still is prime time for numbers.

SETTLING PERIOD (INCLUDES POSTSPAWN AND PRESUMMER PERIODS)

Water Temperature Range: Upper 70°F to Mid 80°F

General Fish Mood: Neutral to Positive

This period, important in fishing for some fish, isn't vital to catfishermen because the catfish spawning period is so extended. Even in ponds where water temperatures and length of daylight are identical for all fish, not all catfish spawn at the same time.

Catfish probably go through a type of recuperative period after spawning, but to an angler, it doesn't matter if a few fish are recuperating because at any given time, some fish are feeding.

This period probably occurs in late June to July in much of the catfish range. Catfish are on the move again, often moving downstream from spawning sites, looking for deep cover-laden holes that offer security and food. Downstream movement isn't automatic. If the spawning area offers good summer habitat, they may linger.

If water levels are high and rising, channel cats move either upstream or downstream during this settling period. More typically, though, water levels are dropping, so they move downstream, often leaving small tributaries to enter bigger rivers. These movements are more pronounced in small creeks than in big rivers.

SUMMER PERIOD
(INCLUDES SUMMER PEAK, SUMMER, AND POSTSUMMER PERIODS)
Water Temperatures: Annual Maximum, 80°F and Above
General Fish Mood: Positive
The Summer Period includes much of July, August, and September in most of the channel cat's range. Summer offers prime fishing. Fish are in predictable locations. They feed aggressively, although not all the time. Plenty of food is available, at least during the beginning of summer, so they add much of their year's growth during this period that doesn't end until water begins to cool in fall. Find the best holes with the biggest catfish and fish them with the right baits at the right time.

COOLING PERIOD
(INCLUDES THE TURNOVER AND FALL COLDWATER PERIODS)
Water Temperatures: Cooling from 80°F
General Fish Attitude: Positive to Neutral to Negative
As late summer slips into fall, longer, cooler nights and cool rains lower river temperatures. In early fall, catfish location depends mostly on river level. During stable levels, catfish continue holding in holes where they spent the summer. Heavy rain during September or October may pull catfish upriver. Generally, though, especially when water temperatures begin to cool into the 60°F range, cats move downstream toward bigger, deeper water and deep wintering holes.

Eventually, the biggest, deepest holes concentrate large groups of catfish. As water temperatures continue to fall, catfish activity is confined to the immediate vicinity of the wintering hole. Catfish location can mean good fishing now. Obviously, though, fishing the right holes is important.

Classifying Catfish Water

CATEGORIZING LAKE, RIVER, & RESERVOIR TYPES

When *In-Fisherman* was first published in the mid-1970s, several overriding principles were offered as part of a learning package that guaranteed that anglers could learn to fish successfully or their money back. Chapter 1 discussed the Calendar Periods that catfish move through as the seasons pass. The ability to identify Calendar Periods remains one overriding factor in understanding how catfish are affected by their environment—where they may be and how they may react to any given presentation.

Calendar Periods also serve as a reference point and therefore a basis for communication. Anglers who understand the system can discuss fish response and place it in context when, say, one person is referencing catfish behavior in a river in Minnesota and another is referring to catfish behavior in a South Carolina reservoir. If the angler in South Carolina is reacting to catfish response during a Coldwater Period and the Minnesota catman is reacting to fish response during the Summer Peak, they're really talking apples and oranges.

The ability to classify lakes, rivers, and reservoirs is another basic critical concept In-Fisherman offers for understanding the structural makeup of different bodies of water. Learning to classify waters helps to note similarities and differences in fish behavior and to place these in context. For example, an angler referencing catfish behavior in a flatland reservoir isn't on the same page as an angler noting catfish behavior in a middle-aged natural lake. Surprisingly, the thousands of lakes, rivers, and reservoirs across North America fall somewhat neatly into little more than a dozen divisions that are easily understood with a bit of practice.

NATURAL LAKES

Obviously, no two lakes are exactly alike. Broadly, though, all lakes can be classified into one of three environmental age groups: oligotrophic (young), mesotrophic (middle-aged), and eutrophic (old). Factors like the lake's

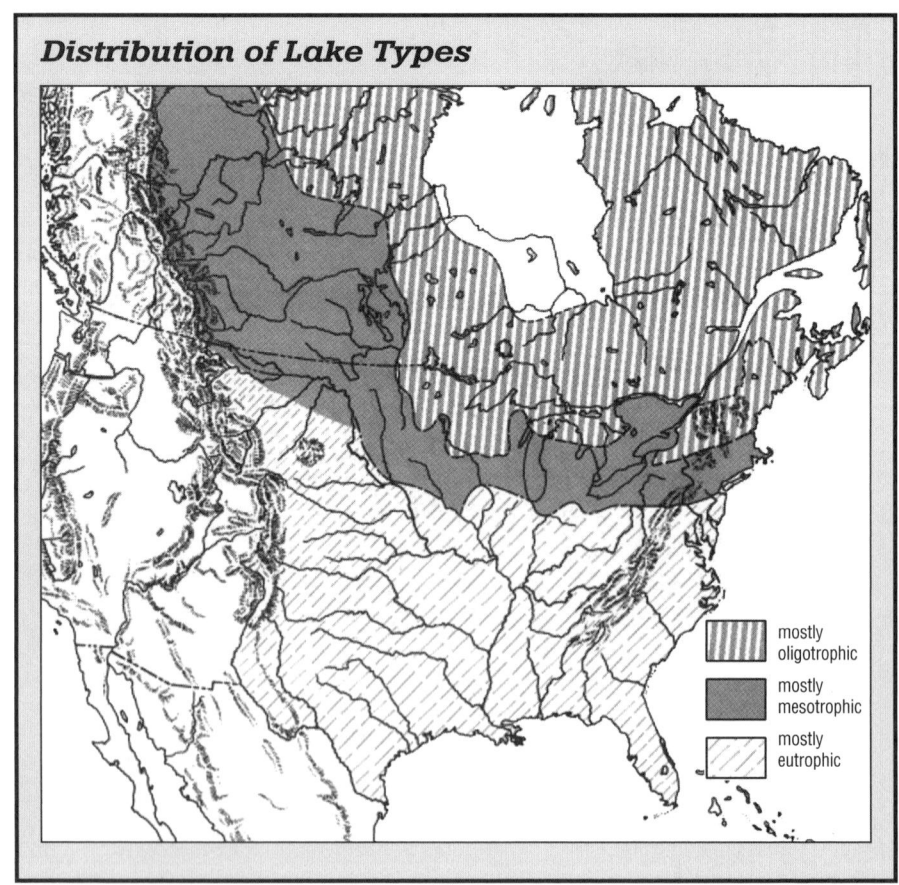

Distribution of Lake Types

mostly oligotrophic

mostly mesotrophic

mostly eutrophic

predator-prey relationships, the amounts and types of aquatic vegetation, and many other structural considerations determine the basic lake classification and ultimately help determine where catfish should be located within each Calendar Period.

No matter where your favorite lake is located, it's changing. In some waters, visible change may take centuries. In other waters, change may occur in just a few years. This aging process is often called eutrophication, and all lakes pass through it. A lake grows older not only in time but in condition. The initial stages of eutrophication may take thousands of years, while the final stages may happen quickly, especially with the addition of manmade factors.

Throughout this process, the lake environment—structural makeup, food chains, vegetation levels, and dominant fish species—changes. Man-caused eutrophication, or aging, is in part due to the expanding human population and waste disposal. Man accomplishes in a generation what may otherwise take hundreds of years.

Because of the manmade changes on most North American lakes, we classify natural lakes according to their environmental condition rather than their chronological age. Each category is a point of reference. Anglers quickly learn to recognize similarities in bodies of water and can readily transfer what they've learned on one lake to another with similar water. This is one method for patterning catfish and applying those patterns to bodies of water not seen before but nevertheless recognizable.

As lakes age, then, their character changes. Environmentally young lakes are deep and clear, while older lakes are shallow and murky. Young lakes are oxygen-rich and support lake trout, whitefish, and perhaps walleyes. Old lakes are weed-choked and oxygen-poor, supporting carp, bullheads, and perhaps catfish. Between these two extremes fall most lakes, each more or less hospitable to certain fish species. Catfish are adaptable enough to thrive in most water conditions found throughout their range, but they prosper in food-rich waters toward the fertile end of the scale.

The three basic categories of natural lakes can be regrouped into nine even more specific categories. First, though, we'll consider the three basic categories.

OLIGOTROPHIC LAKES

The youngest, most infertile lakes typically have rock basins and are almost exclusively found in the northern latitudes of North America. They usually have steep sharp drop-offs, few weeds, and conifer-studded shorelines. The nutrient level of the water is usually low, and oxygen is available in deep water. These lakes usually support low gamefish populations; a few pounds of gamefish per acre is common. We know of few catfish populations in oligotrophic lakes.

Infertile

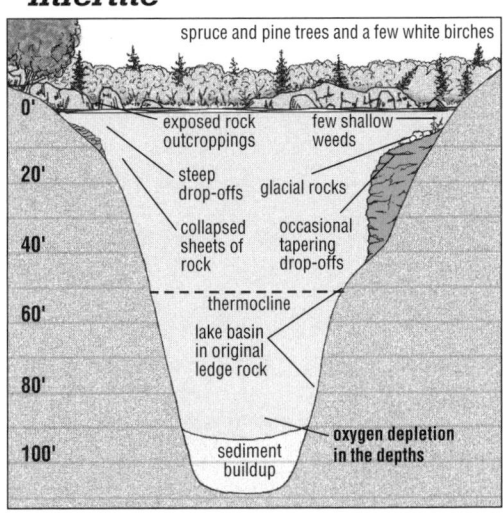

spruce and pine trees and a few white birches

- 0'
- exposed rock outcroppings
- few shallow weeds
- 20'
- steep drop-offs
- glacial rocks
- collapsed sheets of rock
- occasional tapering drop-offs
- 40'
- 60'
- thermocline
- lake basin in original ledge rock
- 80'
- 100'
- sediment buildup
- oxygen depletion in the depths

Moderately Fertile

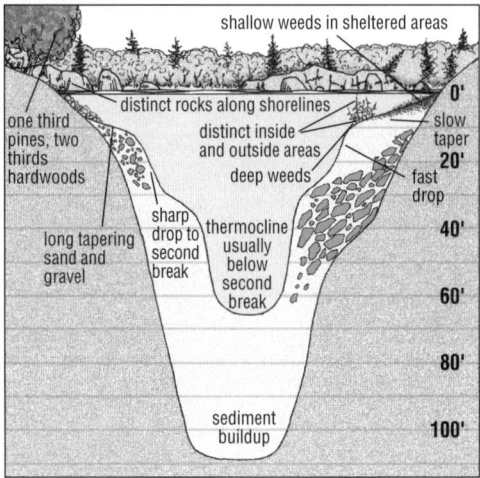

shallow weeds in sheltered areas

distinct rocks along shorelines

0'

one third pines, two thirds hardwoods

distinct inside and outside areas

slow taper

20'

deep weeds

fast drop

long tapering sand and gravel

sharp drop to second break

thermocline usually below second break

40'

60'

80'

sediment buildup

100'

Fertile

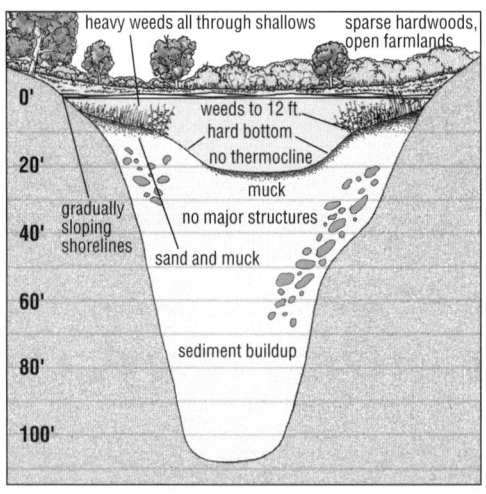

heavy weeds all through shallows

sparse hardwoods, open farmlands

0'

weeds to 12 ft.

hard bottom

no thermocline

20'

gradually sloping shorelines

muck

no major structures

40'

sand and muck

60'

sediment buildup

80'

100'

MESOTROPHIC LAKES

In middle-aged lakes, shorelines are less gorgelike and drop-offs less abrupt. Big boulders give way to smaller rocks, and sand and gravel are more apparent. Weedgrowth abounds. Shoreline terrain is more varied and plant life more diverse. The water contains more nutrients. The lake is moderately fertile, the water cool, with many pounds of fish per acre. This type of lake may support fair catfish populations.

EUTROPHIC LAKES

The environmentally oldest lakes are warmwater environments. Shallow weedgrowth is thick so long as the water remains somewhat clear. Lake bottoms are muck or clay, and shorelines taper gradually to the waterline, often with no secondary drop-offs. Marshy areas usually dot adjacent sections of lake. Hardwood trees and flat shorelines are the rule.

Eutrophic lakes often are called "dishpan lakes" because of their overall shallow depth and uniform shape. Typically, these old lakes are fertile and have large fish populations. Channel catfish are particularly well-suited to fertile lakes, especially when protected from freeze-out with aeration systems. Flathead catfish have been stocked in this type of lake in parts of the Midwest and Midsouth to reduce the numbers of bullheads, carp, and other roughfish.

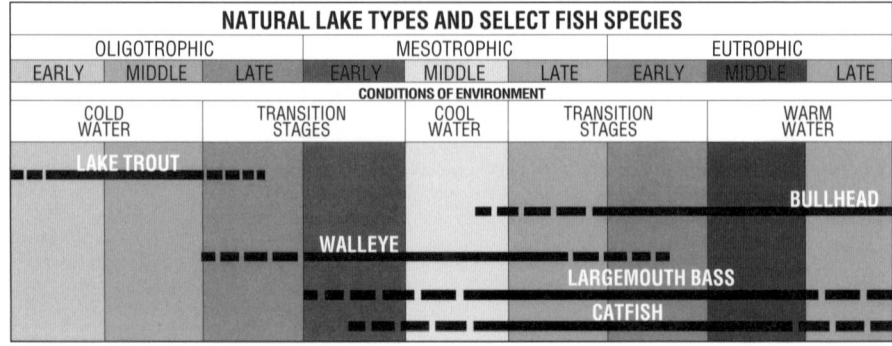

NATURAL LAKE TYPES AND SELECT FISH SPECIES

OLIGOTROPHIC			MESOTROPHIC			EUTROPHIC		
EARLY	MIDDLE	LATE	EARLY	MIDDLE	LATE	EARLY	MIDDLE	LATE
CONDITIONS OF ENVIRONMENT								
COLD WATER		TRANSITION STAGES		COOL WATER		TRANSITION STAGES		WARM WATER

LAKE TROUT

BULLHEAD

WALLEYE

LARGEMOUTH BASS

CATFISH

The Lake Aging Process

STABLE, YOUNG, INFERTILE COLDWATER PHASES
1. Early-stage oligotrophic (no catfish present)
2. Midstage oligotrophic (no catfish present)

TRANSITION FROM COLDWATER TO COOLWATER PHASES
3. Late-stage oligotrophic (no catfish present)
4. Early-stage mesotrophic (no catfish present)

STABLE, MIDDLE-AGED, MODERATELY FERTILE COOLWATER PHASE
5. Midstage mesotrophic (stocked catfish could be present)

TRANSITION FROM COOLWATER TO WARMWATER PHASES
6. Late-stage mesotrophic (catfish beginning to thrive)
7. Early-stage eutrophic (catfish thrive)

STABLE, OLD, FERTILE WARMWATER PHASE
8. Midstage eutrophic (catfish continuing to thrive)

TRANSITION FROM WARMWATER TO VERY WARMWATER PHASE
9. Late-stage eutrophic (catfish may thrive, depending on specific water conditions)

RIVERS

Rivers come in many sizes and provide habitat for many fish species. Different stretches of the same river can exhibit contrasting personalities and support different fish species. For example, a young, clear, coldwater river plunges downhill, flowing over and cutting through solid rock. Here, trout and grayling thrive, but not catfish.

As a river matures, it becomes increasingly fertile, flows more slowly, and begins to meander. A coolwater environment favors walleyes and perhaps smallmouth bass and muskies. Finally, in old age, a river winds through a floodplain. The warmwater environment supports mostly catfish, largemouth bass, gar, and carp.

Middle-aged and old rivers are slow-flowing, shallow rivers with broad floodplains. These wide floodplains create complex backwater areas with abundant habitat. The mouths of flooded backwaters, oxbow lakes, and connecting lakes provide excellent areas for catfish. During spring and early summer, flooded brush, stumps, and timber are common fish attractors.

Channels, meanwhile, provide connections to other prime spots and often attract the majority of catfish during most yearly periods. Since backwaters can be a mile or more from the main channel, they often function more as reservoirs than as rivers.

Distribution of Species by River Age Category

This chart shows the species present in each river category. Notice how a fish's numbers peak and then gradually decrease as the river evolves. Each aging stage favors certain varieties of coldwater, coolwater, or warmwater species.

Young, picturesque mountain trout streams may be unpolluted and unaffected by man. These streams are infertile since they run over rock beds and gain few nutrients from the land. Very young and young streams cannot support large fish populations.

Coldwater species disappear in the adult stage. In sections with less gradient, the water flows slower and warms to a temperature that trout cannot survive. This environment favors coolwater fish like smallmouth bass.

In the mature stage, coolwater fish like walleye, sauger, pike, and muskie begin to dominate. Then, as a river gets older, coolwater species begin to fade. Warmwater fish like largemouth bass and catfish become dominant, and fish like carp become common.

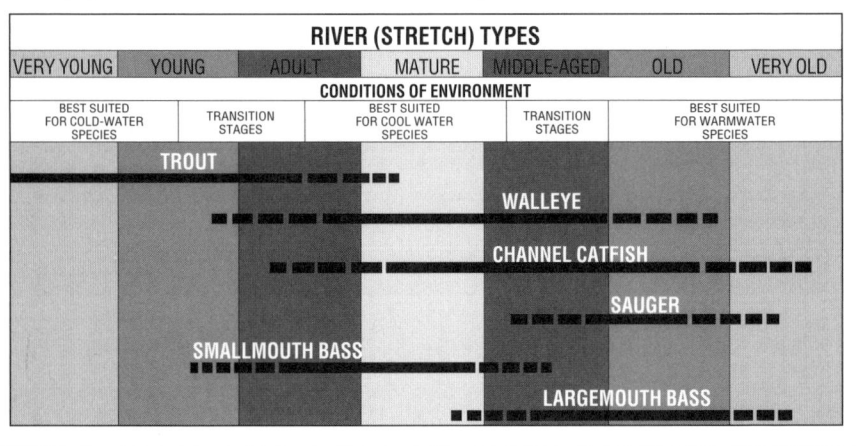

RIVER CLASSIFICATION

Streams must be viewed by stretches. A particular stretch can be young, old, or somewhere in between. For instance, a stream may be shallow with only gradual gradient changes for several miles, with backwater areas, a soft bottom, and aquatic weedgrowth. Crappies and largemouth bass find adequate habitat here. Then this stream may break through a rocky, clifflike area, creating a rapids, and finally pouring into a boulder-based pool. This stretch may hold catfish, walleyes, and smallmouth bass.

Rarely is a stream the same from beginning to end, because few of them flow through regions that are geographically consistent. Because of these variations, we use the following method to classify streams. Most river stretches in North America fall within one of seven categories. River stretches, though, often exhibit transitional tendencies, just as a natural lake may have eutrophic bays while the main body of the lake is mesotrophic.

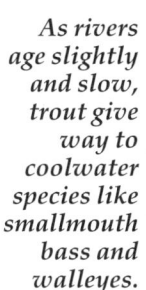

As rivers age slightly and slow, trout give way to coolwater species like smallmouth bass and walleyes.

Young stream sections host trout that thrive as water flows quickly over rock and gravel.

Flatheads and blue catfish favor aging river stretches with greater water volume and slower current.

Channel catfish thrive in mature river stretches.

Habitat In One River Category

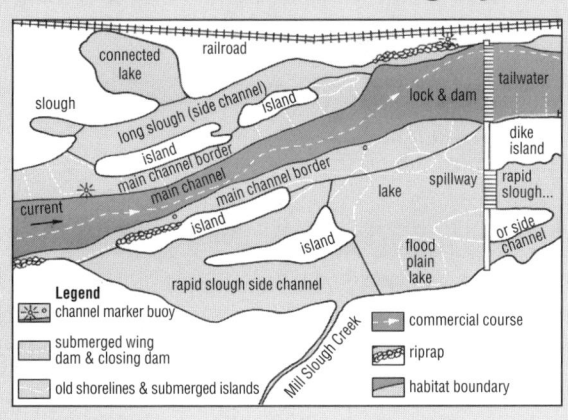

The river category in question determines available habitat, and available habitat determines fish species and their location. This section of the upper Mississippi River shows typical habitat areas in a mature river. Water level and yearly period dictate the movement of fish from backwaters to the main channel.

River Type Continuum

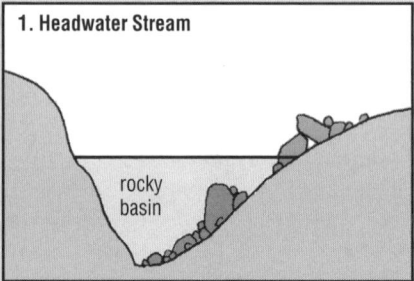

1. Headwater Stream

rocky
basin

Bottom rocky; water cool and clear; depth shallow; width narrow; gradient steep; current fast; no aquatic vegetation. Madtoms may be present but no other catfish species.

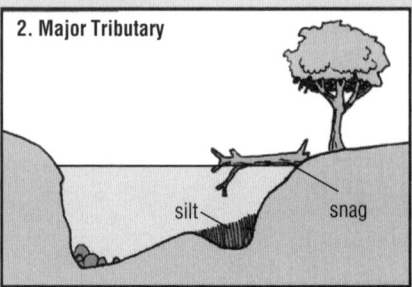

2. Major Tributary

silt   snag

Bottom variable; deeper pools common; water warmer and more turbid, especially after rain; gradient and flow rate reduced; typical riffle-pool-run sequence. Excellent channel catfish habitat.

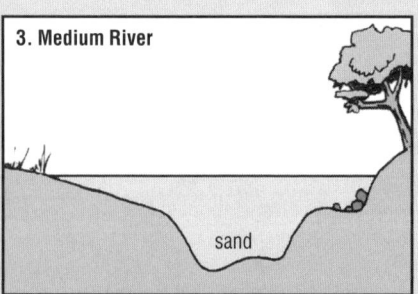

3. Medium River

sand

Bottom variable; riffle-pool-run sequence occurs, but not as well defined; vegetation may be present on shallow banks; tributaries common. Excellent habitat for channels and other catfish species.

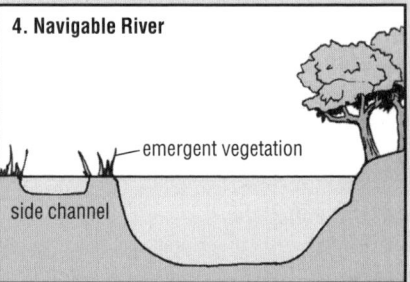

4. Navigable River

emergent vegetation

side channel

Current moderate; channel complex, possibly dredged; aquatic vegetation locally abundant; bottom soft; water murky and warm. Channel cats often abundant; other catfish species also occur.

RESERVOIRS

A reservoir is a body of water impounded behind a dam. Water floods the landscape—marshes, plains, hills, mountains, plateaus, and canyons—depending on the geographic area. In general, reservoirs in the North, West, and Northwest provide cooler water than those in the South, Southwest, and Southeast. Because catfish are warmwater fish, they're more common in warmer regions.

A cross section of North America reveals that some areas are low, swampy, and flat. These are old floodplain regions. Others are hilly. Still others have mountains with highland ridges that form foothills. These usually are low mountain ranges like the Boston and Ouachita ranges in Arkansas, the

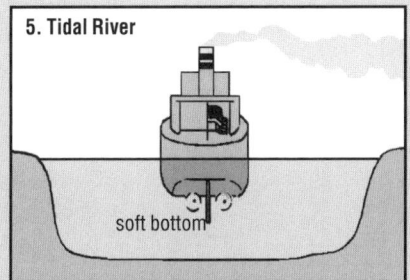

5. Tidal River

soft bottom

Current moderate; channel complex, possibly dredged; aquatic vegetation locally abundant; bottom soft; water murky and warm. Channel cats often abundant; other catfish species also occur.

The force of water is constantly remodeling the riverscape. Over time, rivers change their course. It is this change that constructs adjacent flood plains. If a river stretch does not have an extensive adjoining flood plain, it means that its bed is stable or the river is geologically young. Water is a universal solvent; given time, it can chew away granite, dissolve iron, and move mountains.

In streams, the action of water along with the meandering effect cuts materials on the outside bend where current flow is swift and deposits other materials on the inside bend where current speed and force is reduced. Notice how the current has created a tongue-like structure. The deepest part of any river stretch is always on the outside bend.

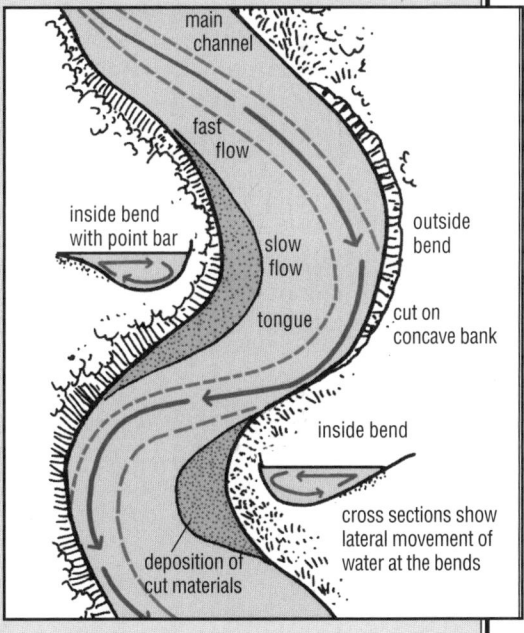

main channel

fast flow

inside bend with point bar

slow flow

outside bend

cut on concave bank

tongue

inside bend

deposition of cut materials

cross sections show lateral movement of water at the bends

Appalachian chain in the East, the Cumberland highlands of Kentucky and Tennessee, and the low coastal ranges of the West Coast.

Reservoirs lying within each of these landforms show the same basic configuration; that is, they have a similar cross section and shape. Canyon reservoirs, for example, are long and snakelike with towering, sharp, almost vertical walls. Impounded waters are wide with expanses of shallow flats.

The shape of an impoundment determines its classification. By studying a topographical map, you can usually determine what classification an impoundment falls into. Other facets of a reservoir's personality include (1) annual fluctuation of water level; (2) water clarity; (3) fertility; and (4) temperature.

Reservoir Types

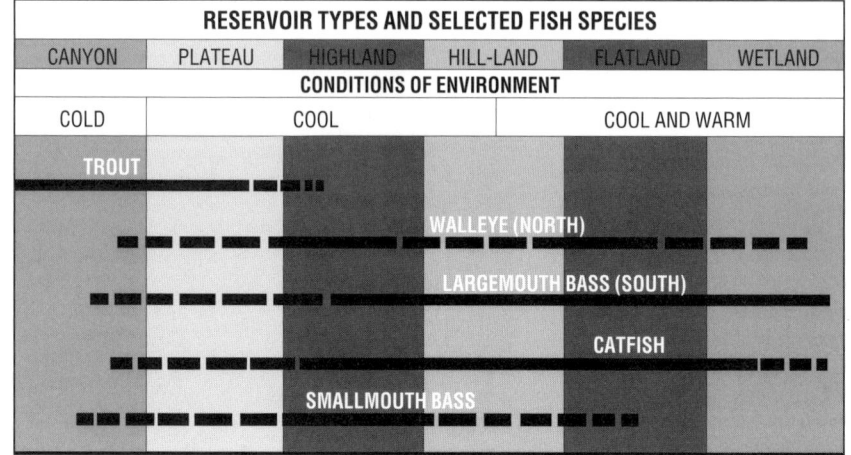

RESERVOIR TYPES AND SELECTED FISH SPECIES					
CANYON	PLATEAU	HIGHLAND	HILL-LAND	FLATLAND	WETLAND
CONDITIONS OF ENVIRONMENT					
COLD	COOL			COOL AND WARM	

TROUT
WALLEYE (NORTH)
LARGEMOUTH BASS (SOUTH)
CATFISH
SMALLMOUTH BASS

Each reservoir category can sustain catfish. Most sections of canyon reservoirs, however, are too deep to provide prime habitat. Likewise, some lowland reservoirs are too warm and fertile to support many catfish. They generally thrive in highland reservoirs, flatland reservoirs, and hill-land reservoirs, and often do well in wetland reservoirs.

RESERVOIR CLASSIFICATION

Rivers flow through diverse land forms. And reservoirs built on them take on characteristics of the land. In-Fisherman has established a system for classifying reservoirs that helps define general fishing patterns and lets anglers communicate about reservoir fishing across the continent.

Flatland Reservoir

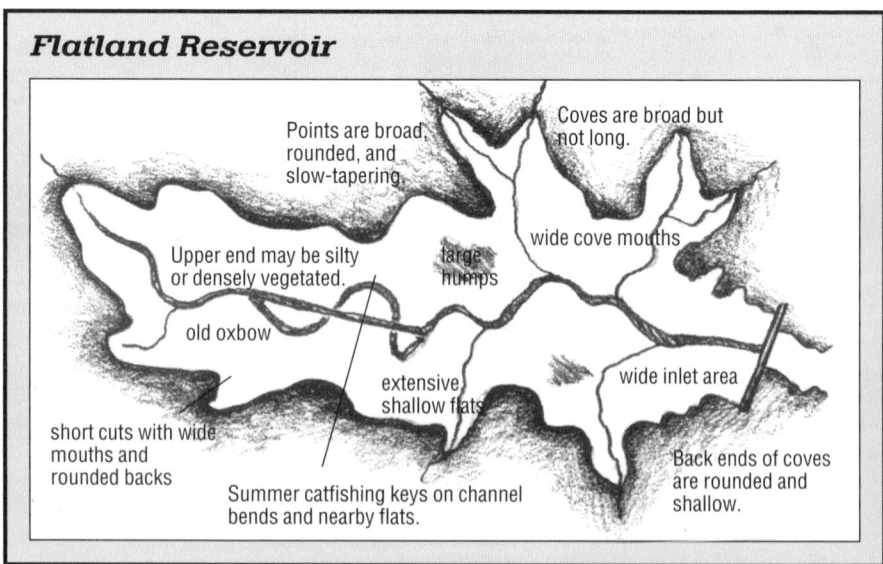

Points are broad, rounded, and slow-tapering.

Coves are broad but not long.

wide cove mouths

Upper end may be silty or densely vegetated.

large humps

old oxbow

wide inlet area

extensive shallow flats

short cuts with wide mouths and rounded backs

Back ends of coves are rounded and shallow.

Summer catfishing keys on channel bends and nearby flats.

Flatland Reservoirs—Flatland reservoirs are those built over watersheds with slight gradients, giving them a shallow basin with maximum depth near the dam of 20 to 40 feet. Their basins typically are soft with brush, timber, and stumps common throughout, unless the area had been farmed before impoundment.

These rounded reservoirs have relatively few major creeks but many small cuts that tend to be shallow and short. Small humps may be present, but the main river channel provides the most prominent depth break, although bridges, road beds, and other manmade structures are important features for fish and anglers.

Large expanses of shallow water make flatland reservoirs productive for plankton, baitfish, and predators. They tend to occur at the lower end of major river systems, and water color tends to be dark unless abundant aquatic vegetation is present to clear the water. Examples of prime catfish fisheries in flatland reservoirs include Lake Seminole (Georgia), Santee-Cooper (South Carolina), Carlisle (Illinois), Ross Barnett (Mississippi), and Castle Rock (Wisconsin).

Hill-Land Reservoirs—These mid-depth impoundments look like typical reservoirs, with a distinct Christmas-tree shape, due to increasingly larger creek arms at the downstream end and a narrowing at the dam. Their diverse habitat provides for a variety of gamefish, often including channel and flathead catfish, and blues in the south-central portion of the United States. Water color tends to be clearer than in flatland reservoirs, again due to abundant vegetation. Examples include Texoma (Texas-Oklahoma), W. F. George or Eufaula (Georgia-Alabama), Shelbyville (Illinois), Kinzua (Pennsylvania), and Sam Rayburn (Texas).

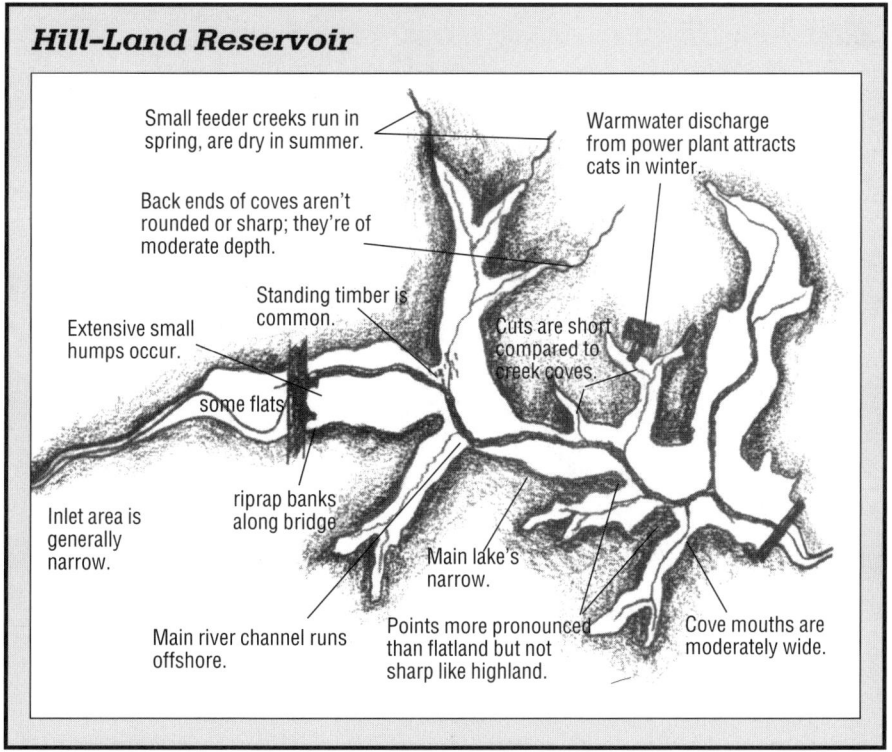

Hill-Land Reservoir

Small feeder creeks run in spring, are dry in summer.

Warmwater discharge from power plant attracts cats in winter.

Back ends of coves aren't rounded or sharp; they're of moderate depth.

Standing timber is common.

Extensive small humps occur.

Cuts are short compared to creek coves.

some flats

Inlet area is generally narrow.

riprap banks along bridge

Main lake's narrow.

Main river channel runs offshore.

Points more pronounced than flatland but not sharp like highland.

Cove mouths are moderately wide.

If power plants release warm water, these thermal plumes attract catfish during the coldest months of the year. Otherwise, catfish winter along the main river channel or in deep creek arms. In spring, some fish migrate to the next upstream dam. They're first caught, however, in deep timber adjacent to the channel. Here they feed on shad, herring, and other baitfish. Other groups of cats move into coves and creek arms with little or no flowing water, as warming conditions there draw prey of all sorts.

Highland Reservoirs—These deep, clear impoundments form when dams are built in mountainous regions, with rock and gravel the dominant substrate. They tend to have many long, deep coves that form over creeks, valleys, and gullies. Populations of all species are less numerous due to reduced primary productivity and limited preyfish.

Populations of channel and flathead catfish aren't large, though individual fish often reach trophy size, also true of other predators like striped bass, walleyes, and black bass in these impoundments. Highland reservoirs are concentrated along the Appalachian Mountains, though some occur in the West. Examples include Dale Hollow (Tennessee), Bull Shoals (Arkansas-Missouri), Amistad (Texas), and Lanier (Georgia).

The deep lower ends of highland reservoirs are predominately much deeper than catfish generally prefer, so fish occupy the shallower headwaters and concentrate around creeks, cuts, and pockets in the lower reaches. In spring, they push far into creek arms and backwaters to feed. Highland reservoirs also feature bluff banks that drop steeply into deep water, although they offer little feeding area compared to the broad flats of flatland reservoirs. Fish hold at the base of bluffs if water isn't too deep (40 feet or so), or along shelves and outcrops along the wall. These areas are effectively fished with banklines.

Highland Reservoir

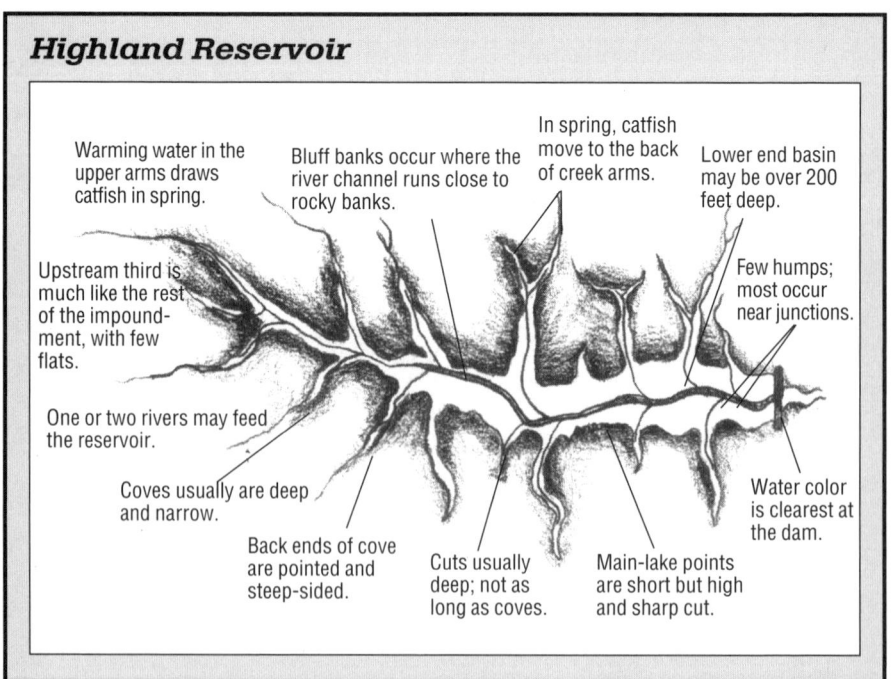

Warming water in the upper arms draws catfish in spring.

Bluff banks occur where the river channel runs close to rocky banks.

In spring, catfish move to the back of creek arms.

Lower end basin may be over 200 feet deep.

Upstream third is much like the rest of the impoundment, with few flats.

Few humps; most occur near junctions.

One or two rivers may feed the reservoir.

Coves usually are deep and narrow.

Water color is clearest at the dam.

Back ends of cove are pointed and steep-sided.

Cuts usually deep; not as long as coves.

Main-lake points are short but high and sharp cut.

Plateau Reservoir

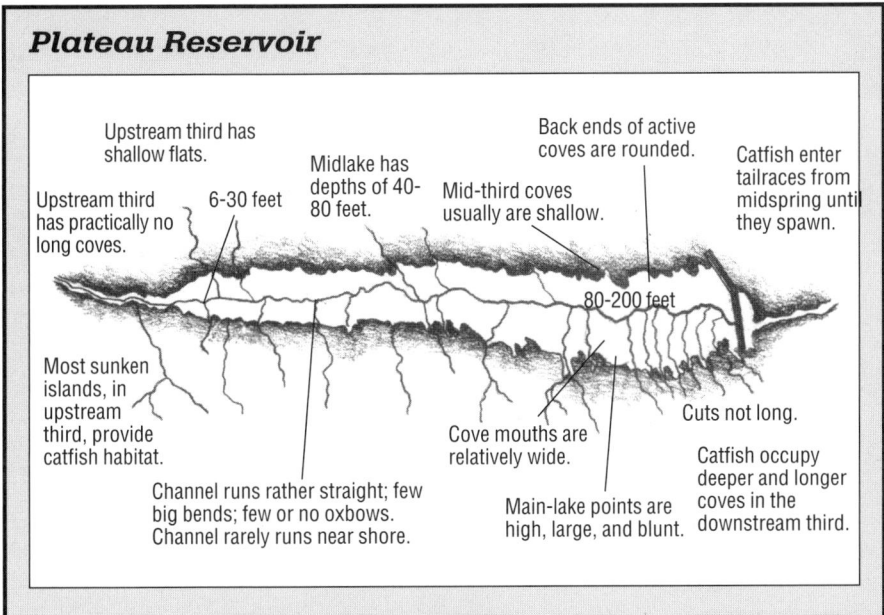

Upstream third has shallow flats.

Upstream third has practically no long coves.

6-30 feet

Midlake has depths of 40-80 feet.

Mid-third coves usually are shallow.

Back ends of active coves are rounded.

Catfish enter tailraces from midspring until they spawn.

80-200 feet

Most sunken islands, in upstream third, provide catfish habitat.

Channel runs rather straight; few big bends; few or no oxbows. Channel rarely runs near shore.

Cove mouths are relatively wide.

Main-lake points are high, large, and blunt.

Cuts not long.

Catfish occupy deeper and longer coves in the downstream third.

Highland reservoirs offer the best opportunity to catch catfish on artificials. First, clear water gives fish plenty of time to react to lures. Also, the relative scarcity of preyfish may make fish less particular about what they strike.

Narrower feeding zones also allow anglers familiar with a reservoir's underwater structure to present jigs, spoons, or crankbaits in high-percentage areas. Highland reservoirs also are conducive to trolling. And artificial offerings pulled along shoreline breaks take cats along with a variety of gamefish.

Plateau Reservoirs—Plateau reservoirs occur from the Missouri River west to eastern Oregon, where geologic formations include small tributaries and flat-topped humps. These impoundments tend to be broad and windswept, with moderate productivity.

Channel catfish predominate due to their location, and populations usually are moderate with a fairly small average size. These waters make prime walleye habitat, but the lack of shallow cover and rock sometimes limits catfish production. Examples include Oahe (South Dakota), Meredith (Texas), Fort Peck (Montana), Roosevelt (Arizona), and Banks (Washington).

As with other reservoir types, some catfish move to the next dam upstream in spring, providing good tailrace fishing for boat and bank anglers. Timbered backwaters also attract cats from spring through fall, with creek mouths and associated points key areas in late summer and fall. Plateau reservoirs feature humps that may rise to within 10 to 20 feet of the surface. Catfish, along with walleyes and sauger, feed on these structures, as well as on sand, gravel, or clay points. Check the deepest side for catfish.

Canyon Reservoirs—These deepest and clearest of impoundments run through western states. Built on major rivers like the Colorado, they're long and narrow with many long tributaries that run over 100 feet deep. The sand and rock substrate make them infertile. And while channel cats exist in many, populations generally are small.

Canyon Reservoir

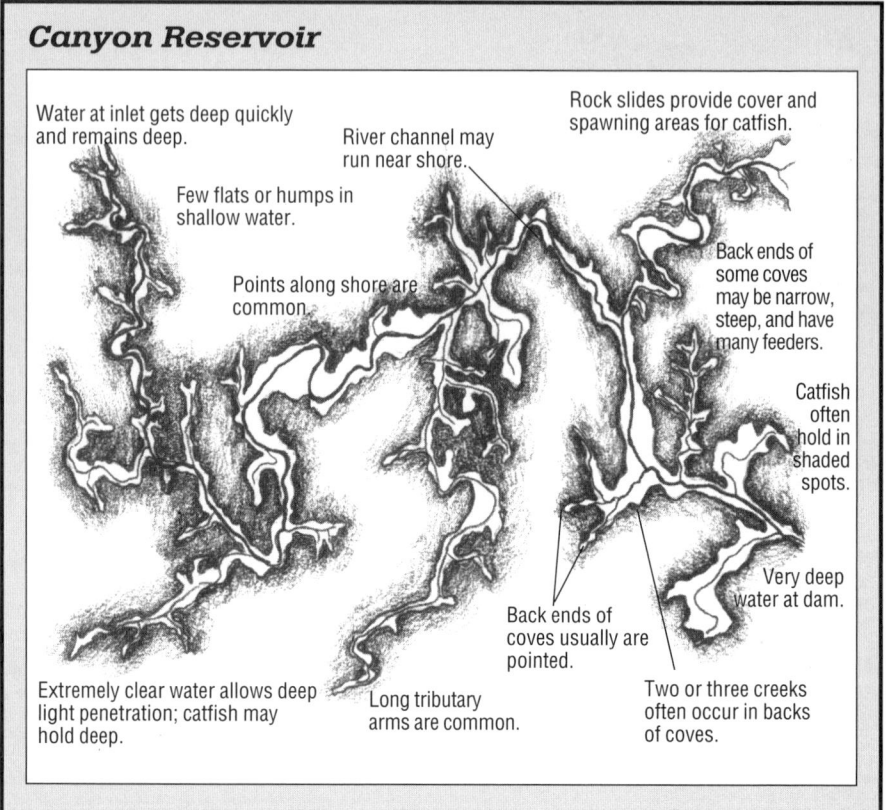

Water at inlet gets deep quickly and remains deep.

River channel may run near shore.

Rock slides provide cover and spawning areas for catfish.

Few flats or humps in shallow water.

Points along shore are common.

Back ends of some coves may be narrow, steep, and have many feeders.

Catfish often hold in shaded spots.

Back ends of coves usually are pointed.

Very deep water at dam.

Extremely clear water allows deep light penetration; catfish may hold deep.

Long tributary arms are common.

Two or three creeks often occur in backs of coves.

Some waters of this type produce outsize fish, though, like southern California's famous bass lakes, where anglers finessing livebaits often are thrilled by channel cats larger than the world-record largemouth. Examples of canyon reservoirs include Powell (Arizona-Utah), Flaming Gorge (Wyoming-Utah), Havasu (Arizona-California), Castaic (California), and Mead (Nevada-Arizona).

In late spring, catfish move to shallow arms that offer rock outcrops or other cover for spawning. At other times, look for cats along deep underwater points, relating to humps or submerged islands, or among deep boulders. While ultraclear water typically keeps catfish deep in canyon impoundments (they've been caught 160 feet deep in Lake Powell), feeding opportunities such as an insect hatch or schooling threadfin shad can draw them to the surface during daylight.

Lowland Reservoirs—Sometimes called flowages in Wisconsin or bayous in Louisiana, these impoundments resemble marshes more than classic reservoirs. They're biologically productive, however, and in catfish country, they're excellent fisheries. Lac Des Allemands in Louisiana contains huge populations of channel, blue, and flathead catfish, at an estimated biomass of 430 pounds of cats per acre.

Maximum depth might be only 20 feet, and creek channels are difficult to distinguish. Abundant shallow cover, stained water, and high organic content that results in a shallow thermocline generally keeps all fish species shallow.

Examples include Black Bayou (Louisiana), Chippewa Flowage (Wisconsin), Bond Falls (Michigan), and Taylor Creek (Florida).

Necked-down areas with increased current concentrate preyfish and catfish. During cooler months, deeper holes hold larger fish. Night fishing generally is most productive, as cats leave thick woodcover and feed on open flats where bait presentation is easier.

Major River Pools—While this category of impoundment isn't included in the original In-Fisherman reservoir classification, the segments of big rivers, divided by locks and dams, provide major catfish fisheries in the Midwest and Southeast. The Mississippi and Ohio rivers are prime examples, while narrow sections of the Missouri, Tennessee, Cumberland, Chattahoochee, and many others fit the pattern.

In spring, some cats, primarily channels, roam quieter spots in the spillways of the upstream dam. As water warms, they move to deeper and faster areas that provide better feeding. During the first half of the season, the upper third of the pool holds most catfish, with fish spreading downstream after the spawn.

Rock dikes and wing dams, built to improve barge travel, hold channel cats from midsummer through winter, though the portion of the rock structure that fish use changes seasonally.

In summer, active fish hold on the upstream side of structures to feed on drifting edibles or to prey on smaller fish using the structures. The deepest wing dams provide wintering habitat by creating deep holes with little current. Other key spots in major river pools are tributaries (fish the ledge off the delta and larger pools near the big river); backwaters, both natural (oxbows) and manmade (harbors); deep riprap banks or points; and major storm drains.

Although the pace of reservoir construction has slowed greatly in recent decades, agencies still build small reservoirs for fishing. In arid regions, however, new reservoirs continue to be built. Nearly all support populations of one or more of the major catfish species, and many have excellent and untapped fisheries to explore.

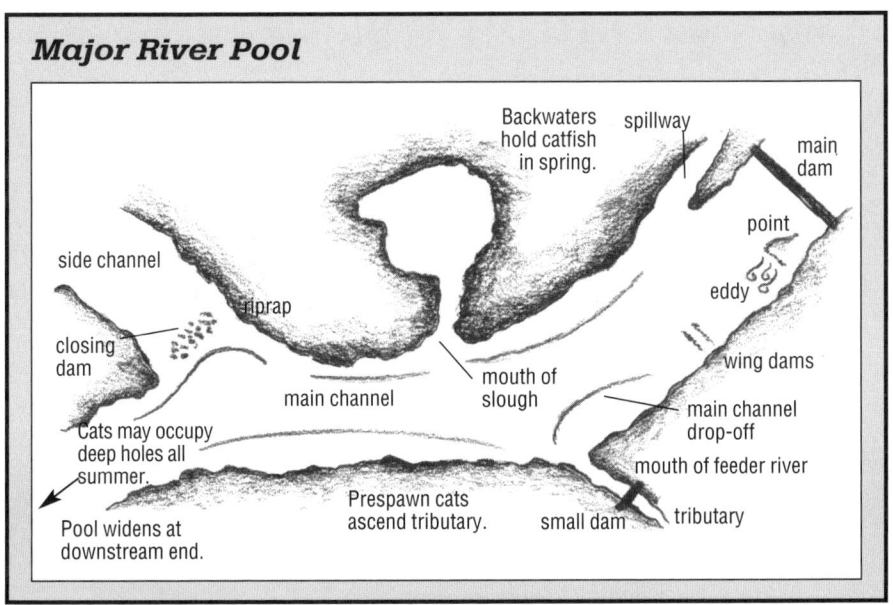

Major River Pool

Backwaters hold catfish in spring.
spillway
main dam
point
side channel
eddy
riprap
closing dam
wing dams
mouth of slough
main channel
main channel drop-off
Cats may occupy deep holes all summer.
mouth of feeder river
Prespawn cats ascend tributary.
small dam
tributary
Pool widens at downstream end.

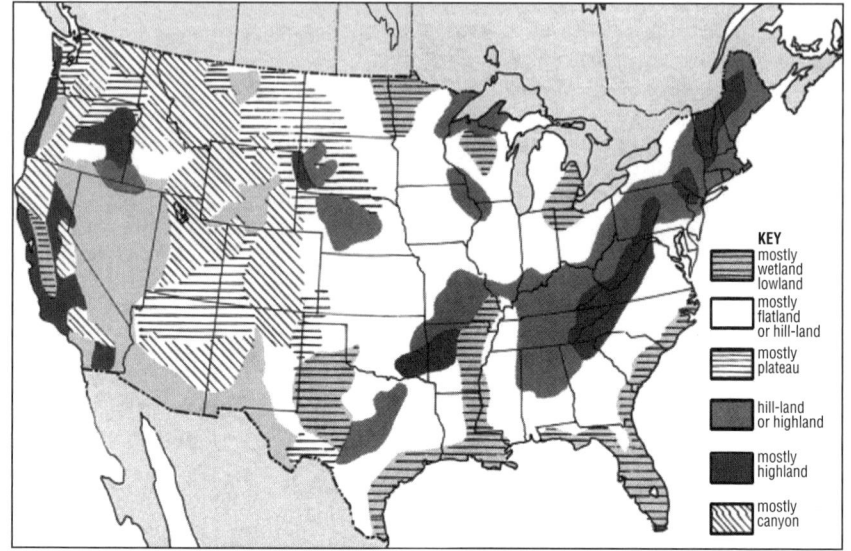

Impoundment Range Map

KEY
- mostly wetland lowland
- mostly flatland or hill-land
- mostly plateau
- hill-land or highland
- mostly highland
- mostly canyon

Reservoirs constructed in similar landforms even when they're in different parts of the country are enough alike to fit into six basic groups: canyon, plateau, highland, hill-land, flatland, and lowland (wetland).

WATER QUALITY FACTORS

Catfish are similar to largemouth bass in their oxygen requirements. They can survive at oxygen levels as low as 2 ppm (parts per million), but at least 5 ppm are required to sustain a healthy population. Most catfish species are stressed when oxygen levels fall below 3 ppm, and at 2 ppm they're forced to gulp air from the surface.

The effect of water clarity on catfish isn't clear, but with their highly developed senses of taste, smell, and hearing, catfish seem well adapted to turbid water. This gives them an advantage over sight-feeding predators in murky rivers and reservoirs, and in fertile lakes and ponds.

Few fish can match the channel cat for tolerating a broad range of temperatures. They survive extended temperatures in the low 30°F range during winter. They usually aren't active for long periods and don't gain weight at such low temperatures, but they continue to feed during extended periods of cold weather. On the other end of the scale, channel cats survive temperatures over 95°F in southern Georgia and Florida.

Two factors affect how fish respond to temperature. Many fish, possibly including channel cats, have genetic sub-types (such as Florida and northern largemouth bass) adapted to different environmental conditions such as temperature. So channel cats in Manitoba may be genetically different than Alabama cats. Fish also acclimate to certain water temperatures. When a fish acclimated to one temperature is suddenly introduced to much warmer or cooler water, it becomes stressed and may die.

Water Quality Needs

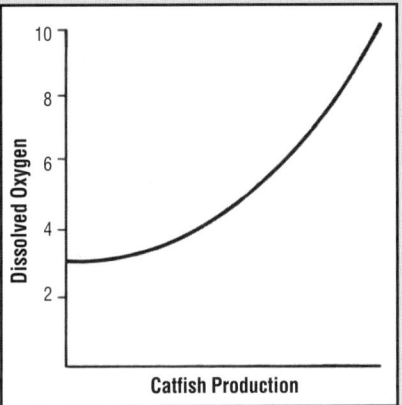

Catfish Production

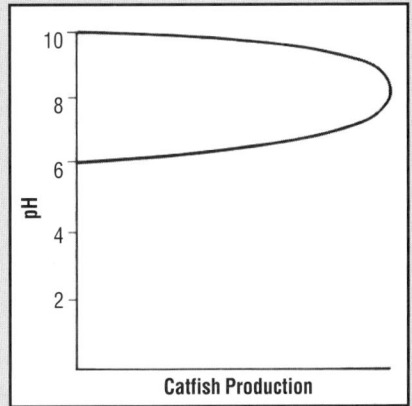

Catfish Production

Besides temperature, dissolved oxygen probably is the most widely studied environmental parameter. Catfish do best when dissolved oxygen concentrations are over 7 mg/l (parts per million). When dissolved oxygen drops to 3 mg/l cats are stressed, more likely contract diseases, and growth slows. Below 2 mg/l catfish and other species often rise to the surface to breathe air. In lab studies, cats have survived dissolved oxygen levels slightly below 1 mg/l for short periods of time.

A measure of hydrogen ion concentration, pH, is critical for maintaining the chemical balance within a catfish's body. Negative effects of low pH (acidic water), from acid rain and other causes, on fish populations have been documented. High-altitude northern ponds and rocky streams are most susceptible to acidification. Such waters aren't catfish habitat. Normal pH ranges of 6.5 to 8.5 seem best for catfish production. Populations suffer as alkalinity increases above 9.5 or acidity drops below 5.5.

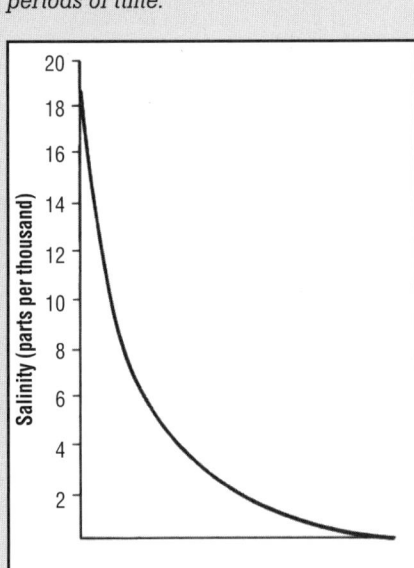

Channel cats are typically freshwater fish. In eastern catfish rivers like the Connecticut and Hudson, channel catfish populations dwindle and white cats, known to be more tolerant of a broad range of salinity, dominate brackish downstream reaches. Yet in the St. Lawrence River, channel cats have been collected in salinities as high as 20 parts per thousand, more than half-strength seawater. In Louisiana bayous, channel cats also occur in brackish areas. In these situations, however, growth is slow, even stunted. Lab studies also have shown detrimental effects of salt.

Truth About Temperature

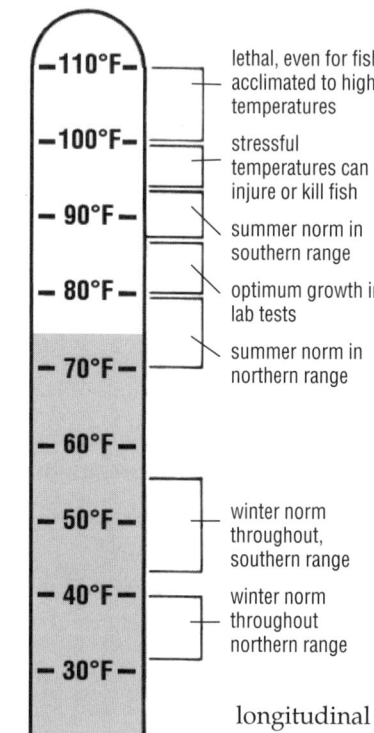

−110°F− — lethal, even for fish acclimated to high temperatures

−100°F− — stressful temperatures can injure or kill fish

− 90°F − — summer norm in southern range

− 80°F − — optimum growth in lab tests

− 70°F − — summer norm in northern range

− 60°F −

− 50°F − — winter norm throughout, southern range

− 40°F − — winter norm throughout northern range

− 30°F −

Fish are poikilotherms, meaning cold-blooded or unable to regulate body temperature. Basically, their body temperature is determined by their surroundings.

Laboratories allow controlled testing of temperatures that fish choose to stay in. Lab tests of young channel catfish generally show excellent survival and growth at 82°F to 87°F as long as sufficient food is provided. Temperatures of 92°F to 94°F can cause damage that belatedly kills fish accustomed to temperatures in the mid-80°F range. Yet for young cats accustomed to the low 90°F range, it may take 100°F to cause large-scale mortality.

In North America, channel catfish are found from southern Canada to southern Florida, a longitudinal range of about 1,900 miles. The Red River population, near the northern edge of catfish range, grows fast, and individuals achieve huge size. Yet water temperatures remain in the 30°F range for five to six months. At the southern edge of the channel catfish range, summer surface water temperatures reach the low 90°F range and rarely drop below 50°F for extended periods in winter, yet growth in many cases isn't faster than in Manitoba.

Channel catfish are highly adaptable and most waters across the United States can support healthy populations, yet it's likely that Florida cats brought to Manitoba wouldn't thrive. Future stockings should be considered carefully so the best-adapted genetic stocks are used.

Catfish are temperature tolerant but are more active and healthy at a specific temperature range. The temperature preference for channel cats—that is, the temperature that produces the fastest growth rate—is from 75°F to 80°F, similar to the ideal range for sunfish and largemouth bass. Don't be too impressed with numbers, though, since channel cats and other catfish species can be caught in water much cooler than 75°F and much warmer than 80°F.

Catfish Movements In Rivers

RADIO TRACKING CATS   Documenting habitat preferences of catfish is a tool in maintaining strong fisheries. And it provides clues to where you should be fishing.

When transmitters small enough to be implanted in fish were developed, a "gee whiz" attitude prevailed. For the first time, researchers and others who read their reports knew precisely where and when fish moved in a body of water. Studies provided new biological information to help anglers understand their quarry.

In two decades since those pioneering studies, biologists have learned to use telemetry as a tool for defining habitat essential to fish. Describing the characteristics of areas radio-tagged fish prefer allows biologists to manage these areas for good fish habitat.

Habitat studies are particularly critical for catfish and other river species because of the great changes made in these systems since European explorers reached the continent. Habitat research demonstrates how much good fish habitat has been lost through dam building, channelization, siltation, urban run-off, negligent dumping, toxic spills, deforestation along stream banks, and pollution from farming.

It might be assumed that such abuses would cease once their effects were documented. On the contrary, plans still exist to dam, divert, alter, and pollute rivers that provide habitat for fish and fishing spots for you. In an effort to preserve these areas, recent radio telemetry studies documented ways fish use different types of habitat.

SOUTH DAKOTA CATFISH STUDIES

For over 20 years, Dr. Chuck Berry, leader of the South Dakota Cooperative Fish and Wildlife Research Unit, located at South Dakota State University, has studied fish populations in warmwater streams in Virginia, Utah, and South Dakota. He has recently completed investigations of catfish populations in the James and Vermillion rivers in South Dakota, rivers that twist through farmlands in the eastern part of the state.

Dr. Berry: "Several sampling methods provide information about habitat needs of catfish and other species. Methods vary for juvenile fish and adults. In the James River (known locally as the *Jim*), graduate student Rick Walsh blocked off sections of river that contained snags, rock dams, tributaries, and rocky stretches, from which he collected fish with a seine.

Walsh found that adult crappie, pike, catfish, and walleye were twice as abundant in river sections that contained complex features than in stretches primarily consisting of runs with little instream structure or cover.

"The Jim originates near Fessenden, North Dakota, and flows south to its confluence with the Missouri River near Yankton, South Dakota, a distance of 747 miles. It's murky, due to its low gradient (about 4 inches per mile) and nutrients and silt from farmland runoff. Catfish are an important species, making up about 25 percent of the total angler catch in the Jim.

"Walsh found that adult crappie, pike, catfish, and walleye were twice as abundant in river sections that contained complex features than in stretches primarily consisting of runs with little instream structure or cover. Catfish were most abundant around low-head dams, pike and walleye abundance peaked in areas with a hard bottom, and crappies dominated around snags.

"The lack of catfish around snags was surprising since catfish anglers frequently do well there. Seines, however, don't fish well around branchy snags. They work well in moderately deep holes below low-head dams and over rocky crossings.

"Seining documented that catfish in the James occupy holes below rocky riffles. Prey are abundant in these spots, and catfish use the structure and cover to prey at opportune times. Catfish also hold in these spots during their seasonal migrations.

"Graduate student Steve Kubeny used radio telemetry to identify preferred habitat of adult channel cats and to describe the physical, chemical, and biological aspects of this habitat. He collected cats with hoop nets and trotline and surgically implanted transmitters in 12 of the largest. He documented over 200 locations of individual fish between May and September 1991.

"Among stream researchers is a belief that 90 percent of the fish live in 10 percent of available habitat. That's about right in the Jim. Ninety percent of the study area lacks instream cover, but catfish were found there only 18 percent of the time. Channel cats spent about 72 percent of their time near some type of woodcover.

"All types of woodcover can be considered snags, but some are more attractive than others. Catfish preferred snag complexes with three or more logs, followed by single fallen trees with branches, then one or two logs without branches, and finally root wads. Kubeny found cats more often in snag complexes than in all other types of snags. But depth and bottom content around a snag also were important.

"Catfish favored complex snags with nearby water from 3 to 6 feet

Documenting catfish habitat preferences helps maintain strong fisheries and provides clues to where anglers should be fishing.

deep. Although most of the study area was less than 3 feet deep, only 2 percent of the catfish locations were that shallow. Cats most often occupied areas with sand or silt substrate. But the Jim has predominately a sand and silt bottom. At times, areas with rock and gravel were favored.

"Radio-tagged cats spent considerable time around rock dams, as Rick Walsh verified in his seining study. Even in this slow-moving river, adult cats favored the slowest water, usually moving less than a foot per second. Kubeny compared nocturnal and daytime habitat preferences and found no major shift in preferred cover type, depth, substrate, or current speed.

"A study by graduate student Pat Braaten documented the importance of snags to juvenile cats in the Vermillion River, a smaller, faster-flowing stream just east of the Jim. Braaten collected fish with an electric seine and determined that channel catfish were the dominant gamefish in the river. Snags near rocky areas rather than snags over a silty bottom were most productive for young cats. The abundance of young cats suggested that the Vermillion acts as a nursery area for the Missouri River."

All snags are potential catfish attractors, though some are more attractive than others. Complex snags adjacent to deep water usually hold the most and biggest fish.

SNAGOLOGY

Dr. Berry continues: "Savvy catfish anglers pride themselves in their ability to read rivers and snags. In some rivers, they find much more reading material than in others. Unfortunately, these observations and good catches fishermen make aren't enough to protect rivers like the James from alteration.

"Engineers view snags as large, dangerous piles of trees that cause flooding and threaten bridges. Proposals to reduce the duration of floods usually involve removing logjams, overhanging trees, sandbars, and low-head dams—habitats catfish favor." Researchers at South Dakota State have been studying 'snagology' to prevent loss of this important cover. In the James, snags provide important habitat for channel catfish and other species of gamefish like crappies, walleyes, and pike. Juvenile gamefish and minnows also used this habitat.

"Fishery biologists recognize that snags also are prime sites for invertebrates. In the Jim, researcher Dave Schumacher found 31 kinds of invertebrates on snags. These invertebrates numbered about 37,000 critters per square foot, a productivity crucial for growth of young fish.

"Snags also seem to create deeper pools through scouring action. Deeper pools may be critical habitat for overwintering or during low water levels in summer. Snags are lost during flooding or through decay, so providing a wooded corridor along the bank of the river is necessary for a continual supply of new snags. As trees die, they provide new fish habitat. And living trees stabilize banks, provide shade and cooler temperatures, and add organic material to the food chain.

"We recognize that snags threatening navigation, bridges, docks, or other structures should be removed. The American Fisheries Society and The Wildlife Society jointly developed the following set of guidelines for removing stream obstructions.

Remove logjams that block flow or are a hazard; leave those that don't cause problems. Cut logs at the waterline to maintain attachment sites for invertebrates and habitat for fish; reposition logs close to the bank to improve flow and prevent erosion. From an angler viewpoint, these guidelines are mostly common sense," Dr. Berry concludes.

Large-scale snagging programs are underway in rivers in other parts of the country. Data from projects at South Dakota State University and others in Nebraska, Minnesota, Missouri, and elsewhere will be useful in protecting snag habitat. Anglers should monitor the streams they fish to check snagging operations. In some cases, political pressure from individuals and angler groups, supported by scientific data, may be needed to keep rivers natural.

Steve Kubeny's study wasn't intended to document how far catfish may swim, but it verified the great distances some cats move in the Missouri River system and other major rivers. During high water, one radio-tagged catfish moved from the James River, down the Missouri, and up the Platte River in Nebraska, a journey of about 400 miles.

Coincidentally, this excursion led it to the Platte River in Nebraska where Dr. Ed Peters and his colleagues at the University of Nebraska, Lincoln, were conducting a telemetry study. Radio-tagged fish often disappeared from study areas, but researchers are unsure if the radio failed or if the fish moved beyond the limits of reasonable search.

Tagging studies also have documented long trips by catfish. In the Mississippi River, a fish released at Lake City, Minnesota, was caught 33 months later in the Minnesota River at New Ulm, about 215 miles away. Another cat moved 111 miles downstream in 36 days during the spring of 1948, averaging 3.1 miles per day and passing three lock-and-dam structures. In 1991, a catfish tagged in the Red River in Manitoba traveled 217 miles in 13 days.

NEBRASKA CATFISH STUDIES

The Platte River of eastern Nebraska, meandering through farm country, is another wide shallow river of shifting sandbars. Corn and soybeans are primary cash crops and their intensive culture demands water. From May through September, irrigation systems suck water from the river, reducing the quality of fish habitat and habitat of endangered birds, including the least tern, piping plover, and whooping crane.

The Platte is an important fishery resource in eastern Nebraska, where water is limited. And channel catfish are the most abundant and popular gamefish in the river. Yet little information about the catfish population existed.

Water management regulations have established limits on water removal during summer, but proposals have been submitted to the Director of the Nebraska Department of Water Resources to withdraw water from the Platte during winter when "excess flows" are present. This water would be stored in reservoirs until summer.

Reducing water levels during winter might severely limit wintering habitat for catfish—deep holes with reduced current.

Dr. Peters and other biologists note that reducing water levels during winter might severely limit wintering habitat for catfish—deep holes with reduced current. In 1984, the Nebraska legislature passed a law giving the Game and Parks Commission and local Natural Resource Districts authority to request that flows be maintained to benefit fish and wildlife.

To determine appropriate flows, the researchers used a set of computer models called Instream Flow Incremental Methodology. The models can predict the impacts of water diversion schedules on fish, once the habitat needs of fish species are documented. Radio telemetry, along with sampling of juvenile catfish, tag returns, growth rates, age structure, and mortality provide data for the models.

During 1986 and 1987, radio-tagged adult channel cats didn't occupy water shallower than 14 inches, but often were located in water from 16 to 48 inches deep. The research team considered depths over five feet most suitable for adult catfish. Deep water is scarce in the Platte, sometimes described as "a mile wide and an inch deep."

Adult channel catfish used areas with cover most of the time, usually logs or snags connected to the bank. The bottom in preferred areas was sandy, and current was rather slow (up to 1.3 feet per second). They avoided faster water.

From 1988 through 1990, Dr. Peters implanted transmitters in 45 channel cats and monitored them during all seasons. During spring, adult cats moved upstream during 54 percent of the observations, with the remainder sedentary or making only local movements. During summer, local shifts were dominant (86 percent). Upstream and downstream shifts were equal, 7 percent each.

During fall, 67 percent of movements were downstream, with the remainder local. During winter, all movements were downstream. Fish moving downstream moved fastest, benefiting from current and perhaps in a hurry to evacuate shallow fast water as it cooled.

Adult catfish spent the coldest months in deep pools with reduced current, where they moved little and didn't feed for weeks. Catfish from the lower Platte moved downstream to winter in deep scour pools in the Missouri River, moving back upstream to spawn in spring. Peters raised the possibility that catfish in the Platte may not spawn every year.

Although catfish growth rates in the Platte aren't unusually slow for rivers of the Great Plains, fish take four to six years to reach 12 inches and 10 years to reach 21 inches and about 3 pounds. Cold winters force migration to overwintering pools and return migrations to spawn. Summer water temperatures, in the upper 80°F range, appear to slow growth. Also, water is generally shallower than ideal for catfish, and large fluctuations are common.

Fish may skip years between spawning when they lack energy reserves to develop healthy eggs and sperm, particularly if spawning involves a migration or the defense of eggs or young, which substantially increases the likelihood of death during the spawn. Further studies are needed to prove or disprove this theory; but if true, it will provide evidence of the further need to improve catfish habitat.

RED RIVER CATS

The Red River, which flows from southern North Dakota to Lake Winnipeg in Manitoba, holds the world's most remarkable trophy channel catfish fishery. In the upper reaches of the river in northern Minnesota, North Dakota, and Manitoba, cats average 18 to 20 pounds. A 30 is possible, and a record 44-pounder has been taken near the dam in Lockport.

Maintaining this incredible fishery is an obvious mandate, and the three governing bodies—Minnesota, North Dakota, and Manitoba—have cooperated with reduced harvest regulations. Yet other forces threaten catfish there. Don MacDonald's initial tracking studies of cats found that many large fish were attracted to a warm-water effluent from a coal bunting station on Cooks Creek. During the winter of 1987-1988, fish kills of giant catfish occurred when the warm effluent stopped in midwinter, quickly dropping the water temperature in the creek.

Dave Tyson, a graduate student, has been following radio-tagged catfish to study their movements in relation to the warmwater discharge. When the water temperature in the Red River falls into the 40°F range, a warm-water plume attracts thousands of big catfish. This unnatural aggregation can lead to disease and starvation, in addition to a threat of huge fish-kills due to falling water temperatures if plant operations stop.

The solution has been to reduce warm outflows during fall, so cats aren't attracted.

The Red River of the North is the premier destination for trophy channel cats.

Once the river is in the upper 30°F range, warm water doesn't attract the sedentary catfish. A fence also keeps large fish out.

Tyson has documented that Red River catfish range widely through most of Lake Winnipeg, swimming upstream through the Lockport Dam when the fishway is operating. Many juvenile catfish live in tributaries on the east side of Lake Winnipeg. Tyson theorizes that this large and variable habitat may be a factor in catfish reaching trophy size.

It takes about 20 years, however, for a channel catfish in the Red River to reach 20 pounds, and 7 to 9 years to reach adulthood, at the large size of about 26 inches. Females apparently don't spawn each summer. In other waters like the James and Platte rivers, cats may spawn at 12 to 14 inches.

The dam at Lockport restricts natural movements of catfish, but is passable most of the time. Proposals have been made to fill and drain marshes and wetlands adjacent to the Red River, to divert the Assiniboine River, and to build flood-control dams. Tracking studies and other biological sampling suggest that these alterations would be harmful and could be disastrous to populations of catfish, walleyes, pike, and preyfish like goldeye. Conservation agencies, angler groups, and environmental advocates can use the data to oppose such projects or to create a water management plan that maintains minimum flows.

OTHER TRACKING STUDIES

Missouri River—The Missouri Department of Conservation conducted a radio-telemetry study of the winter habitat of channel and flathead catfish in the central Missouri stretch of the Missouri River. Ten channel cats were implanted during the fall of 1982 and followed into the next spring. In 1983, eight more were tagged.

During the mild winter of 1982, cats moved mostly downstream, as they did in the Platte River. Some fish moved little while others moved up to 73 miles. Biologist

Catfish Migrations

A recent report on one of the largest channel catfish tagging projects reveals seasonal migration patterns on the lower Wisconsin River and its confluence with the Mississippi River*. Biologists with the Wisconsin Department of Natural Resources (DNR) and U. S. Geological Survey tagged over 10,000 cats during the mid-1980s and collected tags for the next decade. Many fish were recaptured several times, some over a period of several years. The study area extended from the Prairie du Sac Dam on the Wisconsin River to the Mississippi River in Pool 10.

Biologists concluded that this population is migratory. Catfish living in the lower Wisconsin River during summer migrate downstream to the Mississippi River in fall and spend the winter there, with a reverse migration in spring. A segment of the population also migrate to wintering holes below the Prairie du Sac dam.

As migrants, channel catfish can exploit spawning and feeding habitats in shallow rivers during summer and retreat to the safety of deep-water habitats in winter. Wisconsin River channel cats also home annually to specific locations, the first documentation of this behavior by channel catfish in rivers.

Construction of dams on the Mississippi River and its tributaries has, according to researchers, fragmented channel catfish migrations and possibly reduced their numbers. Impassable dams can prevent recolonization of isolated river reaches when stocks are decimated by environmental degradation, disease, or catastrophic events.

*Pellett, T. D., G. J. Van Dyck, and J. V. Adams. 1998. Seasonal migration and homing of channel catfish in the Lower Wisconsin River, Wisconsin. N. Am. J. Fish. Mngt. 18:85-95.

Tim Grace noted a few short upstream movements, including two fish that entered the Osage River. Reservoir releases of warm water upstream at Lake of the Ozarks apparently attracted the cats. Catfish in the warm effluent were more active.

Some catfish moved short distances up tributaries and wintered in 10- to 20-foot holes, while others stayed in deep holes at the mouths of tributaries. During the following winter, which was much colder, catfish moved less. In the Missouri River, channel catfish selected the deepest available holes, some 25 to 30 feet deep.

Deep holes reduced current and provided relative temperature stability. Huge aggregations formed with hundreds or even thousands of cats apparently crammed into a 5- or 10-acre area. Flatheads and channel cats sometimes used the same wintering holes, but flatheads generally favored deep holes behind dikes, rather than holes at tributary mouths.

In late March or April, cats began moving upstream, often into tributaries with potential spawning areas. Upstream movements continued into June when spawning typically began.

Mississippi River, Pool 13—Also during the winter of 1982-1983, Doug Stange and Dr. John Nickum of the Iowa Cooperative Fishery Research Unit radio tagged catfish in Pool 13, which extends 34 miles between Bellevue and Clinton, Iowa. This study was in response to a proposal to dump dredge spoils into deep holes in the river. The researchers feared that such dumping might destroy winter habitat for channel and flathead catfish and other species. Data was needed to support opposition to the proposal.

Several channel cats and buffalo left the pool, moving downstream to Pool 14. All flatheads remained, however. Most channel cats wintered in deep areas bordering the main channel, though some stayed in side channels, and a few entered backwaters. Most channel and flathead catfish wintered over sandy bottoms. Flatheads wintered in the deepest available water (average depth 24 feet) while channel cats held at average depths of 14 feet. Individuals of both species stayed as deep as 38 feet. Channel cats found cover behind sandbars and wing dams while flatheads stayed near riprap and rocky areas.

During spring and summer, the researchers found channel cats in flooded timber in backwater lakes and sloughs. These areas had minimal current and likely served as spawning sites. The researchers recommended that dredge materials not be dumped in deep areas likely used by catfish in winter.

An even closer look at catfish wintering areas occurred when fisheries personnel with the Minnesota and Wisconsin Departments of Natural Resources donned scuba gear during February for a look at aggregations of catfish in Pool 4 of the Mississippi River. Divers reported scores of adult cats huddled in minimal current behind rocks, sticks, or other catfish. They were flat on the bottom, facing upstream in 16 to 25 feet of water.

Variability in movement patterns has been noted in other catfish populations and in tracking studies of other species.

Catfish appeared dormant, with scarcely any gill movement. They could be handled with little response. Some were covered with a layer of silt, suggesting a long period of dormancy.

Wisconsin River—Biologists with the Wisconsin DNR followed 130 radio-tagged channel cats in the lower Wisconsin River from 1983 to 1986. Some fish remained in small home areas while others made long excursions. Variability in movement patterns has been noted in other catfish populations and in tracking studies of other species. In the Wisconsin River, catfish occupied wintering areas similar to those in the Missouri and Mississippi rivers. Some cats shifted wintering areas in midwinter, however. In spring, fish that wintered in the Mississippi typically moved into the Wisconsin when high flows coincided with rising river temperatures. Some fish returned to spawning areas they'd used the year before.

Catfish frequently moved directly to far-flung spots on the river, as though they knew where they were going. During the spawning season, catfish often were found in the shallowest and narrowest stretches of river they occupied all year. These spots offered logs, rocks, and undercut banks for laying and protecting eggs. Summer home ranges often were nearby, usually downstream from spawning sites.

As in other rivers, summer brought generally restricted movement. The fish that swam from the Mississippi River at the mouth of the Wisconsin to St. Louis in less than six weeks were an exception. Catfish used snags and holes, as researchers found in the James and Platte rivers.

Fall signaled a major locational shift, almost the opposite of the spring upstream movement. Cats didn't make a mass migration, but gradually shifted toward winter sanctuaries.

Wisconsin River Survey

A large study of the the Lower Wisconsin conducted by the Wisconsin Department of Natural Resources showed that suggesting a generalized channel cat movement in one direction or the other during fall would be a mistake. While some fish moved downstream from the Lower Wisconsin to the Mississippi, others stayed in the Lower Wisconsin and moved upstream. Thirty-three percent of the fall implants released between Lone Rock and Mazomanie moved upstream to the Prairie du Sac Dam, where they spent the winter. Forty-seven percent of the fish released in the Prairie du Sac area overwintered there as well. The study found no movement of channel cats from the Mississippi to the Lower Wisconsin during fall.

Additional channel cat telemetry studies show that the direction of fall movement of channel cats differs from one river to another. A 1992 study, for example, observed that twice as many channel cats in the lower Platte River moved downstream in fall as those that moved locally. A 1989 project also determined that in fall, all movements of tagged fish from Perche Creek were downstream into the Mississippi. But in 1963, one researcher reported that 60.5 percent of tagged channel cats in the Mississippi River were recovered upstream. Go figure.

These tracking studies document the following trends in channel catfish seasonal movements: wintering in deep, quiet areas of large rivers; upstream movements into tributaries or upper reaches to spawn; localized movements in summer; downstream movements toward wintering spots in fall.

Studies show that catfish populations have tolerated most river alterations, though in many areas, populations are stressed because of environmental effects and overharvest. State and provincial agencies finally are facing the need to regulate catfish harvest as strictly as bass harvest. Growth rates, fecundity, production schedules, and mortality suggest that catfish are as vulnerable to overfishing as any other gamefish.

Continued degradation of rivers, however, is the greatest threat to catfish populations. After a series of river alterations, a single new project can push a population over the edge. Such is the case with salmon on the West Coast, and we have no reason to think it can't happen in our favorite catfish rivers.

SOLVING THE MYSTERY OF THE DISAPPEARING CHANNEL CATFISH

The old river rats have known about it for years. Each fall, channel catfish mysteriously disappear from their traditional warm-weather haunts. Casual catfish anglers continue to halfheartedly probe their favorite river holes for another week or two, then surrender the season and hang up their tackle for the winter.

But the old river rats grin and motor around the bend, only to return a few hours later with a stringer of fat channel cats. They'll confess only to knowing of a secret hole where they regularly catch catfish until ice finally imprisons the river.

A similar scene happens each spring just after ice-out, when casual catfish anglers head for their favorite summertime fishing holes, eager to catch their first stringer of cats for the year. They set up near their favorite logjam or cut-bank, watching the river rat force his boat back into a flooded slough.

The casual angler drowns a few worms, wastes some cheese bait, and gags on rotten shad fumes, but never lands a catfish before giving up and heading home to dine on frozen fish patties. An hour later, the river rat motors out of the slough, a stringer of channel cats flopping at his feet.

Those old river rats know what fisheries biologists now have proven with high-tech radio-tracking studies: While channel catfish generally are homebodies and loyal to small, specific territories during warm weather, they make major migrations each winter and spring. Knowing when and where catfish move is the key to year-round catfishing success.

CREATING A CATFISH CALENDAR

A study conducted on the Wapsipinicon River in northeast Iowa by Gary Siegwarth, fishery biologist with the Iowa Department of Natural Resources, underlines the findings of biologists in other states and rivers. Forty-one channel catfish weighing from one to eight pounds were surgically implanted with small radio transmitters and monitored for up to 2 years in Siegwarth's study.

The Wapsipinicon is a typical small midwestern river with snag-filled holes alternating with sandy flats and a few rocky riffles. As expected, the radio-tagged cats spent their summers dispersed through the 15-mile study area, from a dam at Independence downstream to a dam at Quasqueton.

"The cats showed a strong affinity for a home territory during summer," Siegwarth says. "They generally had a home area and stayed there from late June through the end of September, except for sudden, unexplained movements up or downstream for a day or two."

Vacationing behavior also was noted in a similar study on the lower Wisconsin River and adjacent Mississippi River by Don Fago of the Wisconsin Department of Natural Resources. Fago radio-tagged 134 channel

Continued degradation of rivers is the greatest threat to catfish populations.

catfish and monitored their movements in the Wisconsin and Mississippi river systems. The majority of Fago's tagged catfish tended to stay within a well-defined home territory throughout the summer, but a few took unexplained long-distance vacations.

"Some of our fish that were 70 miles up the Wisconsin River for no apparent reason traveled downstream all the way to the Mississippi River for a couple days, maybe a week, then returned upstream to almost the exact place where they'd started," Fago says. "This occurred in late spring, so it may have been related to spawning, but all we can report with certainty is what they did, not why they did it."

The most striking movements recorded by Fago and Siegwarth were universal migrations of their radio-tagged subjects each fall and spring. "What impressed me about the migrations on the Wapsipinicon was how precise the cats were in where they wintered," Siegwarth says. "On that 15-mile stretch of river, all the radio-tagged catfish went to one of just three wintering holes."

Siegwarth's subjects moved directly to their wintering holes in a matter of days when water temperatures fell to 40°F each fall. "They showed no signs of scouting or shopping for where they wanted to spend the winter," he adds. "Our fish all were several years old, so they could have been using memory or scent to return to those exact wintering holes."

The three wintering holes in Siegwarth's study always were the deepest holes in that portion of river. One hole was below a dam, one was below a bridge, and the third was a dredged sandpit in the river channel. Siegwarth noted that his catfish not only returned to specific wintering holes, but also to specific locations within each hole. "They always were in the deepest part of the hole in an area with absolutely no current," Siegwarth says. "Once there, they remained in that small area pretty much for the entire winter."

Fago found more mobility during winter among his radio-tagged catfish in the Wisconsin and Mississippi rivers. While his fish were equally prompt and universal in moving to wintering grounds when water temperatures approached 40°F, they moved as much as a mile upstream or downstream during winter. "That was a bit of a surprise, because other studies had implied that cats go dormant in one spot during winter," Fago says. "But we were on larger rivers with more flow, and that may have encouraged slightly increased mobility during winter."

As water temperatures warm and the spawn approaches, channel cats migrate toward their traditional summer habitat.

Late Winter, Early Spring—Increased flow and warmer water seems to trigger channel catfish to move from their wintering holes toward their summer home territories. In northern rivers, ice-out is the wake-up call for sluggish cats.

"When the ice goes out, 'boom'—they're out of their wintering holes," Siegwarth says. "That's their dispersal trigger. They'll be a little sluggish, only traveling a couple miles downstream in a couple days. They seem to work the backwaters and sloughs. I assume they're feeding on winter-killed fish in those slack-water areas."

As water temperatures warm and the spawn approaches, channel cats migrate toward their traditional summer habitat. Siegwarth noted that his tagged catfish bypassed numerous logjams, holes, and snags to return each year to a specific home territory, so their journey was not a search for a summer home, but a move toward a specific destination, with a few side trips along the way.

"In late spring, as cats move toward their summer territories, it has been well documented that they temporarily move up into smaller tributaries to spawn," he says. "But after the spawn, they almost always work their way back to the same area in the main river where they spent the previous summer."

Channel cats in rivers usually spend their days in logjams and other cover, and roam at night in search of food.

Postspawn—Once in their summer home, channel catfish behave much as catfish anglers have come to expect. Their days are spent in the shelter of logjams and deep holes, with brief feeding forays to nearby riffles or current breaks. At night they roam the river above and below their home hole. Some cats venture a mile or more upstream or downstream in an evening, but most are back in their favorite logjam before sunrise.

Jamison Wendel and Steven Kelsch of the University of North Dakota tracked radio-tagged channel catfish in the Red River for a year. They noted that most of the tagged channel catfish transported and released several miles from their home range moved toward their home range within a couple days. They didn't always return to their exact summer homes, but tended to move in that direction.

Rainfall and resulting increases in river flow play a significant role in catfish movement through summer. Wendel and Kelsch noted increased mobility of their radio-tagged catfish after thunderstorms. Cats that had been holding tight to specific territories ventured a mile or more upstream or downstream (most often upstream) when thunderstorms raised the river level, but the cats generally returned to their home holes when water levels returned to normal.

They also noted that one of their tagged catfish made a daily run a short distance up a tributary of the Red River during periods when the Red was high due to summer rains. Chances are excellent that their tagged catfish was not alone in his forays. Other studies have shown that channel cats use the lower ends of tributaries, as well as flooded timber, side channels, and backwater areas during periods of high water. Researchers who opened the stomachs of cats sampled from flooded areas found them distended with nightcrawlers.

Late Summer-Early Fall—As river levels stabilize during late summer, radio-tagged channel cats became homebodies closely associated with specific holes and habitats. As summer waned and water temperatures fell, Siegwarth noted a unique behavior among channel cats on several rivers in northeast Iowa. "Both

---

Red River Roamers

One of the most remarkable scientific studies to date on channel catfish movements in rivers during fall was undertaken by the Minnesota Department of Natural Resources in the early 1990s. According to regional fisheries manager Henry Drewes, fish were outfitted with both disc dangler tags and radio transmitters, then recaptured by a variety of methods including angler activity, trotlines, and traps.

"In spring, we found that Red River catfish tend to move upstream when river temperature rises to around 50°F; they would then spawn in the upper reaches of the system," Drewes says. " This is typically followed by a downstream migration to deeper water. During summer,

During summer, many cats would move to holes associated with deeper, outside river bends . . .

many cats would move to holes associated with deeper, outside-meandering river bends, where current velocity usually is lower so the fish don't have to expend as much energy holding in current. Most of these holes are no deeper than about 18 feet."

As the river cooled in fall, however, Drewes and his team noticed that lowering water temperatures generated intense catfish movement, usually upstream. Sometimes the cats quickly covered incredible distances. "Some fish we sampled swam 275 miles in 30 days," he adds. "Whether these fish are even stopping to rest or to eat, we don't really know. All we're sure of is that they're covering a great distance in a short time." This may explain why many anglers report having a hard time finding river cats in fall.

The Red is different from many catfish rivers; it's often shallow, murky, and sinuous. "Seven low-head dams are present on the Red; when the river is filled to the banks, catfish can swim over these obstructions. We're in the process of modifying the dams so the fish can pass over them even in moderate flow."

Channel cats to 28 pounds were sampled. "We noticed that smaller fish used the upper reaches of the system more than the lower, which tended to hold the largest fish," Drewes says. "The lower end of each dammed section held the largest concentration of bigger channels. This wasn't surprising since the river is wider and deeper in these areas and holds greater numbers of mooneye and goldeye, both favorite catfish forage species. Cats that grow over 20 inches in the Red are fish eaters.

"Good snag habitat was especially important in fall and during other seasons as well," Drewes adds. "Locate snaggy areas, anchor down and wait for cats to pass through," he says, "but don't sit on one spot for more than 30 minutes at a time. Keep moving because the fish are moving, too."

---

on our survey river and other rivers we sampled, we noticed concentrations of channel catfish below rock riffles," he says. "They were stacked in there in the middle of bright, sunny afternoons. We never analyzed their stomach contents, but I'd guess they're feeding on some sort of invertebrate or small forage fish concentrated around the rocks. Whatever it is, I've come to expect to find channel cats jammed below rock riffles at certain times in October."

Late Fall-Early Winter—As water temperatures approached 40°F, radio-tagged catfish universally headed for their wintering grounds. In Siegwarth's study, all the radio-tagged catfish from the entire 15-mile stretch of the Wapsipinicon River moved into three wintering holes in a matter of two to three days. On the lower Wisconsin River, 64 percent of the radio-tagged cats in Fago's study moved downstream to winter in the Mississippi River. Twenty-three percent of the tagged cats in the Wisconsin River moved upstream and spent the winter below the dam at Prairie du Sac; 13 percent wintered in holes between the mouth of the Wisconsin River and the Mazomanie.

Fago emphasized that those percentages are averages, collected over several years. He noted that the actual percentage of catfish that migrated to the Mississippi varied from year to year and seemed to be related to water levels in the Wisconsin River. In dry years when the Wisconsin was relatively low, larger percentages of cats wintered in the Mississippi.

"One of the most striking findings in our study was that, despite all the seasonal movements, no catfish moved from the Mississippi into the Wisconsin River to winter," Fago says. "All movement prior to winter was toward the Mississippi and specific locations in the east channel of the Mississippi, relatively close to the mouth of the Wisconsin River."

WHAT THE RIVER RATS KNOW

So what's the take-home for casual catfish anglers from these multiyear radio tagging studies of channel catfish in rivers? Five basic channel catfish behaviors that river rats have known for years and jealously kept to themselves.

"First, this may explain why some stretches of river that look so good for catfish in summer just don't produce as we expect," Siegwarth says. "Lacking good wintering habitat, cats will be absent no matter how good the summer habitat is. Adequate habitat up and down a river has to be available to get the fish through winter.

"We've moved our radio-tagging study to the Turkey River in northeast Iowa because that river lacks manmade holes like the gravel pit, dam, and bridge hole on the Wapsipinicon," Siegwarth adds. "We're curious to learn where catfish and other gamefish winter in a natural stretch of river."

The second lesson for anglers is a reemphasis of how strongly channel catfish associate with woody structure during summer. Siegwarth notes that the only time catfish weren't near or in woody cover was when they were traveling between logjams. "Once they got to where they were going, wood cover almost always was nearby," he said. "The exception to that is in stretches of river with a shortage of wood. In this case, they usually were in deeper water at the base of cutbanks."

The third tidbit gleaned from recent catfish research is for anglers to stay mobile. "One thing I've noticed in our summertime electrofishing is that we average two to three catfish from a log pile," Siegwarth says. "That means that anglers who set up on a log pile, catch two or three cats, then continue to fish the same hole for the rest of the afternoon are wasting their time. Once two or three cats are caught out of a log pile, that's all the active fish, and it's time to move on."

The two final lessons for anglers are to fish below rocky riffles during October to take advantage of that unique feeding frenzy noted by Siegwarth and to follow local river rats when they sneak onto the river in late October or early November. Those old boys probably have located one or two wintering holes that attract most of the channel catfish from many river miles. Follow them to those catfish jackpots, and the mystery of the disappearing catfish will be solved.

TRACKING FLATHEADS

Understanding flathead habitat preference and seasonal movements is of practical importance to fishery managers who must assess and maintain strong populations. But this knowledge also is important to anglers, as it provides clues to where and when you should be fishing.

In the past few decades biologists have used telemetry as a tool for defining

Tracking studies provide anglers with valuable insight into flathead behavior.

habitat essential to fish. Describing the characteristics of areas radio-tagged fish prefer allows management agencies to protect these areas from changes that would decrease their value to fish. It also provides data that enables fishery managers to assess fish populations and establish appropriate harvest limits.

Tagging and tracking studies have provided anglers valuable insight into the habits of many popular gamefish species. While the movements of bass, walleye, and even channel catfish have been widely studied, flatheads, not considered one of the most important sport or commercial species in most states, have been largely ignored. This trend is changing.

During the last decade, increasing angler interest in flatheads has given these fish a higher priority with researchers across the country. Right now, more time, money, and other agency resources are being directed toward flathead research than ever before. Each of these individual efforts provides another piece of information that brings flathead behavior into focus.

But what do we know? We've selected three independent studies that attempt to answer (at least indirectly) questions like, "Where do flatheads spend the winter? How active are flatheads during the day? Why do some areas always seem to hold big fish?" Not all our questions will be answered, but you'll likely learn something that will help you understand and catch more flatheads.

SMALL RIVERS

In a study on the Minnesota River, one of the state's top flathead rivers, biologists with the Department of Natural Resources used trotlines and electrofishing to collect flatheads for tagging. Trotlines were used during the middle of the Prespawn Period in early summer, while electrofishing was more effective in early winter after flatheads had retreated to their cold-water haunts.

Seasonal Movement—The recapture of tagged fish by the study team and by anglers reveals that flatheads in the Minnesota River use a relatively small home range during summer, then move to a separate wintering area sometime during mid to late fall. The data also suggests that catfish use the same areas during each season year after year, so long as the stream topography remains constant.

Researchers found that flatheads chose wintering sites from 15 to 20 feet deep and with many current breaks . . .

Tag returns of fish captured during one winter and one summer showed that flatheads often move considerable distances to and from their wintering areas. At least one fish moved almost 50 miles downstream from its summer tagging sight to spend the winter, then moved back upstream where it was recaptured again the following summer.

Habitat—Researchers found that flatheads chose wintering sites from 15 to 20 feet deep and with many current breaks—rocks, large logs, and snags. When the electrical current brought the catfish to the surface, their backs were covered with silt. Divers, who have noted the same coating on flatheads in winter, say the fish can be pulled and pushed about with little response. In some cases, flatheads also form a chain formation on the bottom, each fish using the next fish upstream to reduce current.

During summer, flatheads usually held in moderately deep holes with abundant snags and other heavy cover. Without radio transmitters, the researchers were unable to define specific home ranges or determine any difference in patterns of daytime and nighttime movement. Based on the success of trotlines set in featureless runs between holes, fishery technician Brad Koenan suggests that flatheads often patrol these areas after dark, particularly during early summer and other high-water periods.

Some of the most productive trotline sets were in the middle of long runs, a mile or more from the type of habitat most flathead anglers prefer to fish. Some of these lines produced as many as 8 fish on 10 hooks, including several of the largest fish caught during the study period. Koenan theorizes that the first fish or two may be attracted by the concentration of baitfish on the trotline hooks, and the struggles of the hooked fish then attract more flatheads into the area.

Summary—Tag return data indicated that flatheads in the Minnesota River use separate home ranges during warmwater and coldwater periods. Both ranges also appear to be small for individual fish, though prime wintering holes may attract and hold a much larger number of catfish than the best summer areas.

Such large winter aggregations raises the possibility of illegal snagging. In some states, snagging catfish still is legal. The possibility exists for a large portion of the big fish in a large river section to be removed. States need to ban winter snagging and look at limiting harvest of large fish during winter.

LARGER RIVERS

A recent radio telemetry study conducted by John Skains and Dr. Don Jackson of Mississippi State University reinforces our feelings that flatheads in rivers carefully select their lair and tend to stay in that vicinity unless a major seasonal migration draws them away. At the beginning of the study, ten flatheads were caught from the Big Black and Tallahatchie rivers in Mississippi and implanted with radio tags.

River Characteristics—The Tallahatchie River, best known for the demise of Billy Joe McAllister, according to Bobbie Gentry's famous ode, is a tributary of the Mississippi and is located in the northwestern part of the state. The Big Black is a tributary of the Yazoo River in westcentral Mississippi. The Tallahatchie is a larger channelized river, with the main channel ranging from 250 to 300 feet wide. The Black is a more natural stream and measures about 100 feet across.

The biologists successfully followed six flatheads in the Big Black from mid-May until early January; they tracked eight fish in the Tallahatchie from early June into early January.

Movement—In the Big Black, the tagged fish moved from .3 to .7 miles, with an average distance of less than half a mile. They moved more in the Tallahatchie River, with ranges from .5 to 1.1 miles. Other studies also have suggested that flatheads move over wider areas in larger rivers, particularly channelized rivers.

Skains and Jackson theorized that flatheads may have to travel farther to feed in channelized rivers because of the absence of natural cover, which influences prey location and abundance. In both rivers, larger flatheads tended to cover larger areas than smaller fish, as three of the largest fish (up to 44 inches long) had the largest home ranges.

Minnesota River Individuals

Brad Koenen, fisheries technician with the Minnesota DNR, is wrapping up an extensive study of flathead catfish movements in the Minnesota River. "Kevin Stauffer initiated this project in 1990, and we're just now tabulating the results," he indicates. "We sampled smaller fish by electrofishing and larger flatheads via trotlines, limblines, and angler activity."

While final results aren't in, Koenen expects the study to reveal data on some 200 to 300 flatheads that were tagged and recaptured, an unusually high number for such studies.

"Fall catfish movement on the Minnesota River wasn't a universal phenomenon, but rather depended on individual fish," Koenen says. "Some fish moved only a short distance, but those that did move tended to roam farther in fall than during any other season. Some moved 20 to 30 miles in a short time. Flatheads tended to favor pool areas separated by current breaks, while channel cats favored deeper water."

Tracking studies indicate that flatheads in rivers prefer middepth holes with current breaks during winter.

Daily Patterns—During daylight, cats generally were sedentary in one of their home areas, which typically had wood cover. Only one fish was found moving during daylight, and this occurred at 3:30 p.m. on a dark overcast day. All the cats had at least one home site, and usually two or three. No radio-tagged fish shared home sites, though the boundaries of their ranges sometimes overlapped.

When flatheads moved at night, they tended to move along shorelines, heading in one direction throughout the night and returning to a home site before daylight. The maximum distance for a nighttime foray was just under a mile, but sometimes they remained in their home site all night. The researchers could detect no seasonal trends in the daily movement patterns of the cats.

Habitat—Flatheads tended to hold in areas with reduced current, day and night, and often in deep eddies. They held in water from 2 to 20 feet deep, and most often from 6 to 10 feet deep. No day or night patterns of depth preference were noted.

During the day, flatheads primarily held in bushy areas or heavy snag cover. At night, their nocturnal activities also kept them around cover, though active fish moved through clear areas. In the unaltered Big Black River, fish held in denser cover than in the channelized Tallahatchie River.

Summary—The authors suggest that management activities for flatheads may need to focus on small units of rivers, as the populations within them seem quite discrete. While the whole large river ecosystem affects flows, nutrients, and the topography of rivers, which directly influences flathead size and abundance, individual cats relate to small portions of the system, likely knowing their home range as well as we know our own backyards.

FALL MOVEMENTS IN RIVERS

Autumn easily is the most delightful of all seasons to be outdoors, but when you're chasing cats, fall can be an extremely frustrating time to fish. The water is cool, the air crisp, and most other anglers have hung up their rods to pursue deer, turkey, pheasant, or other furred or feathered critters. Conditions seem perfect for big-river cats to bite, yet many catmen report disappointing results. Probably because they're fishing where the catfish aren't.

In some rivers, fall is a time when catfish make long-distance runs, while in others, they more likely park in a snaggy spot and wait for the groceries to come to them. Hopefully what we learned about autumn catfish movements in rivers will help you tune into hard-pulling but hard-to-find channels, flatheads, and blues on your home waters this fall.

An age of enlightenment has a firm grip upon the catfish world. In the last decade, many of the grand and colorful myths of the past, stretching back to Mark Twain's days on the Mississippi River, have been squeezed, pummeled, and eventually dispelled. New ideas reign. Yet, despite new revelations, some vestiges from the dark ages still linger—especially about pursuing cats in fall.

At several locales across the nation within the past decade, a burgeoning group of year-round catmen has appeared. Consequently, channel cats are now being caught even through the ice on some northern lakes. On frozen farm ponds across the heartland, some anglers have caught channel cats on tip-up rigs baited with cutbait or live minnows.

Bigger Rivers

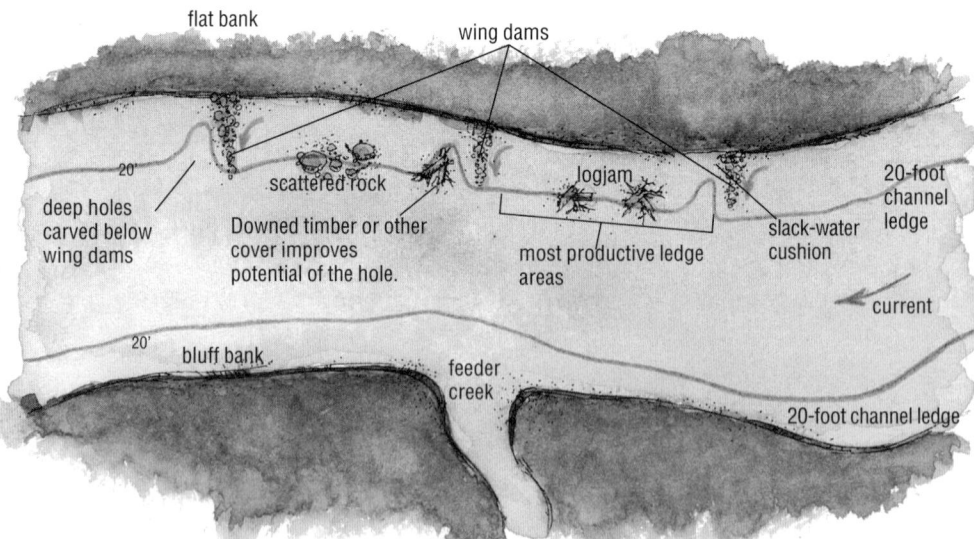

Ledges between wing dams often are productive for flatheads and blue cats, particularly if they contain wood, rock, or other current-deflecting cover. Pockets of slack water above and below dikes also are productive later in fall, especially for blue cats.

On the Missouri, Tennessee, and Mississippi rivers, anglers tangle with blue cats throughout fall and even well after Old Man Winter drives the water temperature down into the upper 30°F range. Since the early 1990s, a myriad of blue cats has been caught at Lake of the Ozarks in November and December.

The flathead catfish, however, remains a cold-water enigma. Anglers and biologists now know that flatheads, as mentioned, sometimes become so dormant that their bodies are covered with silt. And to this day, along the 39th parallel, only a rare catman pursues flatheads past about mid-October.

Perhaps a new cadre of ardent flathead devotees will plumb the cold-water coverts of their quarry and find a way to entice them out of their late fall and early winter lethargy. Already, stories are circulating about flatheads being taken as soon as the ice disappears on the waterways that lie between the 41st and 42nd parallels.

The avid and reflective catmen of the 21st century likely also will discard some of the axioms formulated in the 1990s about channel and blue cats, castigating those beliefs as folklore, a by-product of an unenlightened time.

KEY WINTER AREAS

One axiom, however, seems to be unalterable. This one deals with the movement downstream when the water temperature cools down to around 60°F in fall. Cats on this downstream journey seek deep holes with enough obstacles—jetties, boulders, mud balls, root wads, wing dams, and logjams—to slow the current. During late fall and winter, cats spend most of their days at those slower spots. Blue cats, however, can tolerate a stiffer current than flatheads and channel cats, even in cold water.

Big Rivers—On some of the deep and wide rivers of the mid-South, the best holes contain a series of steep ledges cluttered with massive logs or boulders.

Even along the 39th parallel on the Missouri River east of Waverly, Missouri, anglers work ledges in 15 to 20 feet of water on the flat side of the river. The best spots commonly lie about halfway between two wing dams. These wing dams litter the river from Jefferson City, Missouri, upstream to St. Joseph, Missouri. Anglers primarily fish these ledges for blues, but also take a few flatheads. They bait with live sunfish, goldfish, or bullheads. Most use a slipsinker rig with a 12-inch leader, a 1/0 swivel, a 6/0 to 10/0 hook, and a 3- to 8-ounce egg or bank sinker.

The current on the Missouri River between Kansas City and St. Louis is extremely swift and at times a touch scary. Current velocity can create anchoring problems. To counteract these woes, anglers are experimenting with drift socks to keep the boat from swinging back and forth at spots where the current doesn't flow in a straight line.

Nevertheless, the current at some locales is overwhelming and almost impossible to fish. In fact, it has the power to carve sharp ledges and holes as deep as 60 feet. Untold numbers of these ledges and holes are found in the vicinity of Waverly, and they're waiting to be explored during fall.

Slack-water areas above the wing dams on the Missouri are traditional cat spots. And the holes immediately below the wing dams that contain a root wad or logjam can be an excellent cool-water abode for blue cats.

Since the end of commercial fishing on the Missouri River in the early 1990s and the flood of 1993, a rebirth of the catfish populations has occurred. The blue cats recovered first, then the flatheads began to improve. Today, the best of these ledgy coverts on the Missouri River can shelter a mother lode of cats reluctant to move when Mother Nature drops one of her harshest autumn sorties.

Birmingham, Alabama, fisheries biologist Chris Stephenson participated in several catfish telemetry studies conducted for the U. S. Fish & Wildlife Service and a major utility company on the Coosa, Alabama, and Tennessee rivers. "We found relatively little overall catfish movement in fall in these rivers, probably because the baitfish population was so high— shad spawn in both systems in September, providing an abundant source of food," he says. "In the rivers we sampled, flatheads might move a couple miles a month, but usually not much more. If the bait's plentiful, they really have no reason to move."

Anglers fishing bluff banks in these rivers in fall often report catching big flatheads on bass jigs, Stephenson notes. "This corresponds with what our survey found. We sampled several flatheads over 20 pounds in 15 feet of water at the base of bluffs.

"As the water cools in fall, river flatheads gradually moved upstream to big eddies, where they concentrated in large numbers," Stephenson says. "They also held behind big chunk rock, submerged logs, and old coffer dams, places where they could escape heavy current. The main constant we noticed in fall flatheads was their propensity for shallow water—sometimes they were in 5 feet of water during the middle of the day."

Big blue cats in these rivers tended to hold in eddies under big logs. "Almost every time we electrofished around a log in an eddy, a big blue would float up," Stephenson adds. "Smaller blues, however, tended to roam more and were widely scattered throughout the river."

Channel cats showed a greater propensity for movement than either flat-heads or blues. "They'd move upstream military-style," Stephenson says. " Two or three at a time would lead, then several more would swim past them, then the cats in the rear would pass those in front, and so forth, leapfrogging up the river. Their primary forage, small gizzard shad, stayed toward the bottom of the river. When a group of channels reached a spot with a good concentration of shad, they'd stay there until the baitfish were depleted."

Look for catfish moving in these patterns when a couple cold nights chill the surface temperature several degrees. "Target eddies, submerged cover, and any current breaks. Also, don't fish too deep," Stephenson advises.

Corinth, Mississippi, catfish guide Phil King finds Tennessee River cats schooling heavily during fall. "As the water cools, channel cats congregate on gravel bars at the heads of islands where they can be caught on chicken livers in 10 to 12 feet of water," he says. "They also gather in large numbers below dams, starting in September; by October, big blue cats move to the dams as well. This is a great time to catch a monster blue." King's best day below Pickwick Dam netted him five blues that totaled 109 pounds.

King finds that by anchoring or drift-fishing along natural migration routes, including rock bluffs, ledges, and grooves cut into the bottom by meandering channels, cats can be intercepted as they move upstream or downstream in fall. "These fish tend to go on a major feeding binge, packing in 1- to 3-inch shad and immature skipjack minnows," he explains. "Personally, I like to drift these migration areas, as it allows me to cover a lot of water."

Smaller Rivers—That isn't always the case on some of the shallow sandy rivers in the southern plains. Tom Burns of Lawrence, Kansas, for example, actively pursued cats year-round on the Kansas River from 1932 to 1992. Burns discovered that a heavy, cold rain during midfall provoked the bulk of the cats, especially the flatheads, into migrating downstream to the Missouri River, where they stayed until mid-June. That, of course, totally spoiled Burn's fishing for those months.

This phenomenon occurred on the Kansas River in the fall of 1998, and it perplexed newcomers to the river for more than nine months. They finally stopped spouting the myth that rising water always draws cats upstream.

Yet, when Mother Nature wields a tender hand during fall, the life of a river catman can approach nirvana. The water level is low, which makes locating the best holes easier. Several long spells of Indian Summer days interrupted only by a short-lived mild cold front produce delightful catches. For example, from fall 1993 through fall 1997, several anglers averaged nearly 100 channel cats and blue cats a day that averaged eight pounds. Moreover, during several recent fall outings flathead fishermen have tangled with several fish in the 60- to 80-pound class.

Navigation on the Kansas River and other shallow rivers ranges from difficult to dangerous, especially during low water. In addition, boat ramps are scarce and land access is limited. It's their inaccessibility, however, that makes these rivers such fruitful waters to explore.

During low-water times on these shallow rivers, some long runs are only a few inches deep. Only a few holes measure more than 25 feet deep, and the bulk of the holes are 6 to 10 feet deep.

The most successful anglers usually are the ones who can traverse as many miles of water and probe as many holes as is possible in a day's fishing. These rivers, therefore, are provinces of tunnel boats equipped with jet-propelled outboards.

Smaller Rivers

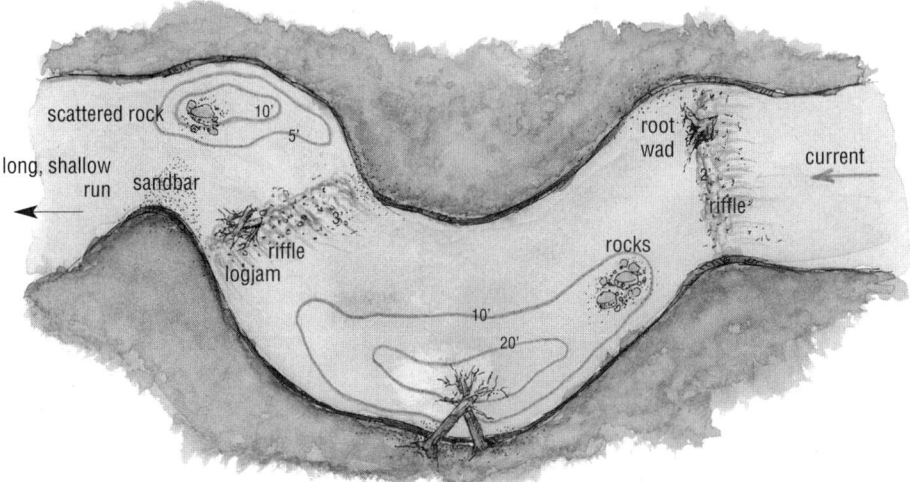

Active channel and blue cats often feed in the riffles at the head of deep holes, while fish in a neutral or negative feeding mood usually hold in the core of the hole. Anchor upstream and present baits in front of wood, rock, or other cover.

Wanted—Dead Or Alive
Hired Gun Takes On Flatheads

Due to their trophy size potential and sporting qualities, flathead catfish have been transplanted by anglers and stocked by agencies outside their native Mississippi River and Gulf Coast drainages. Yet they're vilified by some biologists and angling purists as voracious invaders, capable of devastating native fish populations.

In the West, for example, introduced flatheads and other exotics are accused of pushing rare species to the edge of extinction in the Columbia and Colorado river basins. Endangered species have been found in stomachs of flathead and channel catfish, prompting some researchers to call for catfish eradication in some western streams. And bounties have been suggested.

From South Carolina to northern Florida, non-native flatheads are thought to be edging out native sportfish. In the Flint, Ocmulgee, and Satilla rivers of eastern Georgia, introduced flatheads thrived to a point where traditional fisheries for redbreast sunfish and bullheads were affected.

In 1997, the Georgia legislature established a special position, and the Department of Natural Resources hired catfish specialist Robert Weller to exterminate flatheads. Weller had honed his skills while studying flathead movements on the plains of West Texas. By last October, his shocking program had accounted for 1,500 flatheads in a 25-mile test reach of the Ocmulgee River. The largest specimen shocked was in the 60-pound class. (A limbline angler reportedly pulled out a monster weighing 91 pounds.)

Electrofishing crews will soon learn if the removal program has lasting effects and perhaps whether populations of redbreast and bullhead have improved because of it. Weller hopes that the flathead's immobile nature will prevent quick recolonization of the stretch.

Flathead populations are even greater downstream in the Altamaha River, where Weller's posse collected over three tons of the whiskered outlaws in just five hours of shocking. The Georgia DNR encourages anglers to assist by catching and keeping all flatheads. The state posts no size or bag limits and few restrictions on angling methods for flatheads. And commercial fishermen can sell flathead meat. Fish captured in Weller's removal program are donated to charitable organizations like food banks, soup kitchens, and youth ranches. If successful, the project may be expanded to other streams in Georgia.

Biologists from Florida to Oregon are watching Weller's cleanup campaign to decide if what they see as troublesome nonnative flathead populations in their waters can be reduced with similar methods. Eradication may not be an easy sell in some regions, however, because flatheads have been around long enough in some of these waters to have established their own legion of satisfied anglers.

When blues and channel cats are actively feeding in fall, marauding squadrons have been known to invade riffles above holes. The best riffles on the Kansas River are one to three feet deep and often littered with root wads and small logjams. The current is brisk even when the river is running low, which makes presenting bait difficult.

To fish for channels and blues at these riffles, anchor about 100 feet upstream from one of those wads and jams and place a hunk of bloodbait or a chunk of fresh shad immediately in front of it. Use 20- to 40-pound line and a slipsinker rig sporting a 1/2- to 5/8-ounce flat river or current sinker, and without a leader. The key to catching a bevy of cats during fall around snags in these shallow fast-water areas is to move a lot, never lingering at an unproductive area for more than 15 minutes.

When blue cats and channel cats are less active, probe logjams or other current obstructions near the core of the holes. Those obstructions are also fine places to probe for flatheads.

Since these shallow rivers are so difficult to travel, most anglers fish only during daylight. But flatheads are noted for their nocturnal habits. So flathead anglers who fish at night usually restrict their travel to just a few miles and fish only two or three holes. Even then, a careful angler can wallop a partially submerged logjam or run aground on a sandbar and be stranded there for several hours.

Angling for flatheads on these rivers, therefore, often becomes the domain of line setters. During daylight, limb, log, and throw lines are baited and checked. Then the lines do the work throughout the night. Catmen who set the most lines at the best holes and on the best logjams usually catch an impressive array of flatheads.

Recently some of the folklore about the flathead's nocturnal ways has been discredited, however. As a result, rod-and-reel anglers fishing these shallow rivers are discovering that flatheads can be caught late in the afternoon during fall. Perhaps as the age of enlightenment continues to unfold, more revelations about the flathead will be uncovered, and we'll learn how to entice flatheads at high noon.

Catfish Movements In Reservoirs

**TRACKING
RESERVOIR
BLUE CATS**

The world's largest striper probably wouldn't weigh half as much as the biggest blue cat, but we know infinitely more about locating the migratory rockfish. Then too, almost any trophy trout would look like bait next to an average blue cat. Yet few states have considered managing for blue-ribbon cats.

Millions of anglers fantasize about catching a 23-pound largemouth bass to eclipse the world record. But no million-dollar prize was waiting for William McKinley when he landed a 111-pound former world-record blue catfish in Alabama.

Historically, blues haven't inspired expensive or time-consuming scientific studies. With the field of fishery management now a century old, how is it that this sporting predator, this monster that can weigh over 100 pounds, remains a relatively unknown player? A top predator and sportfish with the potential proportions of the blue cat, native or stocked in most regions of the country, should be well examined by now.

Perhaps both anglers and biologists have taken the species for granted because the blue catfish is so prolific and adaptable in much of its range. The same dams that are responsible for the decline of many native fish species seem to stimulate growth of the versatile blue cat.

Its smaller but more cooperative cousin, the channel catfish, is well-studied and intensively managed in most of the country. The flathead catfish, a notorious distant relative, has been highly scrutinized for its nasty habit of preying on other sportfish. But the ubiquitous blue cat remains a biological and sporting enigma. So scant is scientific literature on the blue cat that little of it sheds light on seasonal or daily movements and prime fishing locations.

Fortunately, a few scientists are beginning to dabble in blue cat tracking and tagging. These pioneers in blue cat study are important sources for angling specialists seeking information on how to locate and catch more blues.

TRACKING BLUES OF THE OSAGE

It's fitting that biologists in Missouri have studied blues more extensively than have biologists in other states, for many of the nation's big rivers that define prime blue catfish habitat merge on Missouri's eastern border. Big blues are legendary in the rivers and impoundments in the Missouri and Ohio river basins. Missouri is one of a half-dozen states producing blues over 100 pounds. The blue cat's North American range is focused in Missouri's "boot heel" region.

Joining the Missouri River just east of the capitol of Jefferson City is the Osage River, fabled for its blues. Impoundments on the Osage likewise have become renowned blue-cat waters.

Biologists have only recently begun to study blue catfish—one of North America's most prodigious predators.

In the late 1980s, biologist Kim Graham of the Missouri Department of Conservation tried to track blue cats in the Osage River below Harry Truman Reservoir. Graham and his associates wanted to know if the important blue-cat fishery below Truman was composed of resident or migrant fish. Their findings would have implications for sportfishing regulations on the species in the Osage system.

After surgically implanting 20 blues with sonic homing devices, Graham found that tracking blues in an open-ended environment like the Osage wasn't going to be easy. "Some of the blues we tagged below Truman moved over 20 miles downstream to Lake of the Ozarks in 24 hours. We couldn't keep up with them. The fish were extremely mobile," Graham says.

Blues migrated back upstream to Truman Dam when water was released, apparently to feed on the smorgasbord of chum and concentrated forage. When the bugged blues returned during power generation cycles, power lines and turbines interfered with the tracking signals.

Fishing pressure was high, particularly below Truman Dam, but anglers were becoming increasingly selective about the fish they harvested.

Switching to "Plan B," over the next eight years, Graham and his colleagues tagged over 5,000 blues throughout the system with traditional plastic ID tags. They encouraged anglers to return the tags, then they compared tagging locations to harvest sites.

Graham characterizes blue catfish tag returns as having "no rhyme or reason," meaning tags were returned from all over the system, nearly at random. "Most of the returns came from trotliners fishing near housing developments," Graham says. He attributes this to increased fishing near these areas, rather than a concentration of blues near residential areas. Graham also noted that many immature blues (less than 20 inches or about four pounds) moved downstream over dams during peak flow periods, supplementing downstream populations if they survived the drop.

When Graham supplemented his tagging study with a short-term jugline effort, he found that jugs were deadly on Truman Reservoir. "We set out 30 jugs and caught about 25 blues up to 30 pounds." Needless to say, Graham finds that areas to set jugs are in high demand at Truman.

Based on tag return results and other blue cat sampling attempts, Graham was positive about the outlook for blues in the lower Osage system. Reproduction and survival of small blues was adequate. Fishing pressure was high, particularly below Truman Dam, but anglers were becoming increasingly selective about the fish they harvested.

"Apparently, more anglers are fishing for large blue catfish because the percentage of anglers releasing blue catfish increased from 1 percent in 1990 to 31 percent in 1995," Graham says. The study concluded with a call for more concerted management of this popular gamefish in order to improve the quality of fishing below Truman Dam. New regulations are now in place to protect this valuable fishery.

THE BLUES OF PONY EXPRESS

In the mid-1980s, biologist Steve Fischer tracked six medium-sized blue cats for up to a year. The 245-acre Pony Express Lake in northwest Missouri ruled out the possibility of long migrations to complicate the location puzzle.

Pony Express is moderately turbid with a maximum depth of 35 feet, and it offers the standard small-impoundment forage base of gizzard shad, sunfish, and crayfish. Like Kim Graham's work on the Osage system, Fischer's movement data in Pony Express confirmed an almost random distribution of blue cats, with a few key exceptions.

Cats spent almost equal time in open water and in standing timber. Spring was the only season when blues were active during the day. In other seasons, their activity was primarily at night.

Depth seemed to be a key element in Fischer's study. "The fish we tracked occupied water over 15 feet deep 70 percent of the time," Fischer says. "When the lake stratified in summer, the fish suspended (over the thermocline) in about 8 to 12 feet of water."

In more temperate seasons, blues were less focused on depth, according to Fischer. In spring, they roamed the entire lake. In summer, they seemed to stay near deeper, cooler water. In fall, the distribution began to narrow to the lower half of the lake. By winter, the fish were tightly focused in deep water near the dam.

From this and other studies on Missouri blue-cat waters, the Missouri Department of Conservation decided to manage for trophy blues in Pony Express and other small waters. Their strategy encourages selective release of blues under a creel limit of four fish. And stocking rates are reduced to allow faster growth under less competition. No juglines or trotlines are permitted in these waters of special emphasis. Under the program, small waters regularly produce Master Angler blues over 34 inches (about 18 pounds).

To The Point (And Other Options For Blues)

Windy reservoir points are like busy street corners on a Saturday night. Predator and preyfish species hang out at these dangerous intersections because that's where all the action is. To understand why turbulent banks and peninsulas attract big sportfish, begin with a lesson at the bottom of the aquatic food chain.

In his textbook *Limnology, the Study of Freshwater Biology and Chemistry*, professor Robert Wetzel wrote that microscopic plankton tend to accumulate at the windward side of a lake, "whenever a strong wind persists for an appreciable length of time." This concentration of food is appealing to planktivores (plankton eaters) like shad. Predators are attracted to the melee like sharks to a chum line.

Shad work their way down windy banks, feeding on plankton piled up on the windward shore. When shad reach points, their predators use shallow underwater cover to ambush the school and pick off disoriented prey. In calmer waters, prey species like shad and sunfish feed fearlessly on plankton, easily recognizing and avoiding blue catfish and other predators. When wave action breaks up the surface of the water, lurking predators are less obvious and use the situation to deadly advantage. It's an example of the give and take constantly at play between competing species in nature.

Many anglers seek calm sheltered coves to fish, but savvy catfishing veterans fish windy shores and points, knowing that active blues will more likely be feeding there.

Thermocline Hot Spots

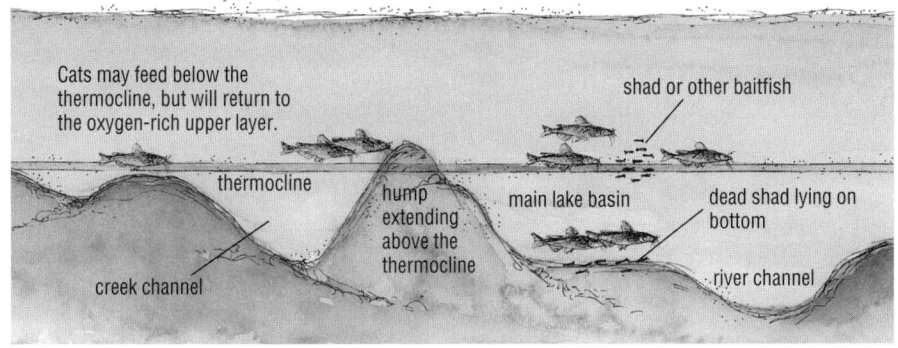

Cats may feed below the thermocline, but will return to the oxygen-rich upper layer.

shad or other baitfish

thermocline

hump extending above the thermocline

main lake basin

dead shad lying on bottom

creek channel

river channel

BAMA BLUES

As a biologist with an environmental consulting firm in Birmingham, Alabama, Chris Stephenson has studied blues and other sportfish in and around the river-run reservoirs of Alabama. His insight is particularly valuable since he also fishes for several of the species he examines.

When operation plans are proposed for hydroelectric dams, federal law requires that managers consider the effects on reservoir and tailwater fisheries. As a top-level predator and sportfish, the blue catfish is an important component of the fish community above and below impoundments.

In one relicensing study of a hydro dam in the mid-1980s, Stephenson resorted to tracking the highly migratory blues from airplanes. Using miniature radio transmitters, he tagged and tracked 15 blues ranging in size from 5 to 35 pounds in the Coosa River system of central Alabama.

Spawning took place in early summer in some of the thickest cover available, like rocks and piers in water less than 14 feet deep. Blues were mobile, moving upstream to feed in spring or whenever flood waters were churning. "In a flood, they almost all did the same thing," he says. "They ran up to the tailrace—particularly the big fish—and positioned like trout behind riprap and boulders, moving back downriver after the flood gates were closed."

In summer, Stephenson found some blues mobile at night, sometimes moving 12 to 13 miles. In that respect, Stephenson suggests, blues are like striped bass, since they rested in the cool water of the thermocline during hot summer days.

Big blues ventured out to feed at night, returning to comfortable home ranges during the day. Some fish, though, wouldn't move at all. Most of these fish were fixed on some form of woody cover like a snag or fallen tree. "Blues are unique," Stephenson says. "At night during summer, we never knew what they'd do."

Prime areas for feeding at night were bends in the reservoir or river with some kind of woody cover, or where a large tributary entered the river. In spring and fall, when water temperatures were more tolerable, blues moved into shallower water (the 15-foot depth range) and fed more frequently during the day.

Then, during winter, Stephenson sometimes found giant blues in shallow water, confirming their reputation as the most active catfish species in cold water. "In winter, the fish were almost split down the middle," he says. "We found some in water 5 feet deep and others at 45 feet."

Stephenson recalls electrofishing in cold weather after hearing about Clarksville, Tennessee, cat guide Jim Moyer's winter exploits with blues. "We went out one time at 19°F—terrible winter weather—and rolled lots of big fish bunched up in huge trees. We found bluegill and catfish in trees together."

Stephenson characterizes blue catfish as highly adaptable, taking advantage of a variety of feeding opportunities. "Flatheads can be pinpointed, and channel cats are well studied, but blues remain mysterious," he says.

Despite their adaptable nature, Stephenson suggests that blue cats are creatures of habit when they find a feeding situation to sustain them. He advises that serious blue cat anglers often can adopt a pattern-fishing style as bass anglers do. If cats are targeting bluegills in brush cover in one reservoir area, the pattern likely duplicates itself in other areas.

Stephenson also says that blues prefer slightly turbid water where baitfish can't see them as well. They also prefer to face current, no matter how slight, and they use cover like rocks, points, and trees as ambush points.

Bigger fish, according to Stephenson, generally don't move as far as small fish. Trophy blues find optimum feeding locations and stay close to them. He suggests that boat anglers should use electronics to find underwater humps and channel bends that hold shad schools, then look for bigger blips that indicate active blues.

But no matter how extensively blues are studied in the future, fishery scientists will at best understand only half the complicated fishing equation. Science is only part of a puzzle. The other part of the mix is a matter of earthy bankside wisdom from veteran anglers.

FINDING RESERVOIR FLATHEADS

Flathead anglers aren't known for trying to impress anyone with expensive gear. Most would rather go fishing after a ball game, rather than trying to squeeze in a trip before it starts. Flatheads are more cooperative under the glow of a Coleman lantern. No sense in waking the neighborhood dogs at deer-hunting hours to track down this critter. And no need to shell out $20,000 on a highfalutin' fishing boat for the chase.

Leathery flathead-stalking veterans would say that "a fish that looks like that won't be out chasin' bait all day." And biologists agree that the external features and internal anatomy of a flathead catfish are reliable keys to its feeding habits and favorite haunts.

THE FLATHEAD PHYSIQUE—PHYSICAL CLUES TO FLATHEAD HABITS

Before scientists begin tagging and tracking fish, they're taught to examine physical features that indicate the habits of the fish. Laboratory tests in aquariums often are used to confirm those tendencies. Fish like striped bass and shad, with their deeply forked tails, for example, are more powerful distance swimmers than fish with round tails, like bullheads and gar. Fish that are flat from side to side, like crappies and bluegills, are adapted to an active lifestyle suspended above the bottom, while triangular fish like suckers and catfish are innately bonded to the bottom.

The flathead, of all the catfishes, is decidedly a creature of the bottom. Whether viewed in aquariums or discovered by divers in the wild, flatheads appear anchored, having swallowed a chunk of lead. Their compressed body form allows them to settle into crevasses that would make a lizard envious. Where the method is legal, noodlers, who prefer to take on catfish bare-handed, seek inactive flatheads in secluded rock cavities or dense brushpiles.

Another tip-off to the flathead's sedentary lifestyle is the squared shape of its tail. As in the bullhead family, the tail of a flathead is made for purposeful, steady propulsion and predatory bursts in tight quarters where accuracy is essential. In contrast, the V-shaped tails of its cousins, blue and channel catfish, evidence their disposition toward constant movement, often against current.

A terse glance at the external camouflage of a flathead suggests that this fish battles in the trenches—between rocks and among branches. An open-water cruiser couldn't sneak up on anything with this dark, mottled exterior—except at night. This is the uniform of guerrilla warfare.

The internal features of this unique fish also offer insight. What anglers call "cleaning fish," biologists politely refer to as "dissection." Viewed under either name, a flathead's flesh is suggestive of a laid-back way of life. Fat deposits, particularly in larger, older flatheads, indicate that this fish is capable of storing energy for seasons of inactivity or periods of low food supply. Fat is less obvious or nearly absent in active big-water predators like blue catfish and striped bass who constantly chase schools of shad or other prey. They can't afford to carry extra fuel to their expansive battlefields.

The strip of red meat so conspicuous in more mobile species is notably absent in the flathead. Red muscle is used by migratory fish for endurance swimming, and the only migration on a flathead's mind is a determined waddle from one side of the cove to another. No, the flathead's anatomy suggests anything but life in the fast lane. This fish lurks in dark corners, often ambushing its opponent, then savors the spoils of the day.

Tail Design As An Indication of Lifestyle

Note the continuing increase in tail fin span as the fish becomes more active, speedy, and mobile.

Body Form And Lifestyle Function

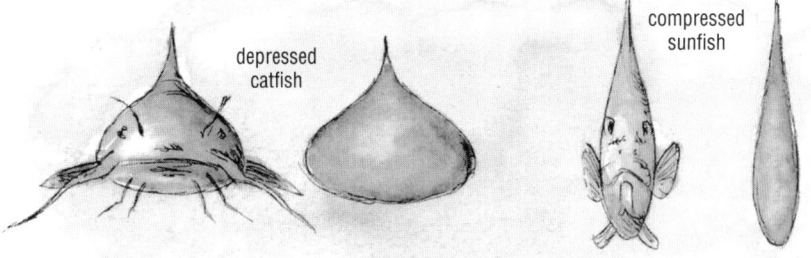

The body form of sunfish species allow them to maneuver effectively in tight quarters. The flathead cat is designed to hold bottom. The flathead cat also isn't designed for speedy travel, although it has lightening reflexes in tight quarters.

FLATHEAD TRACKING—CONFIRMING THE OBVIOUS

Fortunately, in this high-tech age where no problem seems too complex for science, catfish specialists don't have to rely on conjecture to discover successful patterns. Fishery scientists are riding the technology wave to better management of this important sportfish.

If we can send a radio-controlled rover to Mars or pinpoint underwater humps to the nearest meter with global positioning satellites, then we can surely discover where flatheads live—and where anglers should fish to catch them.

As early as 1970, biologists used ultrasonic transmitters (homing devices) to track flatheads. Robert Summerfelt and Larry Hart of the Oklahoma Cooperative Fishery Research Unit bugged 22 adult flatheads and followed their movements in a 3,000-acre reservoir.

The Homing Tendency of Flatheads

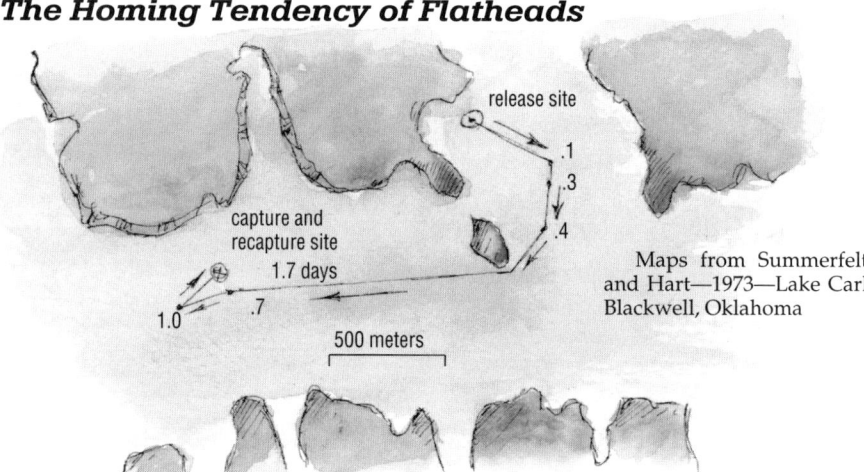

release site

.1

.3

.4

capture and
recapture site

1.7 days

1.0   .7

500 meters

Maps from Summerfelt
and Hart—1973—Lake Carl
Blackwell, Oklahoma

Homing of a displaced female flathead catfish. Numbers represent days after release.

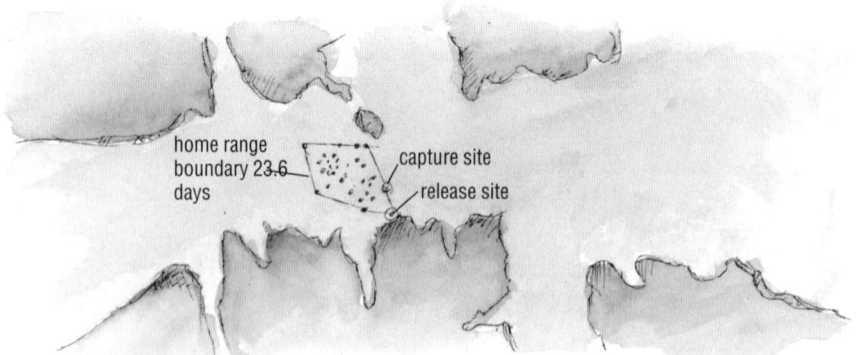

home range
boundary 23.6
days

capture site

release site

This fish established a home range near the site of release and stayed within the home range.

An Early Tracking Study

One of the earliest radio tracking studies on reservoir flatheads was conducted on Lake Carl Blackwell in Oklahoma by a team of researchers led by Larry Hart. Hart implanted 22 adult flatheads from Lake Carl Blackwell with radio transmitters. Six immature flatheads also were implanted with transmitters and released in the study lake for observation.

Lake Characteristics—Lake Carl Blackwell is a small creek impoundment located near Stillwater in north-central Oklahoma. During the study period, the water level was approximately 11 feet below the spillway, and the lake was approximately 3.3 miles long. At this water level, the surface area is about 2,100 acres and the average depth 13 feet. Population assessments yielded an estimate of about 870 adult flatheads.

Seasonal Patterns—This study's average 18-day tracking interval was too short to observe seasonal movements of flatheads.

From December through March, flatheads were located in the deepest portions of the lake basin, or in the deepest channel areas of major creek arms. Fish usually moved into these wintering areas when water temperature dropped to about 50°F. Water temperature continued to drop to near freezing throughout the Coldwater Period, before again warming to 50°F in late March. Fish appeared to be inactive during this period, moving and feeding little.

Flatheads usually began a period of intense feeding in early April and continued until water temperatures reached about 72°F in June. The average home range increased during each month of this period as the water continued to warm, to a maximum size of about 18 acres.

The Spawn Period usually coincided with the warmest water temperatures of the year (around 75°F to 82°F) in late July and August. Spawning usually occurred in rock outcrops near shore or in heavy patches of submerged timber. Average daily home range declined sharply to an average of 5.2 acres, and individual fish appeared to move less often.

Spawning complete, flatheads fed heavily again. Water temperatures at the beginning of September usually were about 75°F, and fish remained active until they moved to wintering areas when the water temperature again dropped to 50°F. The average home range was 5.7 acres and decreased steadily from September through November.

Habitat—Flathead home ranges usually were associated with an old submerged creek channel or steep bank near shore. It was assumed that flatheads usually held on or near the bottom at each location.

Readings with a sonar unit were made at 138 individual known fish locations. Sixty-one percent of the fixes were within submerged creek channels, 38 percent were on steep shoreline drops, and the remaining one percent of the locations were along the upper edge of creek channels. The researchers noted, however, that some fish seemed to swim away from an approaching boat. This could have caused those holding on the channel lip to drop into the channel during an observation.

Summary—The researchers theorized that flatheads probably establish three or four home ranges each year as they make seasonal movements to coldwater, prespawn, spawn, and postspawn areas. Data also indicated that some fish return to the same home ranges year after year, while others establish home ranges in other areas of the reservoir.

After surgically implanting 3-inch-long tracking devices in the bellies of 22 fish, 12 of them were released more than a mile from their capture site. The other 10 were returned to their original capture location. All were tracked four times a day for up to a month.

During the interval the fish were removed from the lake (an average of 3 days), they were anesthetized twice, hauled in covered containers in trucks and boats twice, and held in two different tanks. Even after these experiences, most displaced fish exhibited homing traits after an initial adjustment or reorientation period of 1.5 days.

The researchers determined that 21 of the 22 fish showed some sort of homing behavior. Some fish even returned to the exact spot of their capture. "Reuse of a specific site within the home range suggests a highly developed sense of environmental recognition," the biologists said. After re-establishing home ranges, the flatheads ventured out occasionally on sallies, presumably to feed or search for better habitat. Sometimes these forays covered more than a square mile, but more often were within a few hundred yards of their favorite encampment.

The Summerfelt and Hart tracking study proved that these fish choose and recognize "turf." It emphasized that flatheads are essentially homebodies that prowl within a defined range and return to a specific location within that perimeter.

The lesson here is that successful flathead anglers must also be cover-conscious stalkers. Finding a convenient spot on the bank and casting bait to the vague depths won't cut it for these whiskered maulers.

NEW-WAVE CAT TRACKING

Understanding of flathead location and behavior recently was advanced by Robert Weller, a former graduate student at Texas Tech University in Lubbock. From 1993 through 1995, Weller implanted temperature-sensing transmitters in 29 flatheads in a small West Texas lake.

Besides noting movements, each time Weller pinpointed a bugged fish, he recorded habitat variables, including temperature, depth, and preferred structure or cover. With longer battery life in up-to-date transmitters, he was able to track fish through several seasons.

The percentage of time spent in rocky, woody, or bare-bottom habitat didn't change from day to night.

The fish Weller tracked ranged from 3 to 40 pounds, but he found no size-related differences in the habits of small or large fish. Males and females also chose home ranges basically of similar size and structure.

Predictably, flatheads chose areas with complex cover like rocks and boulders (63 percent of the time) or standing timber and brushpiles (19 percent). Curiously, the percentage of time spent in rocky, woody, or bare-bottom habitat didn't change from day to night.

This conclusion might indicate that flatheads in this muddy West Texas lake were no more active at night than in daylight. The study, however, didn't directly analyze day versus night activity peaks that might have pinpointed best fishing hours.

In the primary fishing seasons, Weller located most fish in relatively shallow water—between 3 and 15 feet. From late spring to early summer, Weller's flatheads chose spawning sites in the riprap along the dam, in water less than 12 feet deep. Spawning began when water temperatures climbed above 75°F.

The average summer home range for the tagged fish was less than 25 acres. One large specimen spent the entire fishing season prowling an area just 200 yards in diameter.

Flathead Diet

With its penchant for lurking in brushpiles and rocky bluffs, it's no wonder the flathead catfish has a reputation as a sporty competitor. Biologists have found crappies and channel catfish in flathead stomach samples.

Truth is, flatheads are opportunistic carnivores that eat whatever is abundant in their chosen habitat. Brushpiles and rocky drop-offs just happen to be favored haunts of other popular gamefish. Despite this obvious overlap in territory, studies of flathead feeding show that they more likely eat more abundant shad, sunfish, and roughfish.

Channel and blue catfish are omnivores that eat live or dead food items as conditions provide. Flatheads, in contrast, prefer live prey. In a food habit study of six Oklahoma reservoirs, 95 percent of the flatheads with full stomachs had eaten fish. Gizzard shad, drum, and carp comprised about 90 percent of that total.

Channel catfish were eaten frequently in one lake where they were abundant, but bass, crappies, and other sunfish made up less than 10 percent of the flathead diet, and less than one percent of the total were harvestable-sized sportfish.

Flathead Diet In Six Oklahoma Reservoirs

Of the 1,329 flathead stomachs checked, 53 percent were empty.

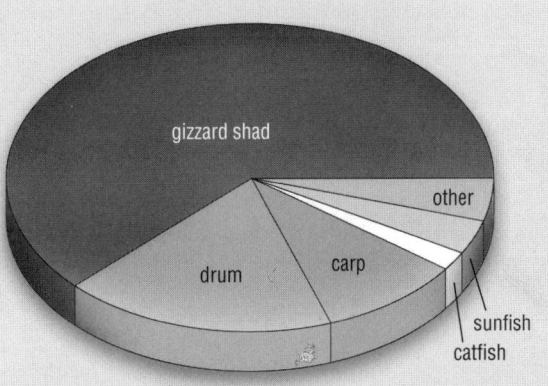

The most notable conclusion from the study was gleaned from the temperature-sensing capability of the new transmitters. By contrasting flathead body temperatures to depth profiles of lake temperatures, Weller found that the fish did not avoid hot water during the extreme West Texas summers. Rather than seeking cooler, deeper water still charged with oxygen, the flatheads seemed right at home in temperatures that would stress other species. Weller concluded that habitat variables other than temperature (such as cover and forage location) seemed to determine flathead behavior during the fishing season.

As water chilled in late fall, flatheads moved deeper (below 15 feet) and established smaller territories. Winter home ranges were minuscule according to Weller's data, implying inactivity (and tough fishing) for flatheads in cold weather.

Like Summerfelt and Hart, Weller found that flatheads are not mobile, schooling, open-water predators. Tough tackle brandished in tight quarters is mandatory.

LOCATING FLATHEADS WITH ELECTRICITY

In the 1980s, biologists resurrected a not-so-subtle way of collecting live flatheads to determine population sizes, feeding habits, and habitat preferences. Old-timers can remember when hand-crank telephone devices using low-voltage electricity were used to "call up" catfish. Researchers at the Oklahoma Fishery Research Laboratory tested the antique gear and confiscated homemade shocking devices called "pacemakers," to discover the secrets of their forbidden success.

They discovered that the kind of electricity generated by those illegal devices could be duplicated by modifying standard agency shockers. Now biologists in catfish country can collect flatheads with an efficiency equal to collecting bass and trout.

Catfish—flatheads in particular—are vulnerable to low-frequency electrical fields. The effect is so hypnotic that cats can be observed surfacing for several yards around a stationary shocker, in a behavior biologists term "motor-boating." Fortunately, the shocking effect—similar to a stun gun—is temporary, and the wobbly specimens can be released unharmed after providing vital statistics.

Flathead Habitat In A West Texas Lake —29 Fish Located By Radiotelemetry

rocks, riprap

other

brush, timber

Ken Cunningham, a research biologist with the Oklahoma Department of Wildlife Conservation, is committed to advancing the science of flathead management. In his home state, flatheads are pursued with rod and reel, by trotline, jugline, spearing, snagging, and noodling. These competing users and the disputes that sometimes arise from controversial fishing styles make the flathead a politically important species. Information from Cunningham's research has been used to set management strategy and flathead law in Oklahoma.

After shocking thousands of flatheads over the last five years in a dozen reservoirs, Cunningham has observed reliable trends in flathead behavior. By mid-spring, he noted that flatheads were already staking claims to cover in shallow water. Shortly thereafter, males moved into prime spawning areas of riprap on dams and bridges, or areas with ample natural rock cavities. Big females are found in spawning habitat only briefly, when water temperatures are prime.

Cunningham agrees with his colleague Robert Weller, that flatheads prefer steep, rocky shorelines and thick brush. In fact, lakes that lack dense cover usually offer poor flathead fishing potential.

The abundance of large fish in shallow water declines somewhat after spawning season, but the really big change in home range, according to Cunningham, occurs when October cold fronts drop water temperatures significantly. "In deeper reservoirs, a flathead could realize all its biological needs in a relatively small area," Cunningham concludes. "A distance of only 50 meters often reveals a considerable difference in habitat—depth and structure—in some lakes."

Predators with home ranges often are territorial, and diet studies prove that flatheads can be cannibals, inferring that catching tons of big flats in one spot on a single night may not be realistic. Obviously, abundant prime habitat improves the likelihood that several flatheads could be prowling within casting range. Prime territories in thick cover are always in high demand, though, and a flathead harvested often is a flathead quickly replaced.

A cultivated crappie fanatic once admonished, "If you don't put your jig in the brush, you're not going to get bit." Likewise, timid anglers that avoid heavy cover for fear of losing terminal tackle or breaking off big fish won't battle many big flatheads.

Finesse anglers can't pull this warrior from his home turf. The tenacious flathead concedes only to anglers of equal character.

FALL MOVEMENTS IN RESERVOIRS

The leap from the rigors of the rivers to the vast expanses of reservoirs can befuddle a catman who is accustomed to plying only running water, particularly in fall. Reservoirs, however, also present the woes of wind. But so long as wind doesn't interfere with presentations, reservoirs can be more bountiful than rivers. This bounty often multiplies once reservoir catmen learn to work with the wind and waves by plying windward shores. In many ways, reservoir angling is easier and less dangerous than what rivermen experience.

The ease and simplicity of reservoir angling for cats is reflected by the number of serendipitous encounters with cats that bass and walleye anglers enjoy. Some of these scuffles with humongous cats have turned several bass and walleye men into catmen.

Such a transformation occurred in the mid-1990s at Cedar Acres Resort on Lake of the Ozarks. Rick Hebenstreit of Kansas City and several other anglers were enjoying their annual fall excursion for white bass and largemouth bass when by happenstance they tangled with several big blue cats. Since then, Hebenstreit and company divide their time among all three species.

To catch catfish, Hebenstreit probes a large cove near the resort. The most productive spot lies about 100 yards inside and is about 35 feet deep. He fishes with

Flatheads and other catfish species are equally at home in rivers and reservoirs.

rods and reels spooled with 25-pound line, a 1/2-ounce slipsinker, and a 7/0 Kahle hook. The bait often is fresh gizzard shad, but a bluegill or even the head of a white bass take their fare share of nice-sized cats.

At times, the fishing can be extremely slow for two or three days. Then, for some unexplainable reason, the 15- to 25-pounders turn voracious, and every once in a while a 40-pounder enters the fray. Of course, these recent converts from the bass ranks say tangling with a 15-pound blue cat on bass equipment is quite a treat, and a 40-pounder nearly blows their minds.

About 100 miles west of Lake of the Ozarks, John Thompson of Ottawa, Kansas, spends some of his autumn days looking for Goliath flatheads that haunt the flatland reservoirs of eastern Kansas. A 90-pounder was caught in 1993 and a 123-pounder in 1998. Thompson also has caught and released a 75-pounder.

He pursues these Titans with log lines that he sets in 7 to 10 feet of water along the edges of channels in small feeder creeks. His line consists of a large piece of a rubber inner tube nailed with a large staple to one of the flooded trees that line the creek channel. To the bottom of the piece of rubber, Thompson ties on a 3-foot length of 300-pound braided nylon line. Then he attaches a 12/0 hook to the line with a snell knot. A large, lively bluegill usually adorns that hook, which is set about 3 feet below the surface.

On these flatland reservoirs, Thompson says the wind can be a catman's salvation. A mild wind blows baitfish around, such as schools of gizzard shad, disorienting them and making them easy for the cats to prey upon.

But too much wind, howling for too many hours, fouls the fishing, breaking up schools of shad and scattering them far and wide. The sort of wind that

Typical Fall Movements

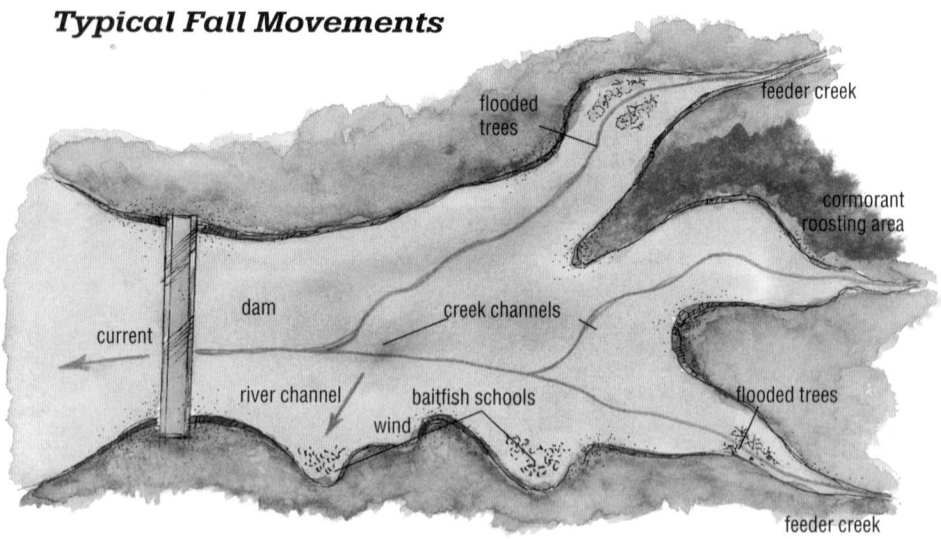

Big flatheads usually frequent flooded creek channels where they're caught on log-lines attached to standing trees adjacent to the channel. Blue and channel cats are attracted to schools of shad driven into shoreline cuts by several days of consistent wind. Channel cats also are fond of the shad-laced excrement so abundant near cormorant roosts.

Channel cats often are attracted to areas below cormorant roosts during fall

blows at 15 to 30 mph for two days and nights is a byproduct of a slow moving low-pressure system or a quick series of cold fronts that moves rapidly across the Great Plains, a common occurrence in September and October.

Thompson says flatheads can be caught on a rod and reel, but the fishing is excruciatingly slow. What's more, to wrestle one of those brutes from its brushy confines would be a devilish task.

Thompson doesn't have the patience to endure that sort of rod-and-reel angling. Instead, he chases the smaller and more plentiful channel cats.

In late October through November, reservoir cats can be caught in water as shallow as 2 to 3 feet deep. At reservoirs that attract massive fall migrations of cormorants, such as Glen Elder Reservoir, Kansas, anglers fish beneath and around areas where cormorants roost. Cats come to these roosting sites to dine upon the shad-laced excretion the birds drop. Bloodbait, sour shad, or stinkbait, entices these scavenging cats.

At lakes that aren't graced with flocks of visiting cormorants, some catmen chum shallow feeding areas with sour grains such as soybeans, wheat, or milo.

On a splendid Indian summer afternoon, chummers can catch 20 to 40 channels between 2 and 10 pounds. A couple fine outings like that ought to supply an angler with enough reveries to last through the harshest winter. But if those daydreams peter out, give wintertime channel and blue cats a whirl.

Chapter 5

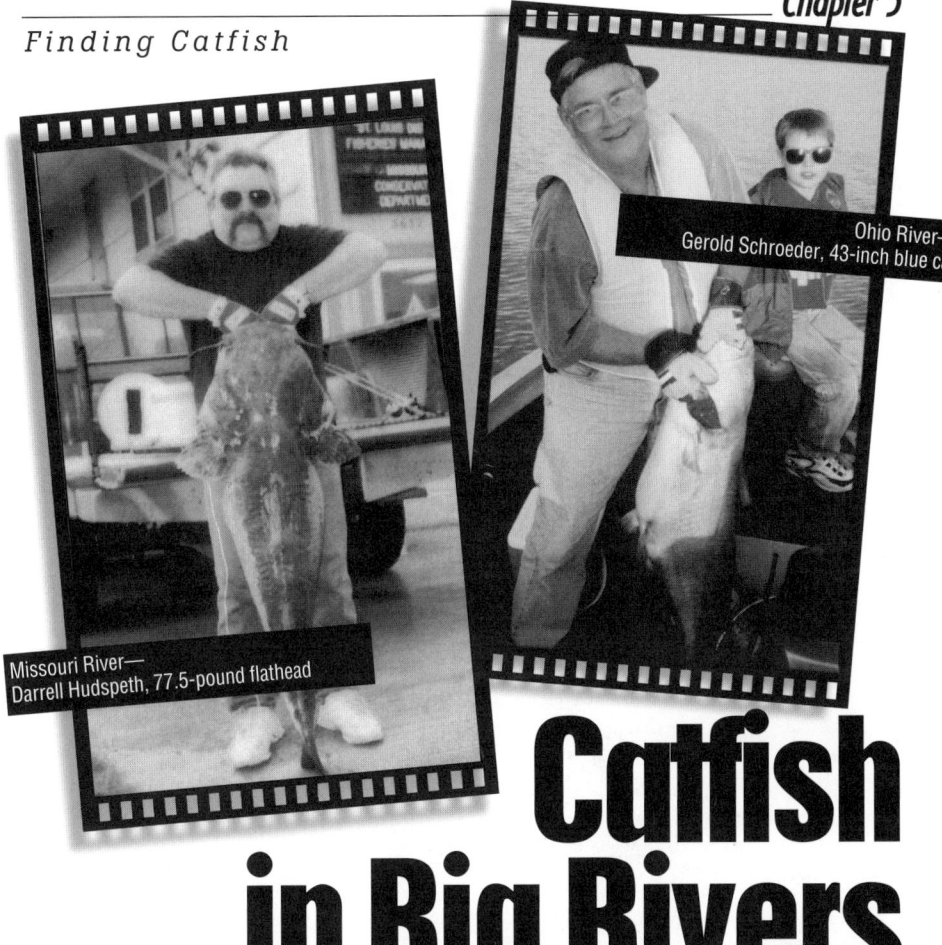

Ohio River—
Gerold Schroeder, 43-inch blue cat

Missouri River—
Darrell Hudspeth, 77.5-pound flathead

Catfish in Big Rivers

**FINDING
BIG-RIVER
CATS**

Big rivers intimidate catmen accustomed to the intimacy of smaller streams. The transition from a small river full of twists and turns and visible riffles and holes to a wide and deep river like the Mississippi, Ohio, or Missouri might seem overwhelming.

But take a closer look at a manageable piece of water—one hole in a section of a big river pool—and you'll likely see many similarities to your favorite catfish river. Snags, tailraces, and other structures hold cats in a big river, just as they do in smaller waters. Sure a hole might be 30 feet deep instead of 10, and 200 yards long instead of 20, but that's just a matter of scale.

Observation and research suggest that catfish location and behavior vary little from one river system to the next. Factors like weather, water levels, and dam generation schedules remain unpredictable, but once you understand how to interpret these factors, finding fish becomes relatively simple or at least straightforward—particularly during the Prespawn Period, when a catfish that can be found usually can be caught.

This is not to suggest that specific locations remain constant from one season to the next, because rivers are constantly changing. Logjams and snags might be deposited at the head of a bend during high flows one season, only to be uprooted and swept away the next. Sandbars shift, grow, and recede beneath the constant pressure of changing currents. And on many big rivers, the Army Corps of Engineers contributes changes of its own in the form of dams, dikes, and levees to control flood waters and maintain a navigation channel for commercial barge traffic.

In spite of these seemingly major changes, though, the overall structure of the river remains constant. All rivers contain a constant series of riffles, holes, and runs. A riffle lying 10 feet beneath the surface of the Ohio River might not be so obvious as one visible on the surface of the Minnesota River, but it serves the same function. The harder bottom resists the eroding force of the current, causing water to accelerate. As soon as this faster flow hits softer bottom downstream, it scours a hole. The current slows at the tail end of a hole, allowing sediments to settle. A uniform flat or run then stretches downstream to the next riffle.

All rivers contain a constant series of riffles, holes, and runs.

Manmade structures like wing dams, riprap banks, and barge mooring stations alter the natural flow of big rivers, but they also contribute to catfish habitat. Dams, for example, often are constructed where a shallow riffle poses a danger to barge traffic. And like the riffle, the force of water pouring over a dam scours a deep hole that provides excellent catfish habitat. Wing dams also function like riffles, diverting current to scour deep holes that offer protection for cats and other species. The piles of downed timber that afford cats cover in many small farm-country rivers are periodically removed by river engineers, but bridge pilings, boulders, and other permanent structures that serve a similar function often are left in their place.

North America's major rivers are much different today than they were a century ago, but many still harbor incredible numbers of catfish. In some river sections, man's alterations may have even improved catfish production by increasing the depth of the channel and the amount of suitable habitat. Finding the most productive locations, then fishing those spots efficiently with proven baits and rigs, is the key to memorable catches of prespawn cats on big rivers.

THE RIGHT TIME

The best time on big rivers is the Prespawn Period. Catfish have the longest Prespawn Period of any North American gamefish. Unlike trout that mate as the first snowflakes fly in fall, or walleyes that spawn shortly after ice-out, cats wait until the water is teeming with enough life to sustain their offspring. To understand why the fishing is so good, though, first understand a little about where the cats have been, where they're going, and why.

Catfish in big rivers winter in deep holes, which provide ample oxygen, slightly warmer water temperatures, and protection from current. In northern

Typical Big River Habitat

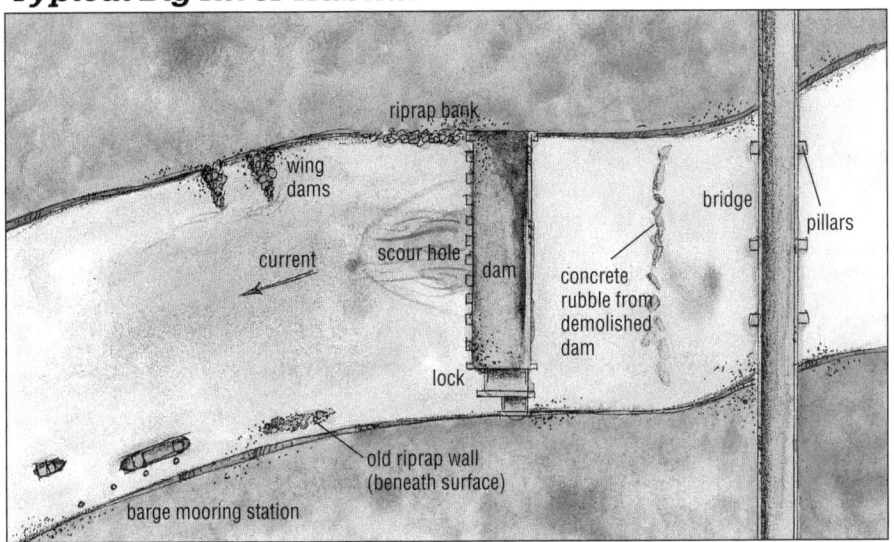

Manmade structure serves as the primary catfish habitat on many big rivers. Learning how cats use the options is the key to consistent fishing.

rivers like the upper Mississippi and Missouri, flathead and channel catfish may remain semidormant for weeks or even months at a time. In more southerly stretches like the lower Missouri or Ohio rivers, channel cats behave similarly during frigid weather. They resume feeding, though, during periods of mild weather, even when water temperatures are only a few degrees warmer than in the North.

It surprises many catmen that blue cats in large rivers often remain active throughout the Coldwater Period. Instead of tucking behind logs and rocks in deep holes, blues often hold along steep channel ledges in heavy current, readily feeding when an easy meal drifts by. Blue cats along the northern edge of their range become less active during extremely cold weather, but we've talked to anglers from central Missouri to northern Virginia who consistently catch big blues from water in the low- to mid-30°F range.

Once water temperatures climb into the low- to mid-50°F range, which often coincides with heavy spring rains, channel cats and flatheads begin feeding. Wintering holes offer plenty of security and comfort but little food, so cats begin to seek areas that concentrate prey. Large minnows, live or winter-killed shad, and any other fish species of appropriate size and abundance—from white suckers to white bass—are important prey. Increasing river flows force prey to hold behind shoreline snags, wing dams, and in deep outside bends. And cats move into these areas to feed and escape the heavy current.

Catfish in smaller rivers often move upstream during prespawn, swimming into progressively faster flows that eventually lead to a barrier like a shallow riffle or manmade dam. An Iowa Department of Natural Resources study documented the movement of several radio-tagged channel catfish in a small interior stream into tiny tributary creeks temporarily swollen with spring runoff. The places where these fish eventually spawn may be several tributaries removed from the river where they spent the winter and where they will return to when water levels begin to drop in summer.

A similar migration may occur in major rivers. Biologists speculate, though, that a percentage of the catfish population in a river can be classified as "movers." These fish bypass lock and dam structures and ascend tributary streams on their way to remote spawning sites. Other fish, though, are more sedentary, spawning and establishing summer home ranges within a few hundred yards of wintering holes. This diversity is important for the health of catfish populations, as it allows fish to colonize new areas and to avoid genetic isolation.

Size and species also determine where fish spawn. A study by the Missouri Department of Conservation of prespawn movements of flatheads and channel catfish in the Missouri River revealed that channel cats tend to move longer distances than flatheads, and that larger channel cats often move farther than small (but sexually mature) channels. These smaller fish, though, more likely ascended tributary streams. Some large channel cats moved short distances up feeder creeks during periods of high water, but no flatheads of any size left the main river to spawn during the study period.

Flatheads and blue cats do move into smaller rivers during some major high-water periods, though. Missouri biologists credit the flooding of 1993 with the recovery of catfish populations in much of the lower Missouri River and its tributaries. Prior to 1993, catfish abundance was depressed from decades of commercial overharvest and habitat destruction, but the high water allowed migratory cats from the Mississippi River to restock the Missouri. Angler catch rates during the last several years indicate that the size and abundance of flatheads and blue cats continue to improve.

During most of the Prespawn Period, though, cats are more concerned with food than with potential spawning sites. They look for easy meals and more likely feed during the day—particularly during the morning and evening twilight periods—than at any other time of year. Set up in the right spot during these intense feeding periods to enjoy some of the fastest action of the season.

Holding Areas On A Typical Wing Dam

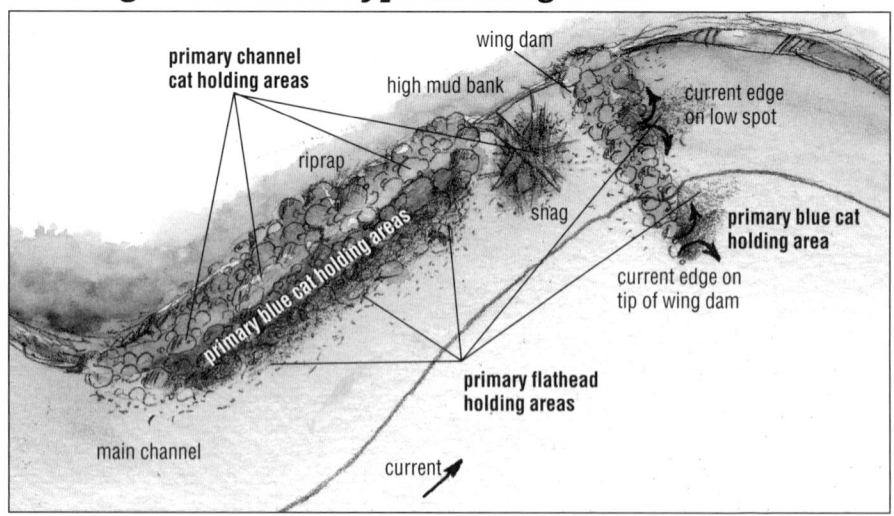

primary channel cat holding areas

high mud bank

wing dam

current edge on low spot

riprap

primary blue cat holding areas

shag

primary blue cat holding area

current edge on tip of wing dam

primary flathead holding areas

main channel

current

THE RIGHT PLACE

Early on, channel cats and especially flatheads are in deep holes near wintering areas. Initially, they stay close to home, venturing onto adjacent flats or moving to the head of the hole in search of a meal, but still avoiding heavy current. As water temperatures continue to rise, they begin searching for larger concentrations of forage. Find lots of forage in the right water conditions and you'll find large concentrations of catfish.

Current Breaks—Ohio River angler Frank Van Winkle believes the resident (more sedentary) portion of the catfish population won't move far if sufficient forage is available near major wintering areas. The best wintering areas on the Ohio River often are in the lower third of each pool, in the deepest and slackest holes. Van Winkle begins his search there, using sonar to locate structural elements that provide cover and deflect current near the main river channel.

Prior to 1993, catfish abundance was depressed from decades of commercial overharvest and habitat destruction.

Some of Van Winkle's favorite spots are old dams. Most of these structures have been reduced to rubble, but the foundations are still intact. Though the top of a dam lies 20 feet below the surface, it's a barrier to catfish and other species moving upstream from wintering holes above the lock and dam. Van Winkle speculates that cats follow the main channel upstream until they reach these dams, then hold along the face of the dam or behind large chunks of concrete. Many cats stay in these areas for the rest of the season, spawning in crevices between rocks and feeding on the many prey species that seek cover around the structures.

When the current is fast and heavy, however, anchoring in the main channel is often too dangerous and presenting baits in deep water too difficult. In these conditions Van Winkle looks for shoreline bars on inside bends or at creek mouths. While the current in the middle of the river is fast, water traveling outside the main channel is slowed by shallow water and numerous obstructions that restrict flow and push the current back toward the channel.

Shoreline barriers are particularly important in channelized rivers like the lower Mississippi and the Missouri. Snags and brush have been removed from large sections of these rivers, and oxbows, side channels, and sloughs have been sealed off from the main river, creating a deep, swift, and turbid river with little cover. Wing dams and riprap banks are primary catfish habitat in these rivers.

A study of the use of wing dams on the Missouri River, conducted by the Missouri Department of Conservation, revealed that active flatheads prefer to hold along the edge where fast and slow currents meet. The most distinct current edges on wing dams occur at the tip of the dam, where fast water from the main channel pours over the slack water behind the dike, and behind low spots atop the dam. Flatheads usually hold behind these current obstructions.

Channel cats prefer similar feeding stations, but in rivers containing flatheads and blue cats, channels are forced into less opportune areas. Most of the channel cats sampled in the Missouri River, for example, were found near snags and riprap along the eroded mud banks in front of the dam. Blue cats were evenly split between the tips of wing dams and snags. Few fish were captured in the deep slack water behind wing dams, but biologists speculate that it could be the result of inefficient sampling gear rather than habitat preference.

The mouths of large tributary streams also act as barriers. Lake Pepin, a 25,000-acre impoundment in Mississippi River Pool 4, is formed by the delta of the Chippewa River. The delta partially blocks the Mississippi's flow, creating a lake-like environment with little current upstream. Similar deltas on major rivers offer relief from current and concentrate baitfish that spawn in smaller rivers. Catfish hold in the slack water of the tributary mouth, gorging on shad and other forage.

Tailwaters—The same water conditions that prompt catfish to move upstream also summon skipjack herring, shad, shiners, goldeye, sucker, and other prey, as well as walleyes, saugers, and white bass. The migration of both predators and prey eventually is blocked by a dam. On major rivers, lock- and-dam structures segment the stream into pools varying in length from about 10 miles to more than 90. In the tailraces below these dams, cats consume fish killed in generator turbines or by lock operations. They also feed on shad and other fish that school in mid-depths or near the surface.

In long river stretches, fresh waves of cats continue to reach tailraces, sustaining the bite as fish from the tailrace are harvested or caught and released.

The migration of both predators and prey eventually is blocked by a dam.

The best tailraces lie at the heads of long pools, particularly if tributary streams and major current breaks don't divert a portion of the catfish population. Blue cats, in particular, on their way to the tailrace, often bypass holding areas that attract and hold large numbers of flatheads and channel cats.

Catfish prefer well-oxygenated water with a steady supply of living and dead baitfish, but they seldom hold in the swiftest current of the tailrace. Instead, cats seek current edges formed where current moving in different directions meet, or where current flows of different speeds and volumes meet. These current edges form tunnels near bottom—areas of relative calm in otherwise turbulent water. Catfish move easily through these tunnels, searching for baitfish and other food items that wash into the tailrace.

The best current tunnels usually are in areas where flows of different volumes meet below the dam. If a pillar separates two dam gates, one running water and one that isn't, the pillar creates a current edge where a large volume of water from the open gate runs over a lesser volume of water moving in the same direction. Current tunnels, though, usually don't coincide with the visible current edge on the surface. Surface currents move much faster than current near the bottom. This allows the faster flow to run farther over the slower flow on the surface than on the bottom.

A word of warning here. Areas of turbulence in tailrace areas can be dangerous. Areas below lowhead dams are particularly deadly. This is no time to guess whether water flow is fishable. When in doubt, don't. No catfish is worth risking your life.

The best way to identify the location of a current tunnel is to use your sinker to feel for it. Anchor in the slow water and cast a bait to the head of the current edge (at the base of a pillar) and let it sink to the bottom. You'll feel the force of the current pushing on the line and bait. Then when the bait settles into a current tunnel, it stops. Keep your bait anchored near the head of the tunnel and a catfish will find it. Usually, though, current bounces the bait along the tunnel and back to faster water. Reel in and cast again.

As waters warm into the upper 60°F range, other species leave the tailrace to spawn. Some cats linger, but their numbers dwindle as they too begin to move toward spawning areas. And after at least a month of predation, baitfish numbers are down, too, and surviving fish are warier and more elusive. The spawning urge also is getting stronger, eventually becoming more powerful than hunger.

Spawning Areas—Some cats spawn in riprap or other suitable areas near the dam, but most move downstream toward slower water with more cover. In the upper Mississippi River, cats enter backwater areas like old oxbows, sloughs, and side channels that contain timber and undercut banks. Shallow flats off the main flow offer reduced current, and manmade or natural cover provides crevices for male fish as they protect the eggs.

John Pitlo, a research biologist with the Iowa DNR, has been netting cats on the upper Mississippi for more than a decade,to determine the effect of minimum-length restrictions for commercially harvested cats. He's identified differences in the spawning habitat of flatheads and channel cats. Before cats begin to spawn, flatheads and channel cats often are caught in the same nets. After spawning commences, though, the range of each species seldom overlaps.

Tackle Specifics

Tackle for giant cats must be strong and durable. Beyond that, choose tackle that complements your fishing style.

For casting into tailrace boils on the Arkansas River, Jim Hart uses 14-foot Fenwick surfcasting rods mated to Ambassadeur 7000C3 reels. He spools them with 25-pound Berkley Trilene Big Game line. That might be overkill for the 3- to 10-pound cats that dominate Hart's creel but is definitely needed when he hooks a 30-pounder.

On the business end, Hart uses a rig weighted with a 5-ounce pyramid sinker. Depending on current velocity, he ties a loop in the line from 6 inches to 3 feet above the sinker and attaches a 7/0 Kahle hook, which he baits with a chunk of cut skipjack.

For drifting and fishing the jetties on the Arkansas River, Charlie Hoke uses 7- or 8-foot medium-power casting rods and Ambassadeur 6000C or 7000C reels spooled with 50-pound-test Spectra line. He starts with a 16-inch leader tied to a 1/0 to 6/0 Kahle hook.

Depending on current speed and the depth of the holes he's fishing, James Patterson uses an assortment of outfits. When fishing 40- to 70-foot holes in light to moderate current, he uses a 7½-foot flippin' stick and an Ambassadeur 6500 reel spooled with 20-pound-test Trilene Big Game. In heavy current, he opts for a long surf rod, Shimano Triton reel, and 30-pound line.

At the terminal end, he uses a three-way swivel rig. To one ring, he ties a 6- to 8-inch dropper ending in a pyramid sinker heavy enough to anchor baits in current. To the other ring of the swivel, he ties a leader and a #4 to 7/0 Eagle Claw Kahle hook.

For fishing big rivers, all three anglers agree that an aluminum boat with a deep-V hull is essential for safety and performance. Boats 16 to 20 feet long best handle the pounding and turbulence of a typical tailrace discharge. Longer boats also accommodate more gear and tackle, and they provide a safe and stable platform for fighting and landing big fish.

The best spawning sites for flatheads in the upper river are old riprap walls built during the early 1900s, before the current lock-and-dam system was built. The walls are about 4 feet deep on top, tapering at a 45-degree angle down to 8 to 12 feet of water. Female flatheads lay clutches of eggs in crevices at the base of these walls. The Spawn Period may last for a month or more in some rivers, but Pitlo speculates that flatheads weeks away from spawning often are attracted to major spawning sites after the first wave of fish begin to spawn.

Pitlo says channel cats prefer snags and timber to rock and concrete. Large rootwads and logjams strewn along undercut clay banks offer good overhead cover and security. Old muskrat and beaver holes are popular spawning sites, too, especially if they're located behind snags or other current breaks. Channel cats avoid inside bends with shallow bars and areas with no current. And, like flatheads, channel cats respond to pheromones produced by other spawning cats. Biologists use a ripe female channel cat to attract other cats to their nets.

THE RIGHT PRESENTATION

Baits—Catfish are omnivores that at times eat almost anything. They're blessed with a unique sensory system that enables them to smell and taste minute concentrations of substances dissolved in water. This offers an advantage in the murky and turbid environment of a big river, where species that rely on sight are unable to feed as effectively. Many anglers believe catfish are best attracted by prepared baits that exude a strong chemical aura. These baits can be effective, but for the sake of simplicity we'll limit our focus to natural baits.

Cutbait works because catfish are programmed to eat what's abundant, and dead baitfish are abundant in big rivers. Cats sense a piece of cutbait drifting in the current or lying on the bottom and immediately recognize it as food. The best cutbaits usually are fresh cut portions of an oily baitfish like a shad or sucker.

Cutbait usually is the best choice for blue and channel cats, but it can also outproduce livebait for flatheads during a portion of the Prespawn Period. Van Winkle, fishing with two lines, one rigged with cutbait and one with a lively baitfish, often catches more big flatheads on the cutbait. This cutbait bite occurs when lethargic flatheads are first emerging from their wintering holes and again when their activity level peaks in late spring or early summer. Several nightcrawlers on a hook also work well at this time. When water levels begin to stabilize and flatheads begin to feed more often after dark, though, they usually prefer livebait.

Wild baitfish, especially those caught by hook and line or by castnet from the river where you're fishing, make the most effective baits for flatheads. This isn't because flatheads prefer native fish species, but because wild baitfish live longer and react more strongly when a predator approaches than do baitfish from a bait shop. Gizzard and

Quick-Strike Rig

12- to 30-inch leader

#2 or 1/0 treble hooks

snell or uni-knot

improved clinch knot

trim tail to reduce aggressive swimming

threadfin shad, bullheads, carp, drum, and panfish all are effective live-baits. Match the size of the bait to the size of the catfish, keeping in mind that a record-class flathead can eat a bigger baitfish than most freshwater anglers can cast with their heaviest rod and reel combo.

Rigs—Use a simple rig that can hold the bait where active cats can find it. Fewer pieces of terminal tackle mean fewer components to fail, and less weight to interfere with a natural presentation.

Most situations call for a live or dead bait presented on or near the bottom. The most popular rig is a sliprig, consisting of an egg sinker, lead shot, and hook. It's simple enough to tie, but the shot usually slips under the weight of a heavy sinker, and the sinker tends to roll on the bottom and snag more often than other sinker designs. To improve the rig's effectiveness, we replace the egg sinker with a bell sinker, and use a swivel instead of a lead shot.

Don't use a longer leader to separate the bait from the sinker. Use just enough leader to attract fish without hanging up. This may mean a 6- to 12-inch leader for anchoring livebaits in front of a snag for flatheads or no leader at all for probing current tunnels for channels and blue cats in a tailrace.

One overlooked option is a standup-style jig. No hair or feathers, no plastic trailers or fluorescent paint; just a plain pyramid jighead tipped with a piece of cutbait. In fast water, a jig offers a good feel of bottom composition and current speed. Even in slack water, though, jigs may provide an advantage. Cast a heavy jig right up to a snag and it will stay there. No leader to wrap around stray limbs or to collect debris. When a cat picks up the bait, tighten the line and set the hook.

Three-way rigs are another versatile option. Use a 6- to 24-inch dropline anchored by a bell sinker heavy enough to keep the bait near bottom. A half-ounce sinker usually is sufficient in shallow water, but 3 to 8 ounces may be needed to drift around the tips of wing dams for blue cats or to anchor big livebaits for flatheads. The leader should be slightly longer than the dropper line—usually 2 to 3 feet.

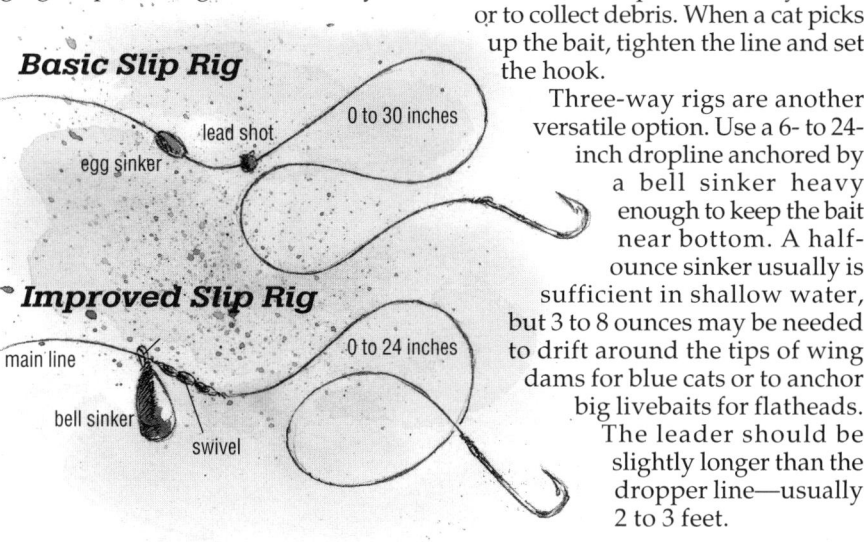

Three-Way Rig

main line
12- to 30-inch leader
swivel
single hook or quick-strike rig
6- to 24-inch dropper
1/2- to 4-ounce sinker

Basic Slip Rig

lead shot
0 to 30 inches
egg sinker

Improved Slip Rig

main line
0 to 24 inches
bell sinker
swivel

Three-way rigs usually are tied with single hooks matched to the size of the bait. Van Winkle prefers quick-strike rigs tied with #2 or 1/0 treble hooks for targeting flatheads. He ties the trebles 3 or 4 inches apart on a 30-pound monofilament leader for 8- to 10-inch gizzard shad. Insert one tine of the lead treble into the flesh behind the head of the bait, the other treble behind the dorsal fin. Set as soon as a fish grabs the bait.

Finally, float rigs are effective for searching areas with slow to moderate current, or for working baits over broken bottoms like riprap that would quickly eat bottom rigs. A small, thin float like the Thill Center Slider works for small to medium-size portions of cutbait. The more bulbous Thill Big Fish Slider works with big livebaits. Weight larger floats with a 1/2- to 2-ounce egg sinker threaded on the main line above a barrel swivel and 12-inch leader.

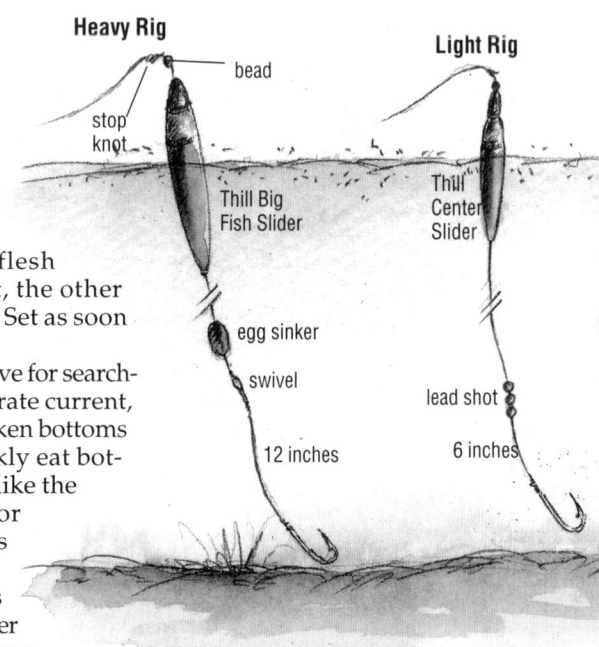

Slipfloat Rigging

Heavy Rig

Light Rig

bead

stop knot

Thill Big Fish Slider

Thill Center Slider

egg sinker

swivel

lead shot

12 inches

6 inches

Ockham's Razor

Ockham's Razor is a principle that states that the simplest explanation, the one requiring the fewest assumptions, usually is correct. The principle's attributed to William of Ockham, a fourteenth century philosopher who saw that medical students would forever diagnose rare diseases in patients suffering from common ailments, not because they were incompetent healers, but because they wanted to test the limits of their knowledge so badly that they often overlooked the obvious answer.

Surely, Ockham's Razor also applies to catfishing. The simplest explanation often is best. To catch more cats, William the Catman might have said, fish the simplest rigs in the most obvious locations when cats are most active. In other words, keep it simple to catch more cats, so long as your simple rigging is placed in top cat water.

Draining about 40 percent of the nation's total land mass, rivers such as the Mississippi, Arkansas, Missouri, Tennessee, and Ohio are among the world's most fertile catfish fisheries. They're exceedingly rich with nutrients, so they support incredibly diverse food chains and all boast terrific numbers of big catfish.

WHAT MAKES A GREAT CATFISH RIVER?

Hutchie Weeks, regional supervisor for the Oklahoma Department of Wildlife Conservation, is particularly impressed by the catfish-growing potential of rivers such as the Arkansas. The biggest blue cat he's sampled with electrofishing gear weighed 40 pounds, and he's handled plenty in the 20- to 30-pound range. One reason such fish are so common, Weeks says, is the river's rich forage base. The most important reason, though, is water quality. Big, muddy rivers aren't the prettiest things in the world to look at, but their fish-growing capacity is astonishing.

"The Arkansas River doesn't stratify," Weeks explains. "It has a constant flow, and the water temperature and dissolved oxygen levels remain constant. Some tailraces, such as those below large highland reservoirs, have problems with dissolved oxygen, but not in navigation systems like the Arkansas, Mississippi, Missouri, and Ohio rivers."

The lower sections of many rivers offer the best chance for a trophy catfish. For example, the Arkansas River, until it reaches Muskogee, Oklahoma, flows mostly over sand. By the time it reaches southeastern Arkansas, however, it flows over rich alluvial deposits of the Mississippi Delta. Phosphorous and nitrogen increase, which feed more phytoplankton, which in turn support larger populations of shad and other baitfish. These baitfish sustain more cats than the infertile headwater stretches. Similar patterns exist on most rivers that flow through fertile farmland.

Ohio River—
Frank Van Winkle, 40-pound flathead

Of course, the growing popularity of catfish doesn't indicate a previous lack of great fishing on big rivers. "The Arkansas has always been a good fishery," Weeks says. "I was raised here, and I remember many big catfish caught before the dams were built. More fish may be in there today, though, and I'm certain that someone will soon catch a new state record blue."

Considering the size of their watersheds and their reputations for churning out giant catfish, the Arkansas and Mississippi rivers adequately represent the great catfish waters of the heartland. Each displays similar topographic and riparian characteristics, and local anglers use similar methods to catch cats of all sizes.

"Channel cats are the least depth-specific catfish species," says guide Donny Hall of Nashville, Tennessee. "I've caught them in water 2, 20, and 50 feet deep on the same day. Particularly in navigable rivers like the Cumberland, the population usually is large enough that distinct populations may gather at several depths to take advantage of different feeding opportunities. But a good number of fish almost always can be found in shallow water, especially during spring."

Hall defines shallow water as "less than about 10 feet, but in river sections with lots of water deeper than 50 feet, a 20-foot flat might be considered shallow. My largest channel cat to date, a 25-pounder, came from a 15-foot ledge. And at times, fish this size or even larger may be found in water barely knee deep."

How shallow channel cats hold depends on several factors. "They hug tightest to the bank in high, muddy water," Hall says, "probably because the shoreline concentrates most of the river's forage species. Many big rivers also have lots of timber and rock cover in the 1- to 10-foot depth zone, and during normal water levels, channel cats often hold near these objects close to the bank. They're usually tight to the cover when the current's intense, less so when it's more moderate."

Tributary mouths also serve as a natural food-delivery system. "When creeks are running high and muddy after a heavy rain, channels move onto the flat at the mouth," Hall adds. "Moving out from the mouth might reveal a ledge or drop-off with a big tangle of woodcover—limbs, brush, or even entire trees—accumulated during high water. This often is one of the best channel cat spots on the river, for numbers and size."

Channel cats also move into the tributary stream when conditions are right, but usually don't move far. "Sometimes a big concentration of cats holds between the mouth and the first major bend in the creek," Hall says. "They usually hold tight to the bank, or in or around big snags and other woodcover. Drifting a float rig through these short stretches can quickly fill a livewell with channel cats."

In clearer water and rivers with little shoreline cover, channel cats are much more reluctant to move shallow during daylight. "Check the 10- to 15-foot zone where light penetration typically stops and cover usually is more plentiful," Hall suggests. "Often a stump row or other seemingly insignificant patch of cover will hold good numbers of fish. The best fishing usually occurs after dark, though, when cats move onto shallow flats to feed."

CATFISH TACTICS FOR A RIVER NEAR YOU

Tailrace Tactics—A turbulent line of churning water marks the point of no return for a fleet of small johnboats below Ozark Lock and Dam on the Arkansas River, but Jim Hart of Poteau, Oklahoma, idles past them with confidence. "Going to the fish is the key to catching big catfish," he says. A sturdy boat designed for rough water allows Hart to get closer to the dam, where large concentrations of cats gorge on dead and wounded baitfish swept through the turbines.

"When the water gets rough," Hart continues, "you need a boat at least 16 feet long with deep sides and a wide beam. I use a 21-foot aluminum boat with a modified V-hull."

To catch big blue cats, Hart anchors about 100 yards below the dam and casts cut skipjack herring upstream into the boils. His target area depends on current, which determines where the fish congregate.

In heavy flow, the water in a tailrace looks like a cauldron of foam and spray.

"On lakes, weather conditions determine fish location and their activity level," Hart explains, "but on big rivers activity level is controlled by the current. In winter, for example, fish avoid stronger flows. They're not as active, so they don't want to fight the current. They just want a place where they can rest and ambush prey with minimal effort."

In heavy flow, the water in a tailrace looks like a cauldron of foam and spray. Look closely, however, and you'll notice subtle hydraulic structures, particularly boils, that function like bottom structure in smaller streams. Learn to identify these elements, and you can fish them as efficiently as anglers in small streams fish visible holes.

"Look for current breaks and eddies," Hart says. "In spring, cats usually hold behind boils. You'll have to cast behind the boil to catch the fish. Drop your bait behind the boil, and the backwash often will hold it there.

"You have to look at the surface to find boils," he adds. "Avoid side currents because they pull the bait away from the dam, where most cats tend to congregate. If baitfish hold near the edge of the side current, though, the cats eventually follow."

How effective is this method? Fishing every Saturday from Christmas Day 1996 to the end of February 1997, Hart says he and his partners caught 1,500 pounds of catfish. Most were between 3 and 10 pounds, but they also caught several in the 20- to 30-pound range.

Drifting The Dikes—In contrast to Hart's anchor-and-cast method, guide Charlie Hoke of Little Rock, Arkansas, searches a 30-mile section of the Arkansas River. Hoke says he and his clients consistently catch their biggest cats by casting toward the dam and drifting downstream at current speed. This technique accounts for some giant blues, including a 60-pounder.

To catch big blues, Hoke prefers freshly cut skipjack herring fillets for their high oil content. Gizzard shad and other oily baitfish also work, but never quite match the attractiveness of cut herring.

"Big rivers are constantly changing," Hoke says. "That's what makes this kind of fishing so enjoyable. You can't always hit the same places year after year, because the layout of the channel is always changing. A structural element like a logjam may produce several big cats this year and be washed away by high water next spring."

When targeting specific areas, Hoke likes to drift baits through the eddies behind the many wing dams that poke out from the banks of the river. There's usually a stretch of slack water behind the jetties and a deep hole gouged out by

JAMES RIVER BLUE CATS

Blue cats probably are the species most anglers in the Midwest and Mid-south associate with big rivers, but growing populations of big blues also thrive in tidal rivers from Virginia to South Carolina. Many of these rivers afford catfish the same kind of habitat as other navigable waterways, though gizzard shad, blueback herring, and other prey species usually are much more abundant. According to guide Jimmy Weir, catfish behave the same way in tidal rivers as they do in inland streams.

"It's important to consider how fish behave in their environment," Weir says. "When fishing secondary channels or feeder creeks, for example, I know the fish are there to eat. I employ a run-and-gun approach by setting up on deep holes or cover like docks and trees for no longer than 30 minutes. If I don't get bit, I move. Since these areas usually aren't as deep as main-river spots, though, I also know that the fish will be more wary. I motor around the core of the hole, then drift back into casting range by releasing more anchor rope."

Tributary streams and side channels frequently are visited by blue cat anglers during high-water periods, but Weir says they usually hold the largest concentrations of fish from midwinter through midspring. "By the time water levels begin to stabilize, I'm looking for fish in the main river channel," Weir adds. "Blue cats have gained something of a coldwater reputation in recent years, but I've taken some of my biggest fish during summer, especially when water temperatures approach peak levels. This is when blues begin to move onto shallow flats adjacent to the main channel to feed after dark."

Even when targeting actively feeding fish, though, Weir says that fresh bait is essential. "I often spend two or three hours gathering enough bait for a day of fishing," Weir adds. "When the bait's not abundant in shallow water, I motor in an s-pattern across ledges in the main river, watching my sonar for schools of shad. I keep an eye out for big-fish arches, too, since this can help pinpoint the depth where blue cats are feeding.

"Many big rivers are blessed with large populations of gizzard shad, skipjack herring, or other schooling baitfish species," Weir says, "which is one reason they produce so many big blue cats. On the James River, one throw with an 8-foot cast net may capture so many shad that I have to struggle to haul it over the gunwale. Shad from about 8 to 14 inches long are the best bait year-round. Cut the bait once behind the gill plate and again in front of the tail fin. On some days, blues seem to prefer the heads, while the body section produces more fish on other days."

the current—that's where the big fish lie. "Holes associated with wing dams are an excellent place for big blues," Hoke says. "To a big cat, it's like sitting at a table and having someone serve you."

Scour Hole Strategies—Guide James Patterson of Memphis, Tennessee, targets similar areas on the greatest big cat river of them all, the mighty Mississippi. Long stone dikes built perpendicular to the current are common on much of the lower Mississippi. In many cases the river has clawed out massive holes behind these dikes, ranging in depth from 30 to 120 feet. These holes offer catfish refuge from the current and strategic ambush points to intercept baitfish. Furthermore, the water in these holes often is slightly cooler in summer and warmer in winter, making it more comfortable to cats.

Patterson catches most of his fish from 30- to 50-foot holes. His biggest fish to date—a 75-pound blue—came from such a hole. He says the biggest fish prefer live shad, but he catches more fish on cutbait. Patterson anchors his boat in the middle of the eddy behind the dike and drops his bait into the tail of the eddy, letting the current wash it into the head of the hole.

As on other rivers, current speed and water volume determine fish activity on the Mississippi. "I like low, clear water," Patterson says. "I prefer the river on the Memphis gauge to be below 10 feet, but I like it best at 6 feet—the kinds of days bass fishermen don't like are my favorites. Couple low water with blue skies and a north wind, and those cats will be belly to the bottom, right where I want them."

The orientation of the fish is important because of the precise presentation required to fish these holes. It's essential for the catfish to be under the bait because they'll come up to eat, but generally won't go down. In the center of the eddy, Patterson explains, a bait suspended high in the water column will be moving, but cats lying on the bottom are motionless.

When a cat senses a baitfish overhead, it will rise up to eat it, then return to its hole. If the current is too swift, however, it's virtually impossible to keep the bait down without 3 or more ounces of weight. That requires heavier tackle and a slower presentation, since baits must be anchored, rather than drifted. Time also is important. Patterson never fishes a hole for more than 30 minutes if he doesn't get bit.

The dynamics of big rivers are essentially the same as those of a small stream, only on a larger scale.

The key to catching giant cats on main-stem rivers lies in the ability to read water and an understanding of how current affects catfish location and behavior. The dynamics of big rivers are essentially the same as those of a small stream, only on a larger scale. Once you learn to identify and evaluate current, you've solved two-thirds of the catfish puzzle—finding fish.

BRACKISH WATER BLUE CATS

Most anglers never consider coastal waters for catfish. Saltwater may seem alien to those familiar with fishing freshwater reservoirs, rivers, and streams, but many brackish (part salt, part fresh water) marshes and bay systems harbor sizable populations of blue cats during winter, creating a virtually untapped opportunity for prime fishing.

Tagging studies and sampling projects conducted by officials with the Sabine National Wildlife Refuge in Hackberry, Louisiana, have found the salt content in coastal waters during winter compatible with blue cats. Blues have a higher tolerance for saltwater than do flatheads and channels, and they fare well in coastal areas during winter when forage is abundant.

The Gulf Coast offers dozens of options for catfishermen in pursuit of these brackish water blues. Some of the best spots are in the vast, lonely marshes and tributaries in southwest Louisiana and southeast Texas. Here a small but dedicated core of anglers move from inland waters toward the coast when water temperatures plummet.

Some of the techniques employed to bag these blues go hand in hand with well-known catfish strategies, while others may seem a little odd. In the right situation, though, they can be deadly.

PRIMARY LOCATIONS

One of the best spots to locate these brackish-water blues is a large marshy drainage where a river and bay meet. These spots offer two key ingredients to success—strong tidal movements and abundant forage.

During incoming tides, look for catfish around points at the mouth of the river. Many of these spots have washouts created by current, which are several feet deeper than surrounding waters.

Cats will bunch up in these holes, which often are filled with potential prey items such as menhaden and blue crabs. Another spot to consider during incoming tides is the river channel itself, which often extends into the bay. When viewing a surface map, it may seem that the river ends where the bay begins, but things can look different when viewed through a depthfinder or when studied on a detailed hydrographic chart.

On Lake Calcasieu near Lake Charles, Louisiana, the Calcasieu River channel gradually declines about 200 yards into what most people consider the bay. Such spots can, at times, be tremendously productive.

During outgoing tides, look to marshy drainages for the most consistent catfish action. As baitfish are displaced from the marsh, catfish gather at key junctures like the mouth of the drain and sloughs that wind into the marsh.

Within marsh systems, one of the most likely locations to find cats is where several small drainages meet. These current-laden spots often form eddies that are natural magnets for catfish. Since crabs, shrimp, and menhaden that dwell in marshes during winter can't navigate well in current, they become displaced into eddies. Blue cats often hold around these eddies, waiting for prey to come to them.

WINTER KILLS, DRIFTING, AND WADING

Air temperatures along the Gulf Coast can range from the 70°F range down to the 20s during winter, so large baitfish kills often occur, especially menhaden and shrimp. Often a warm spell occurs, and baitfish move into the shallows of the bay where the water warms quickest. These warm spells may be followed by a brutal cold front that sends water temperatures plummeting and kills many baitfish.

These fish kills, similar to those in northern waters, attract cats. The spots with the greatest potential for fish kills are where shallow and deep water meet at the mouth of the bay and along shallow, flat shorelines on the main body of a bay. Commercial shrimpers who dredge these areas often bring up tons of dead, rotting baitfish.

Primary Brackish Locations

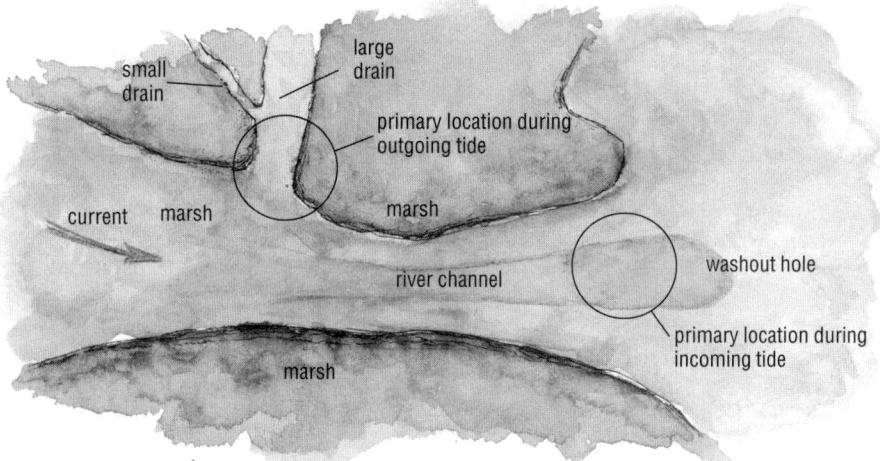

Multiple Drainage Areas

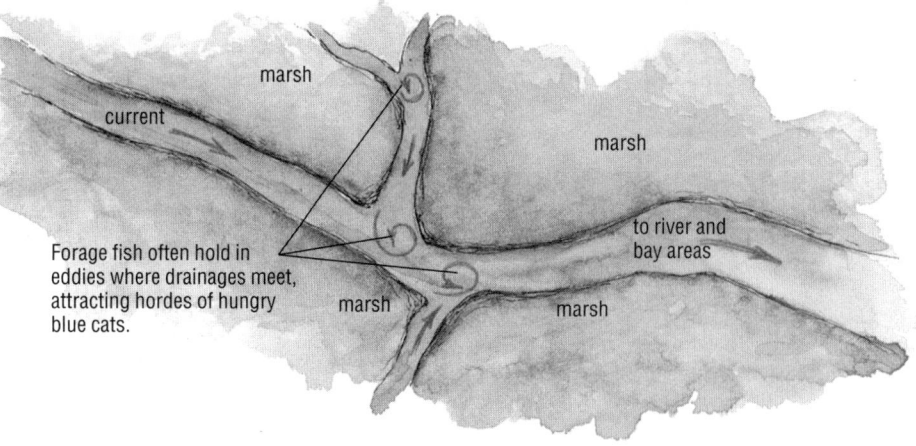

The flats can be especially productive during a high tide on a warm winter afternoon. Since flats usually are barren of fish-holding structure, covering lots of water is important. One way to do this is to freeline a bait while slowly moving through the area with a trolling motor. Another good way is to position the boat along the outer edge of the flat and drift with the tide.

Like any wave, a tide weakens as it moves inland.

Some anglers prefer to don a pair of neoprene waders and wade the flats. This is an especially good method when a falling tide reveals catfish actively feeding in the shallows, their dorsal fins sticking out of the water. At these times, the fish may be caught by sight-casting with popping cork rigs. It's a rare occurrence, but the sheer excitement of it makes it worth looking for.

When wading for cats wear the proper attire. Wadefishing belts like the Wade-Aid give superior back support and plenty of places to carry gear needed for such a demanding method of fishing. Walking through chilly waters can tire muscles quickly and give anglers even in the best of shape sharp back pains.

One warning about wading in coastal bays: don't just find a good looking spot, hop overboard, and start wading. Some spots may have mud deeper than the water. Poke and prod the area with a pole or paddle to test the strength of the bottom. Also, look for areas that have large stands of roseau cane, which typically grows near a hard bottom.

TIDES

Tides are one of the most crucial factors when pursuing brackish-water catfish. Unfortunately, tides are misunderstood by many anglers, especially those who aren't familiar with coastal fishing.

Like other bay dwellers, such as red drum and flounder, catfish usually feed most aggressively during the first couple hours of tidal movements. This most likely can be attributed to a greater influx of baitfish into key areas. But remember that all tidal movements are not created equal.

One question we often hear is: "The high tide was going to be at 11:15, but the water was low at the boat dock. How could the water be so low during high tide?"

Terminal Rigs and Tackle

Hang-ups usually aren't as big a problem in coastal areas as in inland waters. Debris may collect in the mouth of a river, but the marshes and shallow flats usually don't hold many snags. In these areas, the best riggings are simple—a wide gap hook and a slipweight rigged above a swivel.

Floats are useful in some applications, especially for drifting over open flats. The best floats are weighted popping corks used chiefly for speckled trout in bays. These corks work well with the current and displace lots of water when popped, which often draw strikes.

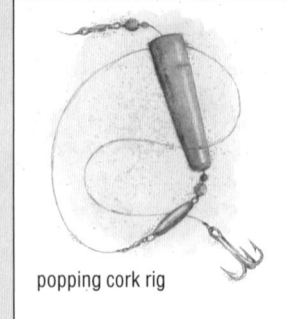

popping cork rig

Tides are the periodic rise and fall of ocean waters, caused by gravity from the moon, sun, and earth. To understand how these tidal movements work, compare them to a wave. In essence, a tide is a large, slow-moving wave that starts in the ocean, moves through a pass, and ends up in the back of a bay or river system. Most waves are influenced by wind, and tides are no different.

North winds, which are common during winter, push water out of a bay. That's why we get low tides during fall. "Blue northers" in conjunction with a strong tidal pull can drain an area and help cleanse coastal marshes. Also, tides at points away from the immediate coastline won't be as strong as those at a pass near the Gulf.

Like any wave, a tide weakens as it moves inland. So the strongest tide will be near the Gulf, with the weakest far into the bay or river.

Another question we hear is: "The high tide was to occur at about 5:00 a.m., but the tide didn't move for hours. Was the tide table wrong?" Probably not. Tides given in papers and on television merely indicate lows and highs. They don't show the change between tides

If a tide table predicts two high tides at 3:35 a.m. and 12:58 p.m., and low tides at 8:55 a.m. and 8:37 p.m., the National Weather Services Charts may forecast a drop of only 8 inches between the 3:35 a.m. high and the 8:55 a.m. low. And it may rise only about 5 inches between that 8:55 a.m. low and the 12:50 p.m. high. But look farther, and you might learn that between that 12:50 p.m. high and the 8:37 p.m. low, the tide is forecast to drop more than 2½ feet, which is a strong tide for the Gulf Coast.

To plan a catfish trip around tidal movements, watch how much change will occur between tides. Blue cats are opportunists, and big tides provide the biggest feeding opportunity. The angler who best understands the tides and other factors related to catching brackish-water blue cats can make the most of this fishing opportunity.

Coastal Bait Choices

Shrimp—One of the all-around best baits for brackish blues is shrimp. Fresh shrimp is difficult to get during winter, but it's definitely superior to some of the dried, frozen stuff that bait shops sell. We usually buy shrimp from fish markets or grocery stores. It's more expensive, but the shrimp usually are larger and in better condition.

Mullet—Mullet are fairly easy to catch with cast nets during winter and are an excellent bait choice. Avoid frozen mullet, though, because it easily tears off the hook.

Menhaden—Menhaden is another top choice for brackish-water blues. It's usually available at coastal bait shops.

Crab—Crab may seem like an unusual choice for catfish bait, but it works. Many catfish caught in coastal ecosystems have a bellyful of crab remains. While fishing in a remote spot in southwest Louisiana called Black Bayou, we once saw a blue cat in the 10-pound range floating dead. When we took a closer look, we noticed it had a large blue crab stuck in its throat. Apparently, the fish died while trying to eat the crab.

Squid—Frozen squid is readily available at coastal bait shops, and it will suffice for catfish bait. Squid isn't one of the best baits, but it freezes well and is difficult to remove from a hook. Use it as a last resort.

Catfish in Small Rivers

FINDING SMALL-RIVER CATS

We say with confidence, after spending a fair amount of time on small rivers, that all remains right with the world. The sky is not bound to fall, nor the earth soon bound to pass; and that rivers still run as they always have, with catfish holding just where they should be during each subsequent season. It brings a smile to think that it really is so terribly predictable. Indeed, even factoring in the unpredictability of weather, catfish will be this season just where they were the last—just where they have been for decades and even previous centuries.

This isn't so in an absolutely literal sense, because rivers are constantly changing. A sandbar right smack there today, might not be there next year or even next week. Permanence is the exception on rivers, not the rule.

It is the definitive parts of a river that never change—the riffles, the holes, and the runs. God created, with only passing exception, all rivers equal in this regard. The rivers in Kentucky alongside which race horses roam have riffles, holes, and runs. Wyoming rivers, like the remaining free-flowing portions of the North Platte, where channel cats swim in near anonymity, have riffles, holes, and runs. Indiana, Arizona, Ontario, Brazil. Rivers there and the rivers you fish have riffles, holes, and runs.

So predictable is this basic scenario that these river elements never even occur out of order. Riffles always lead to a hole, holes are always followed by a run, and runs always lead to another riffle. Yes, each individual element may shift location. Yes, they change shape and size. So too are these elements sometimes difficult to recognize. With time on the water, though, ah yes with pleasant time on the water, these elements become familiar friends who whisper secrets about the catfish that have no choice but to hold there.

It's remarkable how an angler's fishing success can improve once he begins to see river structure for what it is and how it so naturally affects catfish location during each season. Catfishing, after all, like most fishing, remains first a matter of finding fish.

Rivers wind because the earth spins, and as the earth spins, water moves predictably clockwise in the northern hemisphere. Pull the plug in your tub and the water swills clockwise down the drain. River water, though, bends clockwise and then rebounds like a billiard ball from bank to bank, causing curves in rivers that haven't been straightened by man. Even straightened rivers, though, do their best to begin to swivel-hip their way to the sea.

As rivers bend back and forth, they flow over various substrates. Rock and gravel areas do not easily wash away, and these humps in the landscape become riffles—shallow, narrow, hard-bottom spots that form natural dams above which water gathers and then constricts just enough to flow over the riffle and quickly downriver.

Riffles extend downriver so far as hard bottom lasts. Then, as the fast water gathers speed flowing downhill, it meets softer sand and soil, and this substrate is scoured away, creating a deeper, wider section of river. A hole forms. Holes also are called pools.

To add perspective at this point, know that riffles in small rivers might be no more than 20 feet across and might be followed by holes no more than 3 feet deep and 10 feet long. On the other hand, riffles in larger rivers may be a quarter mile across. Such extensive riffles have a series of lesser holes running lengthwise below them, instead of one large hole. Cats tend to gather in the biggest, deepest holes.

Runs are river flats that begin at the tailout of a hole, where water that scoured the hole finally begins to slow before being pushed downriver. Here silt and other suspended debris sinks to the bottom, causing the run to shallow up. Eventually, the river flat may stretch for some distance with no significant depth change. The bottom usually is sand and silt with occasional rocks and patches of gravel, plus other debris. Flats usually form the most extensive areas on most rivers. Soon, the water flowing through a run will again build in front of another shallow, narrow, hard-bottom spot—another riffle. And so continues the series.

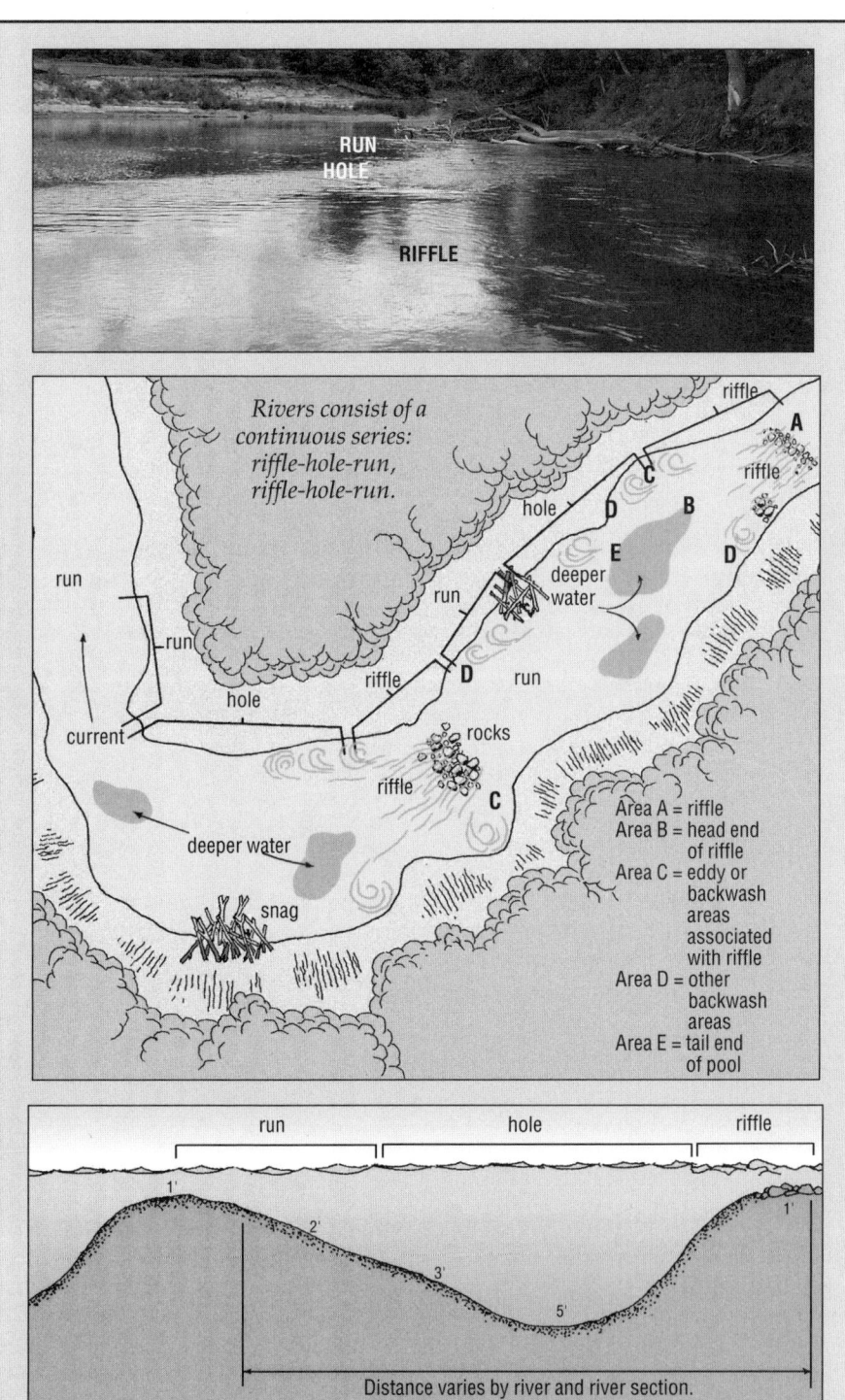

Rivers consist of a continuous series: riffle-hole-run, riffle-hole-run.

RUN
HOLE
RIFFLE

riffle
A
C
riffle
hole
D
B
E
D
deeper
water
run
run
run
run
D
riffle
run
hole
D
current
rocks
riffle
C
deeper water
riffle
C
snag

Area A = riffle
Area B = head end of riffle
Area C = eddy or backwash areas associated with riffle
Area D = other backwash areas
Area E = tail end of pool

run
hole
riffle
1'
2'
3'
5'
1'
Distance varies by river and river section.

Keep Moving, Keep Searching, Keep Understanding

Walk a mile and compare the riffle-hole-run series that occur there. Try fishing in each area. You'll soon see, and certainly your catch will indicate that some of these series are much better than others. Deeper holes with extensive cover often hold the most catfish. Eventually, it becomes obvious that staying long in marginal areas isn't productive. Might even be better to walk right on by until you reach something that's really worth fishing.

Now walk (or float) another mile. And another. And another. Say, over the course of a summer, you eventually cover 20 or 30 miles of river. Now we're really getting somewhere. This is when you begin to realize that some 5- or 10-mile sections of river aren't nearly so productive as other sections. You might even look at a map and realize that a lot of the best sections have narrower, more winding river portions. Eureka. Sometimes you can even narrow the search by looking at a map.

And then, if you stay at it long enough, you'll also begin to view all 50 or 100 miles of river as an entity, where the catfish population shifts during certain seasons. Most of the catfish population might, for example, shift into the upstream third during spring, the downstream third during fall and winter. Then again, in high-water years, the preponderance of fish might stay upstream all year long.

That's looking at river catfishing on a grand scale. At its most basic level, though, once you determine on a grand scale where the fish should be, it's still a matter of going to a river section, finding the best portion of that river section, and then fishing the cover edges in the riffle-hole-run sections in that area.

An old Iowa farmer once said, "Got a hog farm to the east, a chicken ranch to the west, and that feller up north has himself a big feedlot full of cattle. I never have to wonder which way the wind's blowing."

Honestly, river catfishing is a lot like that. Once you understand what to look for, once you've spent time looking and fishing and evaluating, and doing it more and more over the course of a good many years, you can almost sniff the wind—or at least read the current—and just know that fish live there.

You might protest that this continuous series of elements just doesn't exist on your rivers. Not so. In many cases, though, rivers have been terribly altered. Before man entered the scene and dammed, dredged, and diked, even on the largest rivers, these features often were easy to determine.

Even on most altered river sections, though, these features exist in principle if not in easily distinguishable fact. Wing dams may still be seen as riffles, even if they're manmade. And they are followed by holes, which are followed by flats, which extend to the next wing dam. On other altered rivers, a trip upriver or downriver with your sonar running shows subtle changes in bottom contour, depth, and substrate content that reveals the presence of riffles, holes, and runs, again in predictable order.

GOOD, BETTER, BEST

The reason so many fisherman fish at bridge holes is that bridges offer easy access. The car is parked, a lawn chair set out, a forked stick or two pushed into the ground, rods propped up; the angler pops a cold soda and sits comfortably in the shade.

The first anglers to fish a bridge hole often catch fish, too, because bridges usually are built on and over riffle areas, so a hole naturally forms there and often attracts at least a few cats. By the time most anglers get there, however, the fish usually have been fried in someone else's pan. The rule on small rivers during most of the year is that new fish won't move into a fished-out hole until the water rises.

The modern catman is a mobile sort. We have taught for many years that an angler must be prepared to survey at least a 2-, 5-, or 10-mile section of river, in order to determine the location of the best holes. Holes are the homes of catfish. And bigger and deeper holes, and particularly holes with cover in the form of woody debris, usually attract many more cats. Remove these holes from easy access to other anglers, and such holes are gold mines of great fishing, waiting to be discovered. Again, though, keep searching around the next bend in order to finally decide where the best holes are—and where to spend the most time.

SNAGS

Cover often serves as a feeding station or resting area for cats, attractive in part because cover is different from the rest of the river. Mainly, though, cover helps gather food and lets catfish lie comfortably near current, the supplier of food. But cover must be seen in the larger context of where it lies relative to our continuous series of riffles, holes, and runs. Some snags are better than others.

It's not just the size of a snag that determines if cats will be there. Put a great big tangle of trees in the middle of a long river flat, and it probably will attract only small cats. Put that tangle in a big deep hole, however, and some of the biggest fish in that section of the river might be there, both channel cats and flatheads.

Ultimately, the best snags lie in the best holes. As you might also expect, the location of the snag in a hole influences how cats use the snag. Cover in fast current near the top of a hole is primarily a feeding area. Cover in quiet water at the lower half of a hole is primarily holding or resting territory. A snag near the core of a hole is both a feeding and a resting area. The best snags, as you might expect, lie near or just downstream of the core of a hole, where moderate current hits the head of the snag, creates a current edge, as it flows around the snag, and a current break at the rear of the snag.

> Ultimately, the best snags lie in the best holes. As you might also expect, the location of the snag in a hole influences how cats use the snag.

Another way to look at this: rivers are composed of a continuous series of riffles, holes, and runs, and the biggest, deepest holes in an area are the home of the most and largest catfish. A big hole is a big one-room home. In that home, the snag or the core of the hole usually is the bedroom, the top of the hole the kitchen. Catfish usually rest around or under the snag or in the core of the hole, but might occasionally snack there, especially when it's near the kitchen. Active cats move around the hole, checking areas that gather food.

Unfortunately, lots of cats don't always use snags that lie in a perfect position in a good-looking hole. Just as certain snags often gather more cats than other snags, certain river sections sometimes attract more cats during certain periods. A good snag in a section with lots of cats using it has a better chance of attracting lots of cats. This again is one reason for fishing quickly from hole to hole, looking for active cats, at least on your first trips to a river you haven't fished in a while or haven't fished before.

Occasionally, though, you'll also find situations where almost every snag, no matter how small and poorly placed, will have a cat or two using it. This most often occurs during prespawn—when cats are actively feeding and roaming. Or it occurs in river sections with a huge catfish population. Many rivers across the country are like this; that is, catfish populations are booming in many areas. But it won't seem like it if you insist on fishing the same five or 10 holes for the entire season.

BY THE SEASON

Catfish make seasonal movements within rivers and tributary streams. The basic movement is upstream into smaller water during spring and early summer, then back downstream into bigger water during summer and especially fall. During winter, catfish gather in holes with sufficient depth and current where oxygen is available to sustain them. Such holes are most likely in downriver sections.

Soon after spawning and as the water begins to drop during summer, cats tend to move downriver. Tiny stream sections that hold fish during early summer might not hold many fish during late summer; although some cats usually remain in the deepest holes. On the other hand, during wet summers, cats might remain in river sections that run almost dry during most summers. So while seasonal trends apply, weather also plays a part. The point is that we can't just think riffles, holes, and runs, but must also concentrate on river sections that hold the most fish during each yearly period.

The species of catfish makes a difference, too. Flatheads rarely move more than one tributary away from a major river, while channel cats may push into tiny water, sometimes into tributaries several branches removed from a major river. Blue cats, even more than flatheads, are fish of big rivers. Smaller blues may push upriver into the beginning stretches of tributary streams just off big water, but rarely much farther. The biggest blues stay in big water.

Perhaps the watershed of streams and rivers where you fish is something like northwest Iowa. The Little Rock River is a tiny stream only a step or two across as it runs some 60 miles through southern Minnesota into northwest Iowa and enters the Big Rock River near Doon.

Flooding Can Help Habitat

Consider also that flooding helps to distribute timber, brush, and other debris throughout a river. Fallen timber, though, most likely occurs in conjunction with a river hole because of the increased scouring action of current there. Once a tree falls and is held by its roots to the bank, it becomes a prime obstacle gathering floating debris. The biggest snags form in conjunction with river-bend holes. The the most extensive of these become prime holding areas for catfish, usually the best areas in a river.

Meanwhile, the Big Rock River has coursed south for some 100 miles through southern Minnesota and northwest Iowa, beginning as a tiny stream and increasing in size to 100 feet across in the lower section just before it enters the Big Sioux River above Hawarden. The Big Sioux is a major tributary of the middle Missouri, beginning in northern South Dakota as a tiny stream and running almost 200 miles before it meets the Missouri at Sioux City.

Flatheads are common in the lower section of the Big Sioux, becoming less common 50 miles upriver. Occasionally, a blue cat is caught in the lower Big Sioux. Meanwhile, wonderful fishing abounds for small channel cats in Otter Creek, a tiny tributary of the tiny Little Rock River, which again, flows into the Big Rock, which flows into the Big Sioux, which flows into the Missouri. These cats are hundreds of miles and many minute stream sections removed from the Missouri.

What national treasures are these remaining relatively unaltered watersheds. Most tiny tributary streams like Otter Creek, you see, have been straightened and tilled into nonexistence. Where marshes once gathered rain water, filtered it, and then sent it slowly on its way through miles and miles of tiny coursing tributary streams, streams that ran relatively clear and clean, we now too often face a treeless countryside, where arrow-straight chutes carry tiny trickles of water some seasons and raging flood waters the next.

> What national treasures are these remaining relatively unaltered watersheds. Most tiny tributary streams like Otter Creek, you see, have been straightened and tilled into nonexistence . . . We need to protect what remains as we revitalize that which has been damaged.

We need to protect what remains as we revitalize that which has been damaged. Question authority where alteration to any river or stream is concerned, particularly at the county level, where the temptation to ignore state and national mandates concerning national resources often runs strong. To still be able to float for miles along many of our nation's rivers, catching catfish for sport and for our tables, and not be besieged by hordes of other anglers is a great abiding freedom. Reading small rivers right is only part of the equation for continued good fishing.

CLASSIC RIVER EDGES, CLASSIC CATFISH

In one "All In The Family" episode, Archie Bunker stood, cigar in hand, next to his favorite living room chair, lecturing his wife, Edith, on his difficulty in getting her to understand the obvious logic of his ways. " The problem," he told Edith, "is that I explain in English and you listen in Dingbat."

So, too, does the easy logic of the ways of catfish in rivers often pass by the casual river angler. Like Edith, most anglers really haven't a clue. They find a bridge, park their vehicle, walk down and plant a lawn chair—and never move. Or they get permission to drive down to the river through a farm, park at the point of easiest access, and never move. Catfishing can be so much more, particularly if you actually like to catch catfish.

Catfish location is all about identifying river edges, but the game must be played in a larger context than "find a river edge, find cover, find catfish." Every edge, every piece of cover won't attract catfish during each season—yet edges still ultimately key catfish location and, thus, catfishing success.

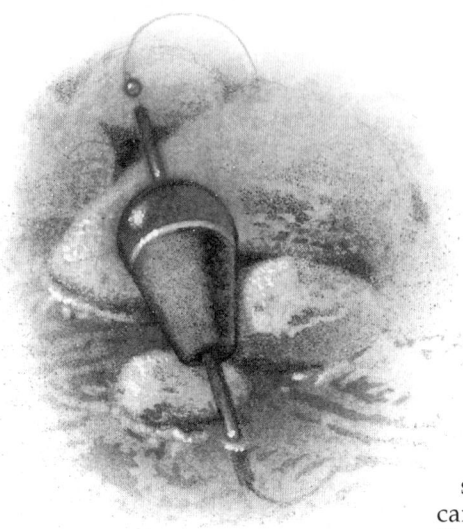

The larger context in question has everything to do with the natural physical layout of rivers as they proceed from beginning to end in a continuous series of riffles, holes, and runs. This is by now an idea often expressed in In-Fisherman publications, including our first catfish book, *Channel Catfish Fever*, published in 1989. We first began to write about river layout in the mid-1970s. We continue to contend that it's just about the most important basic idea in river fishing. Letters from hundreds of you over the years suggest that this kind of fishing success can be learned, although it takes time.

Really, though, it's remarkable how an angler's fishing success can improve once he begins to see river structure for what it is and how it so naturally affects catfish location during each season. Catfishing, after all, like most fishing, remains first a matter of finding fish.

The process is much easier to learn if you start looking at small rivers, where the catfish's world is compressed into a smaller area. In a large river, major holes may be half a mile apart. On a small stream, half a mile might have 10 holes. You can move and see lots of water. More importantly, the continuing combination of riffle, hole, and run, and the cover (or edge) elements that often exist there also are obvious.

Catfishing on small streams relates directly to catfishing on larger rivers. Yet the anatomy of larger rivers is more subtle and confusing. If larger rivers are all that's available, learning to find catfish may take longer.

One Classic River Hole

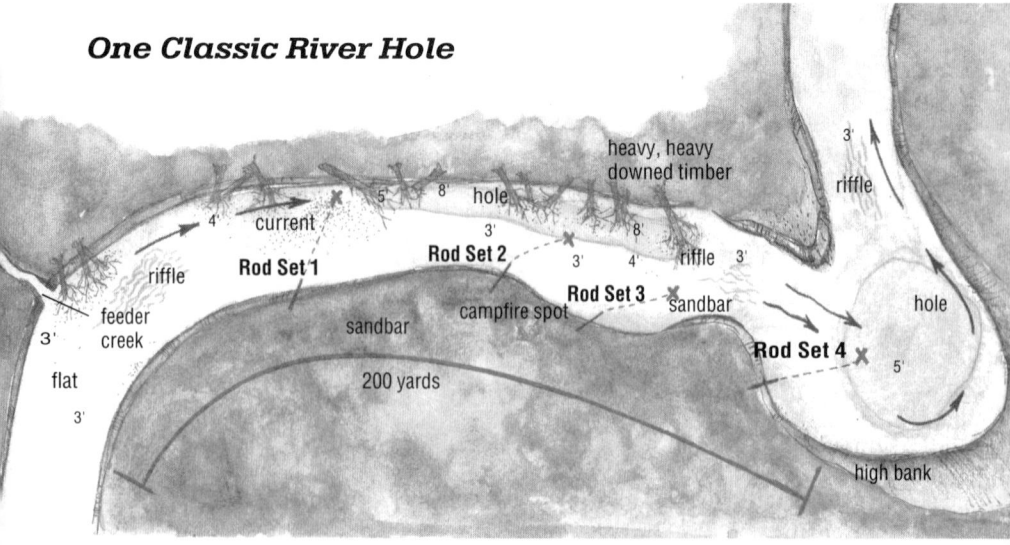

As river water meanders downhill, it flows over bottoms of varying hardness. Riffles form over hard-bottomed areas and are shallower because current doesn't wash away hard bottom. Riffles form natural dams that obstruct moving water. A pool of water builds at the head of a riffle, eventually flows over the riffle, quickening over the constricted area. In most small rivers in farm country, riffles rarely run for more than 30 or 40 feet.

The force of water flowing over and down a riffle scours the softer substrate at the bottom of a riffle, forming a hole, or a wider and deeper river section. Depth in a hole varies according to the steepness of the riffle, subsequent current patterns, and the size of the river. In a small stream, a typical hole might be 30 feet long, 20 feet wide, and about 4 feet deep. The biggest and deepest holes might be only twice those dimensions.

Holes gradually become shallower at their downstream end; suspended materials sink as the current slows. The tail end of a hole becomes a run, which is a river flat, an area with minimal change in depth. The bottom usually is sand and silt, with some gravel, plus plenty of debris like wood and brush. And, you guessed it, at some point the river flat winds and finds its way to another hard-bottom area, a riffle forms, beginning another series of riffle, hole, run.

Free-floating timber and brush also settle easily at the margins of a hole, or at least at the tail end of a hole, as the current slows and a run forms. Boulders that serve as cover (again because of the scouring action of current) also more likely occur in conjunction with a hole. Cover on river flats (runs) is, by comparison, haphazardly placed and, of course, rests in shallower water and therefore tends to draw smaller catfish. Cover in conjunction with a riffle usually doesn't draw catfish unless they're feeding and have moved up from the hole.

Holes, then, are the primary home (or holding area) for catfish most of the time. Catfish tend to spend a major portion of their time holding in or near the cover elements in and around holes. When feeding actively, however, they often move upcurrent into and through riffle areas. At times, they also spread downriver into runs. This is the essence of understanding catfish location in rivers.

ZACKER BRING A BIGGER CAT!
Doug Stange, In-Fisherman Editor in Chief:

When you want information about big catfish you go to people who have caught not just a few, not dozens—but hundreds!—in their lifetime. Problem. You can count the number of fishermen who have done that on four hands, and the number of those who are still alive on one. And if you insist on talking only to fishermen who have done it legally, well, you're not going to be doing much talking. I went to an old-timer big-cat man, little matter how he "learned his fish."

My source must remain a secret, for most of the "old standard" big-cat men are self-described as some of the crookedest ol' polecats you could ever meet. Illegal trotline sets. Snagging. Netting. Anything to catch a cat. Beat the fish. Win. Income and family depend on it. High water, low water, good weather or bad. No matter. Catch fish. Catch catfish.

Yet they tempered the catching with their brand of conservation. Never take every big cat from a hole; never waste a fish, the rules went. And when the market for cats was bad, they went fishing anyway and kept only enough for the family: Trotline catch and release! They lived many a man's dream.

Most of them have reformed, more due to old age and changing times, I suspect, than guilt. But then "guilt" is a paradox, isn't it, for guilty by today's standards wasn't necessarily so by yesterday's. The letter of the law and certainly the spirit of it changes with the times, the people, and the part of the country.

Semantics. Give us reality. Reality is the need to talk to the ol' polecats before they pass on; too many already have. But I won't name names because they don't want you to know, you don't need to know, and it would be the last time I talked with them. Protect those sources!

Catching a bigger catfish, something many of you dream about, is as wretchedly simple in practice as on paper. I use a simple rule to increase the size of my catch, no matter what the environment. Follow the rule and you'll catch some of the biggest cats in any water.

The rules work for me, but again, could I be certain knowing that my catches and your catches combined don't equal what once was the yearly catch of some old-timers? So I had to ask: does this—the approach—make sense?

THE RULE

To catch a bigger cat, the rule goes, fish big-cat spots on big-cat water using big-cat bait at big-cat times.

See? Wretchedly simple.

So the story flows.

Zacker, an ancient, arthritic, short, thin, almost frail man, gnarled as an old oak limb, speaks with a voice like rusty barbed wire. Remember Dustin Hoffman playing the mule skinner, Little Big Man (in the movie by the same name), an Indian-raised white man and the sole survivor of the Battle of the Little Big Horn? Remember the cigarette-harsh, hesitating voice and the sentences constantly accented with jabs from a gnarly hand?

Zacker could be Little Big Man. Someday, Dustin Hoffman should play Zacker. Sixteen to 20 million catfishermen would see the movie. For Zacker knows where big cats go.

"You go down there," Little Big Man goaded Custer at one point before the famous battle, "and there'll be nothing left but a little grease spot." Little Big Man knows, and Custer goes.

Zacker could be Little Big Man. Someday, Dustin Hoffman should play Zacker. Sixteen to 20 million catfishermen would see the movie. For Zacker knows where big cats go.

"Crap," Zacker will growl occasionally as he sits smoking a Camel on a bench on a porch overlooking a tiny creek and cows in a meadow behind his home. Mostly he misses the way things were, or dislikes the way things are.

"Crap!" Mostly he hates being 80 and not being on the river.

"Times ain't good," he'll say. "Damn 'em for changin' the river. No sandbars to hunt geese. No holes to corner big cats. Rivers run like plastic plumbing."

"No big cats left?" I asked one day.

"Course there are," he scowled as he turned toward me. He wanted to be heard. "Maybe more. But 'less you got a free runnin' river, not like these flowing reservoir pieces of crap—they're tougher to find and catch. Course you can still catch 'em, but I'd as soon fish a small river now. You can see holes, you know."

"When you say 'fish'," I began to ask. "Do you mean . . ."

"I mean 'fish'," he interrupted, rising up on the bench. "Fish! Sometimes, just how you catch your fish—with a hook and pole line—but more often with lines [trotlines], nets, or come winter, with snagging lines.

"We caught terrible fish in my day: big mud cats [flathead catfish], plenty of forks [channel catfish], and blues. Like one day we worked the run [a circuit of baited setlines]. Me and Little Lester and Grunt, the fellas I worked with. Great fellas, those guys. Lester was 6 foot 4 and could lift a 75-pound cat in each hand, easy. Grunt looked like a grunt [sheepshead] and was 'bout as smart. I could tell you stories.

"They had set clothesline-cord lines tied up with 10/0 Mustads—O'Shaughnessy I 'spect—early in the evening. We always baited with live carp or big river suckers [2- to 3-pound carp and suckers he later told me] when we wanted mud 'cat, or smaller fish, sometimes, dead, sometimes alive, sometimes cut, when we expected forks or blues. Lots of times we mixed baits on each line.

"Tell you one thing about setlines," he slowly continued as he looked into the distance. "Cats are like deer or 'most any wild animal. They have order. Some of 'em—the little turds—have to feed whenever they can, and others, usually the biggest, feed whenever they want. And it ain't for long.

"To catch 'em you've got to be there then," he emphasized by turning back toward me and poking at me with his skinny arm. "That's why setlines work. They're always there. Danged right!"

ABOUT HOLES

"Tell you somethin' else," he continued. "Don't mean squat where you set a baited line in a hole if there are fish there that aren't feeding when you set the bait. But you got to be patient and you got to have the right bait. A big cat knows what he wants to eat and he knows the hole he lives in like you know your kitchen.

"I've watched them big ones on a moonlit night when the water's clear in June. They lay up in the deepest part of the hole or maybe under a snag. You can fish 'em till hell freezes over and never even make 'em move—until they want to.

"When they start movin' they go 'round the hole a time or two, sort of to warm up before they ever eat somethin'. By that time the healthy fish, including smaller cats, have scattered and only the injured ones or the stupid ones are left. Big cats eat those fish that need eatin'. But if there ain't no injured fish—like on a baited line—they set up in a proper place, and then everything's fair game."

"But what if you were specifically pole fishin'; you know, sportfishing?" I asked. "Seems to me that the head end of a hole, where a shallow riffle or glide flows into the hole, is consistently the best possible spot."

"Sportfishing!" he snorted. "Times sure change. Now some folks say our fishing with lines wasn't right. Now, you gotta race around in a fast boat and catch fish no bigger 'an we used for bait, and win money. That's sport. That don't make sense. But that's fine. Seems to me that folks should just let other folks be, long as there's fish and game.

"But far as where you fish, you're doin' real good thinkin'," he continued. "The place a big feedin' cat checks most often is the head of a hole. That's where they'll find a bait the quickest. Just remember that's where they set up when everything's fair game. Tell you what: I think those big cats can smell what's in the water three or four holes up from where they're at, and they been around long enough to know. Anything that enters the hole from the top side, they know it. And once they're set up, they rarely feed back."

"Back?" I asked.

"Yes, back," he said. "That's what I was tryin' to say. Once they're set up proper toward the front of a hole, they don't much bother with things—baits— anywhere else. Once they start feeding, the head of the hole—where the current comes from—is the key.

"But be quiet," he continued, turning toward me again to emphasize the point. "That's another reason setlines work. Because some dink fisherman isn't standing around pawing the ground like some dumb jackass, or tossing his bait in 50 times an hour like some TV fisherman in women's pants.

"You don't wear those pants, do you?" he asked as he squinted at me.

"You mean shorts—cut offs?" I asked. "Me?"

"Good!" he said. "Toss the dang bait in and let 'er set. A big cat hears a bait tossed in the water. It may be 30 minutes before he feels like feeding.

"About holes," I said as he eased back on his bench.

"Holes! Holes is the home of those big evil-tempered cats!" he said as he raised himself on the bench again. "Mud cats live there and so do big forks. But those blues like to move more. You kin catch 'em in holes, but you can't always predict they're there."

"Prediction," I said, "that's another thing. Lots of catfishermen think old-timer big-cat guys had an aura about them: like you had the ability to feel the presence of big cats like a well digger with a witching stick feels water?"

"Aw, crap! You just want to make me mad," he coughed and wheezed. He took a "proper" spit and proceeded.

"Any idiot can figure out where big cats are. They live in those holes. But not every hole: the biggest ones; the deepest ones; sometimes the one with the most cover like fallen trees.

"Pole fishermen are so dang stupid—and lazy! They walk or float a couple miles of river and then they set their butt down and rest. Resting's fine, but only when I know where a big cat is."

"What you're suggesting," I said, "is that a fisherman should take say a 10-mile section of river and walk it or drift it in a boat, looking—surveying—the habitat. Instead of fishing each hole, just check it out. How big is it? How deep? How much cover is there? How many other holes are nearby? What are those other holes like? How do they compare with this one?

"Once a guy has an inventory of a pretty good-size section of river, he can make a prediction about where the biggest cats are. Once he draws a map, he can make some logical guesses . . ."

"No dang guessin' involved," he interrupted. "No danged guessin' 'tall. You're darn right I had a map in my head. If I knew how every hole in a 10-mile section of river stacked up, I'd know exactly where the biggest cats were. Big cats are easier than little cats, 'cause they're more predictable."

"So," I said, "a fisherman might want to pass by 15 consecutive good-looking holes to get to the one hole that's by far the biggest and deepest hole in say a 5-mile river section?"

"Danged right! Only some jackass city slicker thinks he's gonna catch a big cat without knowing his river. Course those guys think a big cat is 15 pounds. Humph!

"People who used to live on the river knew maybe 50 miles of it. I did. In those 50 miles, they'd know there were really only 10 terrible (great) holes. That's where you fish. That's where you catch terrible fish. City slicker knows one mile of river and four holes and thinks he's what you writers call a 'river rat' Caarap!

"And don't make no difference what size the river is, either. I'll tell you that. Only the biggest size of the catfish change. Show me a creek and the idea for finding the biggest cats is the same."

"But bigger rivers have bigger fish?" I asked.

"Course! Danged right! That's what I'm saying. There are more bigger fish in a hole, too. Bigger river like what the Missouri used to be before they crapped it up with dams, well, a good hole might have 15 big cats. You'd catch 5 or 8 of 'em and then fishin' would turn tough. You wait till the water came up again. Cats—but not always the biggest ones—move when the water comes up. Holes get restocked. When the water's down and the cats can't move, I can catch every fish in a hole. But I never did. We always left some. But catching a big cat is the simplest thing ever.

"Coffee?" he asked. "Too much talk."

"Black. I like mine good and black. But I have more questions," I reminded him.

"Too many questions. Coffee time. Proper coffee—boiled. Cookies?"

"Sure, cookies, too," I said. "Need help?"

He turned and squinted at me. "Jest set your butt down there and shut up."

I sat looking over the meadow as Zacker made his proper coffee. I thought of questions we'd covered in an earlier conversation.

"Aw, crap! You just want to make me mad," Zacker coughed and wheezed.

"Any idiot can figure out where big cats are. They live in those holes. But not every hole: the biggest ones; the deepest ones; sometimes the one with the most cover like fallen trees.

"How big were the fish in those days?" I'd asked.

"Didn't weigh 'em much. Got paid for bulk weight," he'd answered. "Big cats are big cats. But we had lot of fish that weighed 75 pounds. Some maybe 100."

"Mostly flatheads?" I'd asked.

"Mostly" he'd answered. "But plenty of forks weighed 60 pounds and blues, too." I'd told him that the world-record channel catfish was a 58-pounder. He'd shrugged. "So what? We've caught hook-and-line forks that easy weighed 60. Records ain't worth squat on the river. The fish ain't impressed till you catch 'em."

And I'd asked him about the moon—"Do you fish by it?"—and I knew I'd struck upon an important topic by the pause he took before answering.

"The moon—the full moon," he said, "works powerful on big cats. The best days are those before the full moon; maybe starting five days before.

"You know, folks think that all a catfish can do is smell and taste things. But they see darn good, and they like to feed at night in light. But there's somethin' about the full moon that makes them active, too.

"Never cared much for the dark moon, 'cause I think the fish might bite best during the day then; but then I never fished much then because it was too easy to be seen."

"You, mean you didn't want someone to see you fishing, or fishing legally with a pole line?" I'd asked.

"No use ruinin' your reputation," he'd chuckled.

Mostly he was joking, though. Mostly he didn't want anyone seeing his spots. Mostly he fished at night to keep his secrets. The boys would set baits just after dark and pick them up just before daylight, for when big cats first get hooked, they make a terrible noise before settling down and sulking on the bottom. Sure. Leave the lines in for 24 hours on smaller-fish water. But not on big-fish water.

And then he'd said something important, something that reinforced an important observation of my own.

"Too often big cats bite during the early daylight hours," he'd said. "You couldn't afford to leave a line in and make a commotion then. Other fishermen wouldn't turn you in, but they'd sure steal your lines and your fish.

"For my money," he continued, "the best time for big cats runs from 'bout 4 a.m. to 8 a.m. Big cats feed at night, but they need to see, feel, and smell things to be successful. They need light, but not too much light. That's one reason the full moon's so good. But most of the time, big cats that don't feed successfully at night get fed full quickly in early morning. That's the best bite. As morning progresses, the bite gets worse and worse as more and more cats feed themselves full."

Zacker shuffled back, splashing coffee from each large mug as he came. The cookies were stuffed in a very soiled shirt pocket.

"To the girl who lives on the hill," he chuckled as he gave me my coffee. "Know her?"

"Yeah, I know her," I responded.

"'You do?"

"Well, no I don't mean that. I mean I know how the rest of that thing goes."

"Gotcher self into that one, didn't ya?" he coughed. "Here, have a cookie."

"How do you do that?" I asked as I watched him gum a cookie with his five remaining teeth. Crumbs flew as he told me to "Shut up and talk," a difficult assignment.

"About baits," I continued. "Do you use stink baits?"

"Tell you somethin' about baits," he answered. "Little cats eat anything, anything 'tal. Big cats is danged selective. For my money, the bigger the cat, the more he likes fresh bait. I ain't sayin' smelly baits ain't good and they won't take 'em;

I'm sayin' that they just flat like fresh stuff better.

"Take a big mud cat. He's a mean sucker, the meanest fish swimmin' for my money. Danged right! He's the toughest, orneriest, meanest customer that swims in any natural [fresh] water. He won't ever pick up a dead bait, much less a ball of stinky crap. He wants somethin' live and big, like a big sucker or, better yet, one-, two-, or three-pound carp. Mud cats eat carp like peanuts: crack, and a head shake and then he's [the carp is] gone. Only time a big mud cat takes dead bait is spring. They take cut [filleted slabs] carp or sucker then.

"Big forks is kinda the same; I mean they ain't gonna go out of their way to take smelly baits when they're used to havin' the rule of their roost and eatin' live stuff or stuff that ain't been dead long. One-pound suckers or creek chubs—live ones— are good. Or big chunks of fresh-cut sucker or chub. Just cut the side [fillet] off a big sucker and hook it through once with a 5/0 hook. Don't ball the dang thing up or you can't get hooks.

"There's one time big forks like smelly baits, though. In spring you get those ripe carp—the floaters—that died in winter. There's no smell so bad. Cut the side off those fish and you got a good bait for forks of all sizes.

"Don't claim to be an expert about big blues because we never used to catch that many. But they're killers, too. They like livebaits and fresh killed stuff, stuff that smells fresh. And it's just like the other cats. They don't go pickin' 'round with tidbits lookin' for cookie crumbs. They want a meal."

"Where you hooking your livebaits?" I asked.

"Never hook one near the head even when your bait's settin' in current," he replied. "Big cat'll crush that bait and swallow it before you know it; and chances are 50-50 when you set the hook or he swims away from your setline that the hook'll dig back into the bait. I seen it a hundred times before I figured it out.

"You gotta hook a bait in his thinnest part and that's the part farthest away from their head—right in the danged tail."

"Top side or bottom side," I asked.

"No difference, but I always hooked mine in the top. And remember," he said, "only hook it once. Keep the barb of your hook exposed, 'specially with a big slab of cutbait."

"So say we're parked at a good hole and we're going to catch a good fork. No little fish now: a 30-pounder. How would you fish with a pole and line?" I asked.

"It's simple; easiest thing in the world," he said. "First, get yourself a good stout rod and reel, like saltwater stuff, and fill the reel with at least 50-pound line. The reel's got to have a clicker on it so you can set it in free spool, but when the fish takes the line out against the clicker, it makes a noise, and gives constant resistance. Hook your bait on with a good hook, say a 5/0 Mustad. Then toss it in at the head of the hole and wait. Start fishing at dark. If you can't fish all night, get up early and start about 4 a.m. and fish till 'bout 8."

"You fish with a lantern?" I asked.

"Scared of the dark?" he asked back.

"You freelining the bait?" I changed the subject.

"You gotta weight the bait so it struggles. It don't have to struggle all the time, but when a big cat gets close, it does. I usually used a big cork and a slip sinker setup.

"Say an eddy area near the head of a hole is about 4 feet deep. 'Bout 2 feet up your line [from your hook] put a big swivel. Tie good knots. Then add a big egg sinker, like a 2-ouncer if you're using a 1-pound bait. If the livebait's too lively you can trim his tail.

"Big cats crush and kill and swallow," Zacker said. *"When he moves he's got the bait 9 times out of 10. When you get to the rod, engage it, set and hold on. Once I set, I never gave an inch; never let the cat run. Hold him. Turn him over. Make him roll and thrash 20 feet away from you, but never give him his head."*

"Then another 4 feet up your line add a big cork. This cork ain't to keep your bait off bottom. The cork gets blown around in the current and keeps prodding your bait; makes it move and struggle. A big cat'll crunch your bait just for the sport of it."

"And when a big cat takes?" I asked.

"You'll know, you'll danged well know," he said as he scratched the stubble on his chin. He nodded, and a smile crept across his face. "You'll danged well know!

"Big cat'll grab the baitfish with a vice grip and crush him dead. He might give a mean head shake or two. Your drag clicker'll zizzzzz, zizzzzzz. And then zizz,zzzzzzzzzzzz when he takes off. Not,proper manners for a cat to kill and eat in the same place, 'cause they always move."

"Doesn't the drag resistance bother?" I asked.

"Small cat talk," he answered. "Big cats don't care 'bout no pressure as long as it's constant."

"Do we wait to set?" I asked.

"Never!" he shot back. "Big cats crush and kill and swallow. When he moves he's got the bait 9 times out of 10. When you get to the rod, engage it, set and hold on. Once I set, I never give an inch; never let the cat run. Hold him. Turn him over. Make him roll and thrash 20 feet away from you, but never give him his head. You win or lose. And if you start losing you use heavier line. Cats don't care about whether the line is 70 or 80 pounds. Maybe in a reservoir or big river these days you can let a fish go a bit. But we never had such good drags, and my method works. Danged right!

"And use a pick [ice pick] to land fish. Nets ain't worth crap! Or a big gaff. And don't never put your finger in a cat's mouth like you do in those pictures you showed me [of 20-pound channel cats]; they'll crush your finger, sure. Get your hand in there and they'll break every bone. They're the most terrible thing in the water.

"Danged wonderful, powerful fish," he said as he eased back down on the bench. "Say, Mr. Scientist, you know how old those fish are?"

"Experts say the biggest ones may live 50 or 60 years, maybe more," I answered.

"Eighty years. Now that's a lot," he said, pondering his and the lives of big cats. "Times is rough and times is good. Love that danged river. Love them danged cats."

"They're still there?" I asked, searching for something to say.

"They are. Danged right. But there's sure fewer big blues and mud cats. Too many dams. Too much river crap [pollution]. But there's still plenty fish, 'specially forks."

"So I've still got time to catch a 30-pound channel cat?" I asked.

"Catch a 40 or 50 if you want," he said. "Big cats is easy; simplest thing in the world. Course the size of the fish changes with the water. But you find big-fish water, fish it the right time with good bait 'n you'll catch terrible fish. Danged right!"

Catfish in Lakes & Reservoirs

ELIMINATING UNPRODUCTIVE WATER "**D**ese lakes jest ain't natural fer catfeesh," the old-timer muttered, as the young Georgia biologist dipped a netful of juvenile channel cats and released them at a boat ramp. He had a point, though his sentiments against stocking were unusual among most southern anglers.

The old catman apparently favored rivers for his catfishing, which true enough were the original habitat of channel cats, blues, flatheads, and white catfish. But the flurry of reservoir building during the middle decades of the 20th century transformed free-flowing rivers into a series of impoundments separated by dams. These new waters varied in shape, size, depth, water color, productivity, and countless other characteristics.

Fish populations that developed in reservoirs included species that lived in the rivers before the dams were built and other species that were stocked intentionally or entered from tributaries or flooded backwaters. From Wisconsin to Louisiana, catfish became reservoir fish—successful reservoir fish. Stocking catfish in reservoirs rarely is necessary, and the introductions in Georgia were into small impoundments built as public fishing areas.

Catfish are built to deal with current. Their streamlined bodies, strong white muscle, large tails, and flattened bodies allow them to navigate fast flows with seemingly little effort. Yet catfish have adapted to nearly every type of reservoir. Their array of sensory systems helps them feed in waters that vary in clarity from liquid mud to crystal clear, in temperatures from 33°F to 95°F, and in depths from inches to over 100 feet.

Santee-Cooper, A Prime Example

To illustrate common patterns in reservoirs, consider Santee-Cooper Reservoir (sometimes called lakes Marion and Moultrie), arguably the best catfish reservoir in North America. The 60,000-acre lower lake (Moultrie) was filled when the small Pinopolis Dam closed the Cooper River, flooding dikes, swamps, ponds, sloughs, and forests. Soon after, the populations of native channel and white catfish boomed.

White cats in the 6- to 8-pound range became common, and channel cats grew to 30, 40, up to 58 pounds, the largest ever recorded. In 1964 and 1965, blue and flathead catfish, imported from Arkansas, were stocked into Santee-Cooper. Populations expanded slowly, but fish attained trophy size in the early 1980s. In 1991, the reservoir produced the former world-record blue cat (109 pounds 4 ounces) and the state-record flathead (74 pounds). In-Fisherman staff members have made many trips to study seasonal patterns on this fascinating body of water.

Despite its southern location and shallow basin, catfishing warms up slowly in spring in this flatland reservoir. Flatland reservoirs feature many small cuts that focus early-season catfishing. Blue cats are the first to move toward the bank. And in late March, anglers begin catching smaller blues on cut herring fished on bottom.

Blue cats and other species remain in deep haunts through the coldest part of the year, favoring deep holes or creek channels with little or no current. Water warming into the upper 50°F range, though, spurs their appetite to start feeding on live or dead shad. Preyfish concentrate over and adjacent to humps that rise near the surface, often adorned in Santee-Cooper with stumps and brush. They also move into the mouths of creeks and hold along main-lake points.

Blue catfish are more active in cold water than are other species, and they're usually the first to turn on. Channel catfish move into similar areas, though in Santee their numbers are reduced, due to predation by larger catfish species. Finally, flatheads arrive, though by now, prespawn bluegills and crappies may have joined the menu, congregating in coves, creeks, and sloughs.

Catfish activity increases as water temperatures rise and the peak bite moves shallower. Many cat experts on Santee-Cooper and elsewhere find,

Reservoirs typically boost the production of shad and other important preyfish that increase the growth rate and abundance of catfish. Dams create deep wintering areas with little current. And as water spills from the original river channel, it floods creek channels and expanses of level ground, creating underwater flats that become feeding grounds for catfish of all sizes.

But this abundance of catfish habitat makes life harder for catfishermen. Spring feeding areas abound and prespawn movements to these shallow areas are less synchronized than in rivers. The same is true of spawning holes and summer feeding locations.

Fish populations that developed in reservoirs included species that lived in the rivers before the dams were built and other species that were stocked intentionally or entered from tributaries or flooded backwaters. From Wisconsin to Louisiana, catfish became reservoir fish— successful reservoir fish.

however, that the biggest fish rarely move to the 2- to 4-foot-deep flats used by smaller fish in Santee-Cooper's dark waters.

All this feeding prepares catfish for the spawn to follow, when water temperatures nudge into the 80°F range. At this time, perhaps two months after the initial movement toward shallow water, catfish choose spawning niches to lay their eggs. In flatland reservoirs like Santee-Cooper, hollow logs and undercut stumps, culvert pipes, and rock walls provide plenty of places for fish to spawn. In other types of reservoirs, rock bluffs, undercut tributary banks, or riprap shorelines provide cavities for nesting.

The spawn brings a midsummer lull in catfishing, as male fish remain in their nesting cavity for a week or two until fry can venture into the reservoir. Females remain near spawning locations and seem to need a recuperation period before they resume heavy feeding.

After the spawn, the focus for catfish feeding shifts deeper, particularly for large cats of each species. In reservoirs of all types, predators often become most active on wind-blown shorelines and points, as plankton and shad concentrate and orient in a particular direction. Channel cats, blue cats, and even flatheads key on these concentrations, often feeding off bottom.

Anglers on Santee-Cooper and other productive reservoirs often find groups of flathead catfish suspended under schools of baitfish at first light, and cats immediately snatch a bait dropped through the school. Groups of mid-size blue cats also cruise midwater in flatland and river-run reservoirs, moving vertically in response to baitfish location and light levels. In this manner, blue cats behave like striped bass, and many of the best waters for blue cats also offer good striper populations (Tennessee River impoundments, California reservoirs, Santee-Cooper, and Lake Texoma, for example).

During summer, chemical stratification also drives catfish from the bottom of deep channels, since the deepest, coldest layer of water (hypolimnion) gradually loses oxygen as summer progresses. Less-active cats hold along the upper edge of channels or on flats adjacent to channel bends. In reservoirs like Santee, fishing deeper than 20 feet can be fruitless for this reason. If livebaits die from suffocation, fish shallower.

RENDEZVOUS WITH RESERVOIR CATS

A glance at the National Fresh Water Fishing Hall of Fame record book confirms the productivity of reservoirs as catfisheries. The all-tackle world records for channel, blue, and flathead catfish came from impounded waters.

Sheer size often allows reservoirs to produce more catfish than the rivers they back up, but that same size creates a larger playing field for anglers. Locating hot spots in tens of thousands of surface acres is tougher than finding a deep bend in the river. Fishermen who learn to read reservoirs, however, soon discover that persistence often pays in fabulous fishing.

Reservoir anatomy depends on the lay of the surrounding land, but all operate pretty much like giant beaver ponds. Water running downstream through one or more rivers backs up behind a dam and floods the river basin as high as the dam. From the headwaters to the dam and well up every creek along the way, the original series of channels is important for locating reservoir cats, which remain river fish even in impounded water.

As a reservoir ages, channels become less defined as water causes erosion, softening miles of ledges. Silt settles in the channels, eventually filling them. Old reservoirs, therefore, offer less habitat than younger reservoirs, and finding good spots is more difficult. Any remnant channel in such a reservoir, however, is apt to hold catfish.

Dam operations usually turn current on and off, making it necessary to recognize the roll of water movement, just as in rivers. Some riverine reservoirs, especially those with dams at both ends, flow almost like unimpounded waters when water moves through the dams. But many vast flatland impoundments have no discernible current in most areas.

Along with channel drops and current patterns, spawning habitat and food sources dictate catfish spots through the seasons. Although hot spots vary, certain patterns remain consistent almost anywhere catfish swim. More varied are the seasonal holding areas of different species of cats.

FLATHEADS

Efficient as predators and not so selective about the kinds of fish they prey on, flatheads spend less time than blues and channels following forage fish. Often they find cover that suits them in areas with forage, then feed on whatever comes through. Typical forage includes small catfish, sunfish, and perch, plus a variety of shad and herring.

Flathead catfish prefer big rivers, slack current, and plenty of cover. While they use a range of depths and many kinds of cover in reservoirs—stump flats, rock bluffs, brush-covered points, and channel drops—they usually prefer habitat near the original river channel or in a major creek.

Topographical maps and electronics are used to locate bends in river channels, creek-river confluences, submerged humps or stump rows near the edges of channels, and other combinations of cover and structure.

Most flathead fishermen don't set up over their favorite hole in their favorite reservoir without marking at least a few big fish. Flatheads don't roam far, so if a hole is full of fish, it's time to set up and wait.

Anglers on South Carolina's Santee-Cooper lakes often spend an hour or more winding back and forth across the original Santee River channel in search of a good group of fish to set up over. It's tough to spend so much time with your bait in the

---

livewell, but veteran fishermen know that on reservoirs, this can be time well spent.

In spring, some flatheads are drawn into major creeks and up the rivers, while in summer and fall, they tend to hold closer to the dam in deep water. Through winter, flatheads come as close to hibernating as do any popular gamefish.

Flatheads also are the most nocturnal catfish species, moving out of the channel onto flats to feed at night. Day or night, therefore, the best areas in any reservoir are where a major channel pushes close to a flat and where some unusual feature adds appeal to that part of the channel.

Flatheads, like many other species, often feed best when water is being pulled through a reservoir. When the current is running, however, they may hold downstream of a hump, under a ledge, or somewhere else that protects them from the current.

BLUE CATS

Native to larger rivers, blue catfish do best in major rivers or impoundments of major rivers. While not so tightly keyed to actual channel ledges as flatheads, blues almost always stay in the largest tributaries, whether downlake in open water or well upriver.

Blue cats feed on live or dead fish and mollusks, and they're especially fond of oily schooling forage fish like threadfin and gizzard shad, and blueback and skipjack herring. Various clams and mussels constitute an important part of a blue's diet in many reservoirs, but shad and herring more often dictate where blues are found.

Flatheads, like many other species, often feed best when water is being pulled through a reservoir.

Bottom structure, current, and schools of shad or herring are reservoir elements that blue cats seek. Much like striped bass, blues relate to humps and drops, and they move with the food. When baitfish are spread through large sections of a reservoir, blues are equally scattered. Special conditions, however, create great concentrations of baitfish and catfish in many reservoirs.

In the Deep South and Midsouth, winter conditions leave narrow zones of suitable temperatures and oxygen levels for threadfin shad. Shad ball up in the lower ends of reservoirs, and the blue catfish lie among them and beneath them, feeding at will.

Where reservoirs lie in succession on a river, the tailwaters of one become the headwaters of the next, and that zone draws concentrations of baitfish and catfish. When shad are washed through the turbines, coming out minced or at least stunned, blue cats downstream enjoy a smorgasbord.

On any reservoir with blue catfish, the first hints of spring warming draw baitfish and blues into the shallows. Any section that warms a degree or two higher than the rest of a reservoir—windblown bank; shallow, stained cove; rocky shore with a southern exposure—is a likely early-season spot.

Tools of the Reservoir Trade

Much of the best structure and bait in a typical reservoir lies well beneath the surface. Prime catfishing zones represent small portions of large acreages. Location tools and a knowledge of how to use them become essential for success.

Topographical maps, studied prior to a trip, are the first essential tools. Beginning with major creek and river channels, catmen should seek structure lying adjacent to those channels, giving consideration to the season and the behavioral differences among flatheads, blues, and channels. Mark several potential holding areas and establish an order for giving each spot a closer look with electronics.

Electronics are next, and a high-resolution graph or liquid crystal display unit is beneficial for finding and following channel ledges, searching for stumps, rocks, brush, or baitfish, and for identifying catfish in or around holes. Units with Global Positioning System capability save searching time by pointing straight to spots that have produced catfish in the past. Thirty-year Santee-Cooper guide Don Drose pulled his two biggest catfish from the same hole, which he marked using GPS coordinates.

Floating marker buoys are important, too. If a graph shows several big catfish atop or just below a ledge, a buoy or two tossed into strategic spots makes it easier to circle back, set anchors, and put out lines among the fish.

The most overlooked fish-finding tool, and in the minds of many veteran catmen, one of the most important, is a well-kept journal. The same conditions that once caused certain spots to be covered with catfish are apt to repeat. For folks who don't have GPS, landmarks for relocating midlake hot spots by triangulation are among the most important notes kept. Where topo maps aren't available, veteran anglers create their own reservoir maps marked with noteworthy features.

In summer, current becomes important. Blues feed better when water is moving through a reservoir, and they opt first for narrow passes, areas around islands, upriver spots, and structures near the dam, where the water's pulled when the turbines are turning.

When baitfish and blue cats are scattered, drifting covers a lot of water. Make passes across open water with bottom-bumping rigs baited with preyfish, bumping the baits down into and then out of the main river channel.

CHANNEL CATS

Smallest of the big cats, channels also occur in the smallest rivers and creeks. Channel catfish can be found almost anywhere in a reservoir, but the best fishing often is up tributaries not large enough to attract blues or flatheads.

Like blues, channels feed on both live and dead fish, and are even more fond of mollusk meals than are their larger cousins. Like flatheads, channels prefer to stay out of current most of the time, although they prefer to hold just barely out of the flow, a good vantage for hunting fish or grabbing scraps.

Where The Birds Are

We've often written about the connection between birds and fish. Flocks of gulls or other birds locate schools of baitfish and attack them from above while predators like largemouth bass, stripers, and hybrid stripers push preyfish to the surface. It's a hot bite when you get there in time. But it seems birds may attract fish by a more direct means.

Catfish angler Jeff Rader, a hunting and fishing guide on Glen Elder, a large reservoir in northcentral Kansas, uses the "cormorant pattern" to find fish. "One day a few years ago, I fished where a flock of cormorants had perched and had great success on channel cats. I followed the cormorant pattern and continued catching loads of fish," Rader says.

"Catfish concentrate under the cormorants to get an easy meal," Rader theorizes. As expected, cats bite best on familiar forage, so Rader concocts a stinky paste he dabs on a short ringworm often used to deliver dip-bait—"matching the hatch," so to speak.

More so than the other cats, channels in reservoirs tend to move seasonally. While they don't all migrate together, and some may not travel significant distances, enough fish move predictably to warrant targeting certain areas through the seasons.

The first warming days each year put channels on the same banks as blues, feeding on concentrations of baitfish, often in the windward parts of the reservoir. Winter-killed shad are the primary target of these fish. Soon they begin moving up creeks and into rivers. Through most of spring and early summer, channels are in a prespawn mode, feeding heavily and providing some of the year's best fishing. Cutbanks draw channel cats, and riprap often does, too.

A few weeks after the spawn, as summer kicks in, channels move back toward deeper water. While they generally don't make heavy use of open-water structure well out in the main body, they do hold over points and along flats at the mouths of creeks and coves as they intersect open water.

A hump or gradual point that drops into a major creek channel near where it opens into the main lake often is a hot spot for channel catfish (and blues) during summer. A vast flat in a similar location, with deeper water nearby, offers all the elements for excellent after-hours catfishing. In Kansas, Oklahoma, Texas, and other parts of the Midsouth, anglers often chum portions of reservoirs with sour grain to draw fish.

Locations of mollusk beds often dictate the best spots for catching channel catfish. If a sandy shallow bar is loaded with mussels and has deep water nearby, it likely holds channels, especially during summer when their metabolisms run high, and their other food sources have spread across deep waters.

Channels generally are less food selective than flatheads or blues, and they follow their senses of smell and taste to find food. Marking fish, therefore, usually is much less important than for flatheads. Most anglers anchor on a good-looking point and fan out lines at various depths. Trolling with walleye-style livebait rigs is another option.

FINDING AND CATCHING CATS DURING SUMMER

From 1930 to 1990, Tommy Burns worked a 30-mile stretch of the Kansas River as a commercial fisherman. Gete Hibdon, meanwhile, plied Lake of the Ozarks as a multispecies guide from 1930 to the mid-1960s, a workplace that spanned nearly 100 miles.

These two observant catmen were afloat so often that they saw catfish do things that few fisheries biologists (or others for that matter) have ever seen. And some of the antics that Burns and Hibdon witnessed continue to defy modern wisdom.

For instance, Burns once saw thousands of flatheads frolicking on the surface over submerged sandbars during their spring migration from the Missouri River to spawning sites on the Kansas River and its tributaries. Some years, the schools covered almost an acre of water.

After spawning, the flatheads commenced their migration, following creases in the current, moving single file in a long column. As they moseyed upstream, they often swam so near the surface that their dorsal fins poked out of the water like sharks.

Burns once saw thousands of flatheads frolicking on the surface over submerged sandbars during their spring migration.

Likewise, Hibdon watched cats at Lake of the Ozarks perform antics that most men will never see and probably wouldn't believe even if they did. During his many late-night forays in mid-December to gig suckers, buffalo, and carp, Hibdon often witnessed countless blue cats surfacing like porpoises over some of the deepest parts of the lake. He was one of the first anglers to note that blue cats in reservoirs spend much of their life far above the bottom.

Hibdon also discovered that the blues, when stimulated by hunger or the urge to procreate, are able to move many miles in a day. From his days of plying the Osage River immediately below Lake of the Ozarks, Hibdon learned that the blue cats were attracted to raging current. Strong flows could draw them from miles away, perhaps as far as the Missouri River some 75 miles downstream.

The late Hibdon's ghostly presence still wields an influence on a small cadre of contemporary anglers across the northern plateau of the Ozarks, but he died long before biologists became curious about the ways of cats.

Burns, however, has coached several biologists about the ways of catfish. In June 1994, he showed three of them the Kansas River routes channel cats follow upriver and downriver. Burns says the biologists were dumbstruck by the number of cats he hauled over the gunwales of his boat, but they've yet to employ the methods he showed them. And that's the way it often has been in the catfish world—science lagging behind the wisdom of savvy anglers like Burns and Hibdon.

Nevertheless, many of Burns' observations about catfish were published in several venues during the 1990s. And thanks to Burns and several other masterful anglers, our understanding of the ways of catfish has expanded exponentially. In addition, more biologists are attempting to study and understand catfish.

A NEW ERA OF CATFISH RESEARCH

This new age of understanding was exemplified at the First International Ictalurid Symposium at Davenport, Iowa, in June 1998. This catfish symposium was the first meeting of the minds between ichthyologists and savvy catmen. Despite these advances and the pioneering work on reservoir cats performed by biologists like Kim Graham of Missouri, Chris Stephenson of Alabama, and Larry Hart of Oklahoma, though, we still know little about the ways of reservoir cats.

We are however, hearing an emerging clamor from some catfishing quarters, a plea for biologists to conduct more radio telemetry surveys, tagging studies, and other scientific investigations. But what impedes the biologists is their dogged insistence that anecdotal evidence can never replace scientific proof. Biologists remain reluctant to publish their inclinations about catfish without reams of supporting data.

Until a new generation of biologists emerges to build on the rudimentary explorations of Graham, Stephenson, and Hart, we will have to employ our own wits to glean a better understanding of catfish behavior. Even if biologists begin their research today, though, it will take years to determine the movements and habits of cats in big reservoirs like Lake of the Ozarks, Texoma, and Santee-Cooper.

TOURNAMENT PERSPECTIVES

Perhaps one of the quickest methods to garner a better understanding of reservoir cats is to listen to anglers who fish catfish tournaments. Some observers maintain that tournament anglers can expand our piscatorial vistas wider than biologists can. These contests continually reveal that numbers of big blue and channel catfish can be caught from different environments in the same reservoir at the same time. One angler, for instance, can catch five blues from a mussel bed in 8 feet of water, while another can catch five more from a hump that tops out at 25 feet. They also may be taken on varying baits and presentations.

Tournament anglers Keith McCoy and Tom Lawrence traverse the tournament trail from March through October, fishing reservoirs around the country. And wherever they fish, McCoy and Lawrence contend that channel cats and blue cats behave the same. A catfish is a catfish wherever it lives, with a few minor environmental exceptions.

These inconsistencies, however, shouldn't perplex us; in fact, they should open a grander vista from which we can better understand how catfish survive in different environments. With that perspective in mind, McCoy and Lawrence maintain that an intelligent reservoir angler eventually will learn that at certain times, cats have a symbiotic relationship with gar, white bass, and other schooling species.

SPAWNING BEHAVIOR

Channel Cats—Lawrence thinks that one of the easiest ways to observe these variations is to examine the spawning behaviors of reservoir cats. At Merritt Lake, Nebraska, for instance, channel cats spawn when the water temperature ranges from 75°F to 80°F, usually around June 15 in shallow water along the riprap of the dam or in flooded weeds in the back of coves and feeder creeks. He has seen channel cats spawn so shallow that their dorsal fins break the surface. Some anglers are fooled by the lustful cats wallowing in the weeds and wrongly assume they're carp.

Hibdon said the water in some coves would turn a milky hue from milt ejaculated by the male cats during the heat of the spawn.

Catmen at Lake of the Ozarks, though, seldom witness channel cats spawning in shallow water. Perhaps because Lake of the Ozarks is devoid of flooded weeds. There's no riprap either, but the lake is graced with hundreds of miles of boulder-strewn shorelines and an inestimable number of driftwood piles in relatively shallow water. Channel cats in Lake of the Ozarks spawn at the same water temperatures, but this usually occurs about 15 days earlier than at Merritt.

Blue Cats—Santee Cooper blue cats, according to Lawrence, are known for spawning in shallow water around stumps or slight depressions in hard clay banks. Santee Cooper anglers say, "If you can't see your bait, you're fishing too deep to catch a spawning blue." Lawrence has found Santee Cooper blue cats in spawning areas when water temperatures were in the 60°F range.

Lawrence suspects that some blue cats migrate a long distance to reach preferred spawning sites. Gete Hibdon noted the same phenomenon at Lake of the Ozarks, where he regularly found them spawning in a large cove about 70 miles from the dam. Hibdon suspected that some of those cats had traveled more than 40 miles to reach the cove. We should note, however, that Hibdon also found blue cats spawning in a cove about six miles from the dam.

Hibdon never found blues spawning as shallow as they do at Santee Cooper, though, and he never found them near spawning areas when the water temperature was still in the 60°F range. But when blue cats did move in, there usually were lots of them. Hibdon said the water in some coves would turn a milky hue from milt ejaculated by the male cats during the heat of the spawn.

POSTSPAWN MOVEMENTS

Once the spawn ends, Lawrence and McCoy say that big blue and channel cats quickly move to deep-water lairs. Submerged creek channel bends, the confluence of submerged channels, and deep humps usually are attractive to both species. Smaller cats, though, often can be found near a variety of deep and shallow structures around the reservoir. This is especially true of cats under about 8 pounds.

At Lake of the Ozarks, Hibdon intercepted blue cats in late June or early July as they migrated from their spawning sites in upper reaches of the reservoir to middle and lower portions, where many of them spent the rest of the year. The raging current of a midsummer flood on the Osage River and its big tributaries, though, often summoned blue cats from considerable distances. But once the flows calmed, blues again returned to their main-lake haunts. According to Hibdon, these radical moves befuddled many old-time catmen. And many of today's catmen are equally confused by the roaming penchant of blue catfish.

As their bellies fill, cats turn around and slowly meander back toward deep water. Some of them continue to forage as they move back across the flats, but usually not with the same intensity.

McCoy and Lawrence maintain that the best deep-water lairs on such lakes as Merritt or Kentucky Lake on the Tennessee-Kentucky border are large flats where big blues and channel cats feed. Furthermore, the best flats are as shallow as 10 to 15 feet and within a quarter mile of a deep-water sanctuary such as a submerged creek or river, where the big cats spend more of their time during the hot, bright daylight of midsummer. In this sanctuary, channel cats often linger along the bottom in 25 to 35 feet of water.

McCoy enjoyed his finest tournament catch at Santee Cooper. At that 30-hour event, his winning catch of blue cats weighed 235 pounds, the biggest at 70 pounds. But most notable is that all the fish came from the same depth where McCoy targets channel cats across the county—15 to 35 feet.

That's not to say that McCoy and Lawrence haven't probed water over 35 feet. In fact, Lawrence caught a channel cat in 67 feet of water at Merritt. Then one September at Santee Cooper, sonar revealed a handsome congregation of fish in 60 feet of water near the dam. They immediately plumbed that deep lair and eventually tangled with some titans. Unfortunately, those brutes merely took all the line off their reels and broke the arbor knot.

Daily Patterns—During summer, Lawrence says that big channel and blue cats usually leave their deep haunts at about 10 p.m. They move from the creek channel, usually in 25 to 35 feet of water, to the edge of the channel (15- to 20-foot range) where they begin feeding. On the best summer nights, the feeding hits a Wagnerian crescendo at about 1 a.m. On those rare nights when the big cats feed with extreme abandon, Lawrence has seen them move as far as 2,500 feet across a flat in water as shallow as 10 feet.

As their bellies fill, cats turn around and slowly meander back toward deep water. Some of them continue to forage as they move back across the flats, but usually not with the same intensity. Sometime around 8 a.m., Lawrence believes most of the cats have returned to their daytime holding areas where they again await the cover of darkness.

Environmental Variables—According to McCoy, the most voracious feeding spells erupt when a fierce storm front is in the offing. On those occasions,

McCoy has followed channel cats, as well as blue cats, across mudflats into water as shallow as 5 feet. Lawrence adds that the approaching storm front may cause many of the blue cats to suspend in 10 to 15 feet of water, where they feed aggressively.

After the front passes, though, channel and blue cats in reservoirs often turn sullen. They may confine their movements to a small area—perhaps moving only a few yards from their deep sanctuary—and feed with little gusto.

In addition to storm fronts, Lawrence says that wind can dramatically affect the location and attitude of cats—especially blues. Wind often pushes plankton to various parts of the lake, and shad follow. Blue cats follow the shad, often suspending as shallow as 5 feet beneath the surface, depending on the depth of the baitfish.

In comparison to windy days, Lawrence finds that a hot and calm midsummer day sends cats to deep water, where they seldom suspend. When cats are holding in deep water, Lawrence notes that the thermocline affects their location, but not so much as it does other species. Lawrence suspects that some big cats periodically penetrate the thermocline into the hypolimnion (cooler layer of water below the thermocline).

In reservoirs with strong striped bass populations, like Santee-Cooper, Lawrence also has found that blue cats and stripers often pursue the same baitfish schools. The schools of stripers, though, usually are larger and more concentrated than the congregations of blue cats.

To catch these suspended blues, Lawrence initially employs a vertical presentation with a large jigging spoon, which he drops directly over the side of the boat to the exact depth of the cats. Then he uses his rod to lift and drop the spoon about 2 feet. Once he determines that the fish are blues and not stripers, he switches from the spoon to a slipbobber and bloodbait rig, which he drifts through the school. Lawrence says the slipbobber outfit works well if the blues are suspended in 15 feet of water or shallower.

As Hibdon discovered at Lake of the Ozarks, Lawrence has found during his tournament outings that blue cats spend a lot of time moving nearer the surface than to the bottom. He says this phenomenon occurs at every reservoir that contains a large population of blues. McCoy, however, says that he seldom attempts to catch suspended blues, because for every suspended blue, he suspects two or three are on the bottom.

Even when blues are on the bottom, though, McCoy and Lawrence have found that they seldom hold tight to the bottom as channel cats do. They more likely hold within about 2 or 3 feet of the bottom.

Lawrence says the best method to determine the location where blue cats and channel cats are feeding at 1 a.m. is to find the shad. To do that, Lawrence makes a quick tour of the reservoir, using his sonar to pinpoint the depth of the shad. Then if the preponderance of shad are in 15 feet of water and they remain at that depth throughout the day or night, most of the channels and blues will be at that depth, too.

THE MYSTERIOUS FLATHEAD

Despite their many days of chasing blue and channel cats, McCoy and Lawrence readily admit that they know nothing about the habits of flatheads in reservoirs. Across his many years of tournament fishing, McCoy says he's caught only one flathead. In fact, most tournament anglers don't pursue them. McCoy and Lawrence conjecture that the reason the flathead is shunned by tournament anglers is that the number of flatheads in reservoirs is significantly lower than the numbers of channel and blue cats.

From biological explorations conducted by Larry Hart at Lake Carl Blackwell, Oklahoma, McCoy and Lawrence's contention about the paltry number of flathead that abide in reservoirs is correct. Hart's survey revealed about two flatheads per acre and, that during summer, each flathead's monthly movement encompassed only 18 acres. This limited range is much different from the pelagic nature of blue cats who chase schools of shad for many miles.

Spawning Movements—In contrast to the great and long spawning migrations of flatheads that Tom Burns witnessed on the Kansas River, the spawning journeys at Lake Carl Blackwell were short, only a short distance to shorelines cluttered with boulders or patches of submerged timber in about 3 feet of water.

At Lake of the Ozarks, Hibdon found that some of the best flathead spawning areas were small indentations on bluff walls with a slide of large rocks. It was at such a spot in the Soap Creek arm of Lake of the Ozarks on a day in late June during the 1960s that Hibdon's son Gail landed a flathead that broached 100 pounds. Back in the 1940s, Hibdon used to bait such spots by sinking a cage that housed a ripe female flathead. This caged critter occasionally attracted a bevy of nice-sized males.

Once the spawn ended, Hibdon discovered that flatheads spent the summer along the same bluffs where they spawned. And at Lake Carl Blackwell, Hart noticed that flatheads summered either along steep banks or in submerged creek channels.

At flatland reservoirs in northeastern Kansas, John Thompson of Ottawa, Kansas, finds flatheads spawning during mid-June in four locales. One spot is in 3 to 5 feet of water in flooded timber along a submerged creek channel. Second is along the riprap of the dam. Third is along a steep bank occasionally cluttered with big rocks. And fourth is in the main river that feeds the reservoir, where flatheads spawn in logjams.

Postspawn Movements—After the spawn, Thompson suspects that flatheads move to deeper abodes along submerged creek channels. Like the blue cats and channel cats that Lawrence and McCoy pursue, flatheads spend daylight hours in the creek channel, venturing to adjacent flats to forage on shad and other baitfish after dark.

Even though Thompson has chased flatheads in these parts for 40 years—and long before that his father suffered a flathead fixation—he readily admits that he's not sure what reservoir flatheads are doing about 65 percent of the year. In Thompson's opinion, the easiest time to catch reservoir flatheads in northeastern Kansas is in April and May. The rest of the year is a crap shoot.

Until fishery managers across the country develop ways to nurture and protect flatheads, Thompson says anglers will remain uncertain about what the fish are doing and why. Not enough fish are around today, he adds, because too many are being killed. Reasonable creel limits that allow anglers to keep only a small fish or two should be mandated until we better understand this mysterious predator.

RIVER-RUN WISDOM

Looking back now on all those days of catfishing with the late Toad Smith on some secluded river, and satisfied that there was nowhere else we'd rather be than right there right then. Well, it's almost not right to sit here now and tell the truth, that sometimes fishing with Toad was exasperating.

Know how those TV sports commentators are always talking Big Mo (Mo being Momentum)? As in this team or that team will for no apparent reason suddenly get everything going its way—base hits just seem to drop, pitches just seem to pop—and Eureka! Big Mo's picked a side. Well, as ol' Diz used to say, that Toad and Big Mo were bosom buddies, best friends, permanent partners.

Big Mo. You'd be drawn into a minor league cat contest, a pleasant little friendly one-on-one with Toad. Suddenly, it was as if all the wind would be sucked from the world, while all the good vibes from heaven above would gather on Toad's behalf, and he'd go on a 10-cat run while you stood there all puckered up and pathetic.

And after setting the hook, Toad would pronounce his success with a, "Waaaaaaaaaal, nowthere'sanotherone!" He had this way of really squealing through his mischievous gap-toothed Toad Smith smile, really hanging on the Waaaaaaaaaal, for about 10 minutes, and then finishing the "nowtheres'anotherone" in a millisecond. "Waaaaaaaaaal," he'd say, "nowthere'sanotherone!"

Toad wasn't just good, he was lucky. Or maybe it was angels. Toad used to talk about angels as he sat next to a fire on some riverbank, darkness focusing thoughts, night sounds bolstering wonder, stars above pronouncing peace, while mosquitoes added a realistic measure of frustration into even this portion of the best of life.

Many of you have asked where Toad stood on religion. Toad could be a downright religious sort, even a fair (but unorthodox) biblical scholar; but always out of ear shot of everyone, because when it came down to it, he had big-time trouble rectifying his behavior with biblical standards. Many of us have the same problem. With Toad, though, it was always like heaven and hell were implementing their latest and greatest battle plans right then and there, using Toad as the battlefield (and a big battlefield it was); and as Toad often observed, the winner of the ultimate battle may have been predetermined, but often as not when it came to hour-by-hour reckonings, well, hell could get on a real winning streak where Toad was concerned.

We're not glorifying that Toad occasionally wandered the corner of 5th street and hell. Just the facts, Ma'am. Many of you have wandered there from time to time, too. Yet love conquers all, and Toad knew it and lived his own daily sacrifice, bore his own cross, lived that love in his way. Perhaps that's the reason he could gather legions of angels to sit on his side when it came to cat contests. And for those of you who don't understand the reason for any of this in a fishing book right here right now, maybe someday you will, when grace calls for no reason at all and a tear rolls down your cheek for the pain and the joy that others share with you.

Cats are cats are cats, and pretty soon big rivers look like small rivers look like ponds look like small reservoirs look like flowing reservoirs look like natural lakes.

We have met many great catmen in our travels. Toad was the dean of them all because he had reached that stage in his life when he understood who he was and what catfishing meant. On a practical level, it didn't take Toad weeks on a body of water to understand. He'd seen so much, done so much, experienced so many catfishing situations that what took others years to figure seemed obvious to Toad in a trip or two.

Toad was pretty much a small-river man. But cats are cats are cats, and pretty soon big rivers look like small rivers look like ponds look like small reservoirs look like flowing reservoirs look like natural lakes. So it was that Toad knew in a half-dozen trips to "flowing reservoirs" where channel cats and the occasional big flathead held during summer.

Don't think that in his life Toad ever caught a blue cat. Never fear, though, because according to Glen Stubblefield, a Toadlike figure of sorts in his part of Kentucky, blue cats act a good bit like channels and big flatheads. Long time In-Fisherman contributor Don Wirth, who gathered the information from Stubblefield, likes to tell the story of a guy pulling up a '66 Oldsmobile from deep water in a reservoir in Oklahoma, opening the trunk, and pulling out two 75- pound flatheads. "Cats like cover," Stubblefield concludes. That the Olds came from deep water in current during summer further illustrates important connections.

Cats, structure, current, and deep water go together in river-run reservoirs, which are impounded bodies of water with noticeable current. Stubblefield fishes Kentucky Lake and reservoirs like Guntersville and Pickwick on the Tennessee River system. Toad fished parts of the upper and middle Mississippi and middle Missouri. Could just as well have been parts of the Ohio and its tributaries.

Toad would tell you that the quality of the current was the chief factor affecting catfish location. Stubblefield harps on deeper water, water as deep as 45 feet, where he has tangled with cats big enough to pull his boat upstream. Indeed, he's hung some that, as he puts it, pulled harder than the Midnight Express to Puducah.

The Mississippi and Missouri, and reservoirs like them, though, are more riverlike than the reservoirs Stubblefield fishes. But the connection remains constant between current and deeper-lying channel-related structure and current. Sometimes though, channel cats and flatheads move shallow, too, so long as it's shallow relative to deeper-lying areas where cats spend most of their time.

When cats drop deeper, they tend to consolidate. During summer, fishing may actually be better during the day and into early evening because the fish are grouped. Of course, you have to find the fish in deeper water. For Stubblefield, deep is 45 feet. For Toad, deep was 25 feet.

WHERE FOR RIVER-RUN CATS

Stubblefield: "The old riverbank keys catching big blues in a river-run reservoir like Kentucky Lake. Check the banks of a river near you. See the rockpiles? See the small creeks cutting into the river? See the ditches, rock slides, and trees lining the bank? Now flood that area, put it 20, 30, or 40 feet down, and you have prime blue cat territory during summer—so long as you also add current. The best spots aren't in dead water."

Toad would tell you that for channel cats and flatheads, it's only slightly different. The channel remains the key. In this case, though, picture yourself at the base of the channel drop-off being carried along downriver by current. Whoosh, current washes you into a depression in the channel. Whoosh, current washes you against a bank with sunken logs. Whoosh, current washes you past the deep edge of the tip of a wing dam and then behind the wing dam. Whoosh, current washes you past a secondary channel cut coming from a backwater area or an area closed off by a closing dam. Whoosh, current washes you along a riprapped bank. So long as the channel moves distinct current past structural elements, all these locations mean catfish.

Current's the key. The best bites occur when water is moving from upstream. Generation usually begins midmorning and continues into sunset. Again, this is a daytime pattern. Want to fish 24 hours a day? Well, cats also move shallow after dark. That's a different story. The daytime story is consolidation. Find the fish and fishing will be better during the day than at midnight.

The best bank structure for Stubblefield is what he calls a "bench." A secondary bank, he explains. "Say the original bank ran from 15 to 18 feet, then dropped down to 25 or 30 feet before dropping into the river," he says. "A bench like this may only be a few feet wide, but cats really stack up here sometimes."

> *The channel remains the key. . . . Whoosh, current washes you into a depression in the channel. Whoosh, current washes you against a bank with sunken logs. Whoosh, current washes you past the deep edge of the tip of a wing dam and then behind the wing dam. So long as the channel moves distinct current past structural elements, all these locations mean catfish.*

Stubblefield says these areas hold cats moving from the deepest parts of the channel where it's difficult to fish, to the deep-lying bank structure where they feed some of the time during the day. Toad, though, would rather have spent time probing another type of cat territory. Of all the other possibilities, channels running from backwaters or creek arms into the main river may be best. Benches aside, Stubblefield agrees.

Stubblefield: "The trick is to fish these cuts at the right depth and follow them out until they form a V where they intersect with the old river channel. Sometimes all the cats are on the creek side of the V. Sometimes they're all on the river side. Most of the action comes in the 30-foot zone where the two areas connect."

The main channels in Toad's waters are shallower than in Stubblefield's waters. Toad usually reversed Stubblefield's procedure, starting in the channel and working his way back into the creek arm. He looked for a lip, a bench-like structural element at the junction of the channel and the feeder cut.

Both Toad and Stubblefield considered this mainly a summer pattern. Today, well, we're not so sure. Folks using those tactics are beginning to catch cats during spring and fall, too.

A NOTE ABOUT PRESENTATION

For the most part, this is not an anchor-up deal. Move to find consolidated cats, the way walleye fishermen move to find walleyes. Sit comfortably in the bow of the boat, bowmount motor in the water to move the boat. You're looking for catfish via electronics as you probe vertically below the front of the boat. Before dropping the bowmount, motor around the area and thoroughly search with electronics to get a sense of the layout.

The cats are on the bottom. Stubblefield uses a modified swivel rig with a small livebait. He prefers a stout 6-foot casting rod and a Garcia 5500 reel loaded with 17-pound line. The main line connects to a barrel swivel with an 18-inch dropline of 25-pound test and a 1-ounce bell sinker on the end.

The leader consists of an 18-inch section of 17-pound line, also tied to the swivel. This section has a #1 or 1/0 hook threaded into a 2- or 3-inch minnow. Pinch the head of the minnow to kill it, then thread the minnow on the hook, leaving the hook point inside the tail of the minnow to discourage white bass from stealing the bait. Freshly killed minnows are vital; blue cats prefer them.

The surprising part of this advice is minnow size. Toad would have agreed with Stubblefield. "These fish eat bigger stuff when they forage shallow," Toad observed. "But during the day, they prefer smaller stuff."

Toad, though, opted for a slightly larger fresh minnow, usually a freshly killed sucker about 4 inches long. He fished the same rigging he would have used for walleyes; that is, a medium-power fast-action spinning rod, an old Garcia Cardinal 4 reel, and 12-pound line. Our favorite combo, by comparison, is a flipping stick, baitcasting reel, and 14-pound line.

Toad used unpainted and untied leadhead jigs weighing 1/2 to 1 ounce. His favorite weight was 5/8 ounce. He'd tap the minnow on the head and slip the hook into its mouth and out just behind the head.

Stubblefield keeps his rig bumping along, his bait always within 18 inches of bottom. Toad fished the jig as vertically as possible. He'd drop the jig so it just touched bottom, then he'd lift it slightly so the current would sweep it along. Toad's jig was always within 12 inches of the bottom.

That's about it. Sleep in, eat a leisurely breakfast, and go after those cats when the sun's high in the sky. Fish hard and Big Mo more likely will get moving your way.

Toad never fished too hard. Often as not, didn't matter if we were into catfish big time, Toad would be flat on the floor, snoozing and snorting like an old Kentucky race horse. So dutifully, we'd reel up our bait, swivel around, and dangle a minnow on his lips. "Uhrrluup!" he'd grunt. And then, because his big hairy bellybutton was always poking from between his shirt and pants, well, we'd dangle the minnow there a moment, too. Tickle, tickle, tickle. "Uhrrluup!" he'd grunt.

We digress from time to time because you cat guys never seem to mind. Occasionally, though, bass fishermen will run out of reading and wander these waters and immediately wonder what's going on. They will be the ones who write that we can't write about angels in a fishing book.

Toad was a great catman, not because he could catch so many cats, but because he symbolizes for a generation of catmen the great glory found in the simplicity of the pursuit of catfish.

Chapter 8

Finding Catfish

Catfish in Ponds

FINDING POND CATFISH The streamlined shape of a catfish, their feeding strategies, and their spawning behavior are adapted to life in current. But the same characteristics that enable catfish to thrive in current also enable them to adapt to a variety of other waters—many more accessible than fine catfish rivers.

Across the country, more fishing opportunities for catfish exist in ponds than in any other kind of water. The U.S. Agricultural Conservation Program of 1936 gave farmers subsidies to build ponds, and in 30 years the number of ponds grew by more than 5,000 percent. While financial incentives to build ponds have been greatly reduced, land owners continue to construct ponds for agricultural, aesthetic, and recreational reasons.

Today, the number of ponds in the U.S. probably exceeds 3 million and continues to grow. Within the "pond belt" region from northern Virginia to southern Montana, more than 1,000 new ponds are built each year. Unless large natural lakes predominate in your area, several ponds usually are within a 10-mile radius of your home. To catch catfish in the 10-pound class, locate and gain access to the most productive ponds in your area.

Unlike large river systems and big reservoirs, the ecosystems of ponds are fragile. A healthy pond that provides good fishing usually results from a good pond management plan. Stocking rate, species composition, harvest levels, and fertilization

Dug Pond

Farm ponds with shallow, featureless basins often are dug with earth-moving equipment. Water runs off adjacent land to keep them full, but supplemental pumping from wells may be necessary in dry periods. When water is pumped into a pond, cats often are attracted to the flow.

Although dug ponds generally are less than 5 acres, management can make them productive for channel catfish.

Active cats roam shallow banks and hold near structural elements like fallen trees, docks, and weedbeds, or in shade produced by shoreline trees and bushes.

Corners and depth breaks attract cats when better cover is scarce. During summer, when the deepest areas lack oxygen, fish avoid them despite the cooler water.

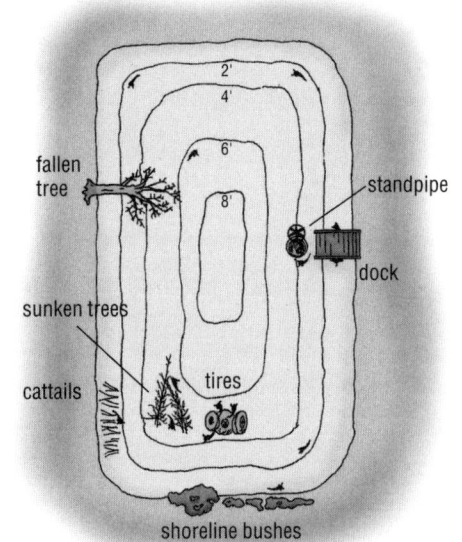

Built Pond

Building a dam across a low area creates a pond if the watershed and soil type have been accurately surveyed. The dam backs up runoff, forming ponds of up to 100 acres.

The area near the dam is deepest. Cats winter there, moving in spring toward shallow areas with cuts, points, and flats with wood. As the spawn approaches, they search shallow areas for hollow logs, natural crevices, and manmade structure like tires, drums, or cans in which to lay eggs.

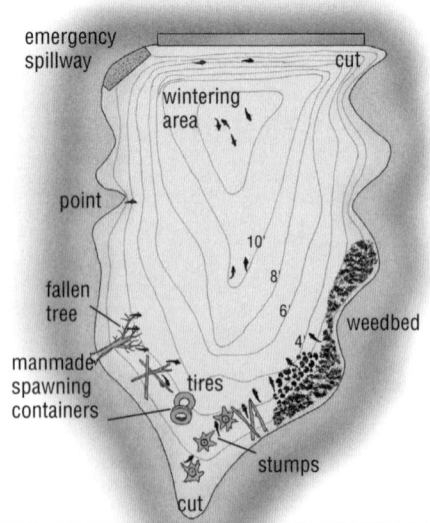

affect the pond's productivity and quality of fishing. Building a pond, stocking it, and leaving it to manage itself is like a gardener throwing seeds in the soil and expecting to harvest a basket of vegetables. Like a garden, ponds that are weeded, fertilized, and planted—in other words managed—produce better results.

POND CATEGORIES

We define a pond as any manmade body of water ranging from about 1 to 50 surface acres. Ponds differ in fishing potential, so in addition to management strategies, a pond's structure, function, size, and shape should be considered. A pond's construction determines the number of fish it supports, the maximum size the catfish will likely attain, and the area of the pond they'll favor during each calendar period. The size and type of watershed—the area surrounding the pond that provides runoff—also is important, as it affects water level, clarity, and fertility.

The most common type of pond in most parts of the country is the dug pond. Earth moving equipment is used to dig a tiered basin that resembles stair steps descending into progressively deeper water. Most dug ponds have a surface area of less than 5 acres and are relatively shallow, but proper fertilization can make them more productive than much larger bodies of water. Most dug ponds are fed by runoff from the adjacent watershed, but auxiliary pumps from wells may be needed to keep the pond full during droughts.

Borrow ponds, a simpler variation of the dug pond, are constructed by a bulldozer shoving earth from the center of the pond. A broad low spot is scooped out and surrounded by the displaced fill. The resulting basin is generally shallow, with no significant variation in depth.

Dams constructed across low-lying areas with adequate soil quality back up runoff and create a built pond up to 100 acres in size. Built ponds are significantly more complex than dug ponds, but their basic structure is still predictable. The deepest area of the pond is usually near the dam, with the basin gradually becoming

Dammed Creek

Creeks are dammed for fishing and to power mills for irrigation. The creek channel is a focal point for catfish during all seasons, with standing or submerged timber along channels particularly attractive.

Creeks often prevent ponds from stratifying, so some cats move deep in summer. Species diversity usually is high, and structural elements are diverse.

Low fishing pressure on creeks can provide superb catfishing.

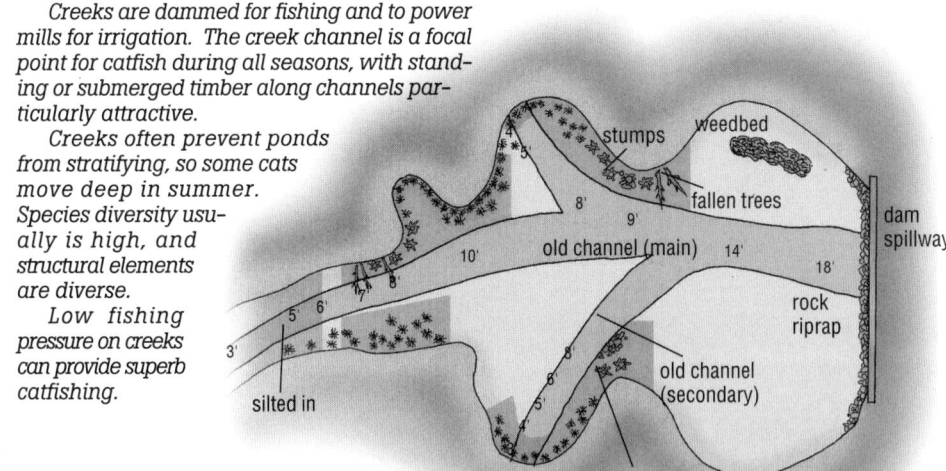

shallower as the land rises away from the dam. Structural elements that key the fishing on built ponds include cuts and points, ditches, and shallow flats with weeds or timber.

Colonial settlers built thousands of dams on small streams across New England to power mills and irrigate crops. These small reservoirs are still being built today, but modern landowners are more likely concerned with creating a quality fishery than with providing a source of power.

Dammed creeks create ponds from 10 to several hundred acres in size, depending on the size of the feeder stream and the size and type of the watershed. Similar to large reservoirs, main and secondary creek channels usually are key structural elements in these ponds. Current may keep dammed creeks from stratifying in summer, but they also make the pond vulnerable to invasions of many species of wild fish—especially during periods of high water.

POND BALANCE

The diversity and abundance of forage depends on the type of pond and its management. In ponds where catfish coexist with bass, bluegill, or other species, cats eat young fish along with aquatic insects and other bottom-dwelling invertebrates. In mature ponds, especially dammed creeks, wild species like shiners, bullheads, and crappies provide additional forage. Growth rates lag on this diet, however.

Many pond owners supplement natural forage with commercial catfish pellets. In the South, managers feed sinking pellets throughout the Coldwater Period, switching to floating pellets when the water warms. This provides an opportunity to observe the number and size of the fish in the pond.

Managers trying to increase the carrying capacity of northern ponds through supplemental feeding may cause more problems than they solve. In-Fisherman editor Steve Quinn says, "Feeding increases the organic load in the pond, possibly causing winterkills from oxygen depletion when the pond is ice-covered. Of course, pond depth,

Across the country, ponds provide more catfishing opportunities than any other kind of water.

current, water color, and duration of ice cover affect oxygen levels. Pond owners forget that channel cats, unlike bullheads, require high levels of dissolved oxygen to survive."

Channel catfish don't successfully spawn in most small ponds because lack of cover offers few nooks and crevices that cats need to lay and guard eggs. In highly managed situations, however, lack of spawning doesn't hurt the fishery since small catfish (6 to 10 inches) are stocked to compensate for harvest and natural mortality. Stocking provides control over catfish density and can prevent overpopulation problems that slow the growth of the entire catfish population.

Adding barrels, tires, or old-style milk jugs help catfish reproduce naturally. This avoids stocking costs, but relinquishes control over catfish density.

CATFISH LOCATION

In ponds, as in rivers, holes often key catfish location. Catfish winter in the deepest holes of the pond and prowl adjacent structure like points, cuts, and flats during the open-water season. In ponds without feeder creeks or other sources of oxygen, the pond might stratify in late summer. With the depths devoid of oxygen, small channel cats often roam the shallows, but the biggest fish usually suspend over deep water. Current areas created by creeks, springs, or pumps always are worth checking.

In ponds, as in rivers, holes often key catfish location. Catfish winter in the deepest holes and prowl adjacent structure like points, cuts, and flats during the open-water season.

Quinn has observed that in ponds without definite holes, catfish tend to roam. "Without any current to influence their movements," he says, "catfish location becomes less predictable. In barren ponds, look for active fish along banks that drop off quickly into deeper water, or near visible cover like docks and weedbeds. Cuts, corners, and sharp depth breaks also hold fish when better cover is scarce. And if food is provided, catfish hold in the feeding area, in anticipation."

FISHING STRATEGIES

The biggest cats in ponds often are tough to catch. Usually, though, many traditional presentations produce fish. Set rigging with crawlers, cutbait, dipbait, or crawdad tails, weighted with a simple slipsinker, is the most common approach.

Slipfloats, however, remain an overlooked option. A slipfloat allows anglers to change the level at which a bait is suspended by moving the stop knot up or down. Channel cats often suspend in ponds, particularly over the deeper portion of the basin. But floats also work as a strike indicator when a bait is fished deep enough to lie just on the bottom in shallower water.

Fishing at night with natural baits provides an edge for catching difficult cats, or other, more refined approaches can be employed. Randall Akin, a former member of the U.S. match-fishing team (featured in past issues of *In-Fisherman* and *Catfish In-Sider Guide* for his success with European catfish tactics), is a frequent visitor to commercial pay ponds across the country. These ponds are small waters where fishing pressure quickly teaches catfish to avoid hooks, and floating pellets condition them to feed on the surface.

Akin addresses difficult fish by using light line, small baits, and lots of chum. When fishing on the bottom, he usually begins by introducing small pieces of bait mixed with groundbait—a dry blend of fish-attracting ingredients—into the area he intends to fish. A weighted swim feeder, a small plastic cylinder filled with groundbait, keeps his bait on the bottom and sustains his cloud of chum. Later in the season, when the bottoms of clear ponds are covered with a foot-thick layer of algae and the depths lack sufficient oxygen for fish, Akin uses floats and chums with small pieces of bait.

"Nothing attracts fish and gets them to feed," Akin says, "like other feeding fish. Attract them to the area you're fishing and keep them feeding." He has found live maggots an economical and effective bait for pond cats, especially in cold water. Akin: "There's something about a live, wriggling maggot that catfish can't resist." He uses up to three maggots on a #12 hook. "Once catfish are feeding in a competitive environment like a pond, they take small baits with confidence."

As the season progresses, Akin may switch to more traditional baits, but he still presents them in a nontraditional way. "I've been experimenting with cutbait and bloodbait on hair rigs," Akin says. The hair rig begins with a #6 octopus-style hook on a standard sliprig. One end of a short piece of light monofilament is secured to the eye of the hook with several half hitches, and a small loop is tied in the other end to form the "hair."

For the cutbait rig, Akin threads the hair through a small piece of meat with a bait needle and secures it with a hair stop—a short, stiff piece of plastic specifically designed for this purpose. When the rig is properly constructed, the bait is nearly flush with the bend of the hook, but the hook itself is free and ready to penetrate catfish flesh.

To prepare chicken bloodbait, pour a generous amount of blood onto a screen so the runny liquid passes through. The caked blood can then be sliced into quarter-inch-thick strips about an inch wide and four inches long. Akin packages the strips in the spawn sacs steelhead fishermen use to bag salmon eggs, and he ties the sac to the end of his hair rig. "This rig is especially effective in ponds because the blood disperses into the water, attracting catfish from a considerable distance," he says.

Knowing whether pond owners feed the catfish in their ponds can help determine the best fishing approach. Visit a commercial catfish farm, where channel or blue cats are raised for sale, and you'll see the extreme effect conditioning has. The vibration of the truck's tires draws droves of hungry fish.

We know a pond owner in Iowa who buys 5-gallon pails of fresh chicken livers as a treat for the catfish in his pond. A few times a week he walks out on the

dock and lobs the livers into the pond where they're quickly devoured by the resident flatheads. While natural baits surely would produce on a pond like this, fresh chicken liver is effective because the fish are used to eating it.

If you fish big natural lakes and reservoirs or heavily pressured sections of a river, you'll be amazed at the kind of fishing a well-managed pond provides. But it's a delicate balance—an invasion of wild fish or a severe winterkill might require draining or restocking the pond. Selective harvest must be practiced, and most importantly, comply with the pond owner's management strategy to ensure the long-term health of the fishery.

Ponds may never replace rivers in the hearts and minds of most catmen, but they are an enjoyable and accessible alternative. Take time to identify productive ponds by talking to pond owners. Helping them with routine chores like stocking, fertilizing, or removing excess weeds will help you understand the unique ecosystem and make you a welcome visitor.

EXPLORING FARM PONDS

Dave McClure will take you to his favorite catfishing holes, but you'll have to be blindfolded during the trip.

"I've worked too hard and too long to get access to these spots," he says. "If you won't wear a blindfold, then be prepared for a long ride, because I'll go 10 miles out of my way to make sure you're lost and won't be able to find your way back there again."

It's worth wearing a blindfold or enduring a long ride to fish for cats with McClure. The 36-year-old resident of Cedar Rapids, Iowa, has caught in three hours as many as 50 channel cats ranging from 4 to 10 pounds. He views 5-pound cats as average, and considers catching fewer than a dozen cats as a slow day. He does all this using the same bait, tackle, and presentation spring, summer, and fall.

"It's where I fish that makes the difference," he says. "Nobody else fishes where I fish because nobody else knows about the spots. Even if they do, they probably don't have permission to fish the spots, so I have the cats all to myself."

McClure specializes in fishing in farm ponds, and has made a science of locating and getting permission to fish these private angling paradises. He is neither related to nor close friends with any of the owners of the Iowa farm ponds he fishes, but on any given day he has access to nearly 100 ponds. The privilege to fish those ponds came as the result of days of research, travel, and salesmanship, and required the combined skills of a psychologist, a private investigator, and a computer geek.

Ponds are accessible to millions of anglers and offer some of the finest and most secluded fishing opportunities most catmen will ever experience.

FINDING PRODUCTIVE PONDS

"I never mess with any pond within 30 miles of a large city," he says. "Plain and simple, the average angler doesn't want to travel more than a half hour to fish, so anybody who owns a pond within a half hour of a good-sized town probably is tired of having people ask to fish. Here in Iowa, I've had good luck getting permission to fish in ponds in the southern two tiers of counties. There are lots of ponds down there, but few large urban areas, so the pond owners aren't tired of being asked all the time."

McClure always is on the lookout for new ponds as he travels in rural areas, but he normally avoids any pond visible from a rural road.

"What I want is a pond that's over a hill, that you have to walk or drive along a cornfield to get to," he says. "Some of my best ponds are at the ends of dead-end roads—less traffic, and fewer people have stopped to ask permission to fish."

McClure locates hidden ponds by studying county plat maps or by downloading satellite photographs from the Internet. He regularly visits the library and photocopies page after page from plat maps for rural counties. Plat maps don't show individual ponds, but reveal roads, building sites, landmarks and, most important, who owns all the tracts of land in the county.

From the Internet he collects satellite photos of the same counties, then studies the images to identify potential ponds.

From the Internet he collects satellite photos of the same counties, then studies the images to identify potential ponds. McClure uses *www.terraserver.com* to get satellite photos, and he also uses the U.S. Geological Survey's Web site, *www.usgs.gov,* to access detailed topographic maps that show ponds larger than 3 acres. Another Web site that offers detailed satellite photos to subscribers is *www.globexplorer.com.*

"Then I get in the car and go scouting," he says. "I don't bring any fishing poles or tackle, just the maps and photos. My goal is to find the ponds, figure out who owns them, and get permission to fish them.

"I try to make my trips during the middle of the week, during the months of July and August," he says. "Farmers are busy and hard to find in the spring and fall. Once I locate a pond and figure out who owns it or who rents the ground and has management of it, I drive in, knock on the door, and see if I can get permission to fish it."

Salesmanship and good people skills are a critical part of gaining access. An unfamiliar car with out-of-county license plates raises suspicions that McClure works quickly to dispel.

"I go up, introduce myself, tell them where I'm from, and explain that I'd like permission to fish in their pond," he says. "I tell them right up front that I'm a catch-and-release fisherman, and that I won't leave any gates open or leave trash or litter. I always offer them my name, address, and phone number. It seems to help if they know exactly who I am and how to contact me if they ever need to.

"If they show the least interest in letting me fish, I find out what kind of fish are stocked in the pond, how deep the pond is, and if the fish are worth catching. If I actually get permission, I ask for their rules. Do they want me to come and check in at the house every time I come to fish? Do they want me to call in advance? Do they have certain routes they want me to use to walk or drive back to the pond? I never ask for more than they are willing to offer, because I want them to know that I consider it a privilege to be on their property."

McClure continues to practice salesmanship for as long as he fishes each pond. He tries to find some special way to thank each pond owner. Some like a meal of fresh fish. He discovered that a few of his pond owners didn't object to a gift of an occasional bottle of Jack Daniels. "Whatever it takes to let them know that I appreciate being able to fish their pond," McClure says. And each of his nearly 100 pond owners gets a Christmas card each year, whether McClure fished their pond that year or not.

"I spend a lot of time researching and finding these ponds, and then I spend as much or more time on the care and maintenance of the owners," he says. "But it's worth it. I was a guide in the Boundary Waters in northern Minnesota for 12 years. I've caught 20-pound pike, 20-pound lake trout, and walleyes by the boatload, but I've never seen anything to compare with the fishing that's available in farm ponds.

"Travel across southern Iowa, eastern Nebraska, Missouri, southern Illinois, eastern Kansas, Oklahoma—there must be hundreds of thousands of farm ponds. Most of them are stocked with fish, but few of them get any kind of serious fishing pressure. If you can get permission to fish them and develop a string of ponds to hit on a weekend or over a week's vacation, you'll experience some of the best fishing in the world."

That's what McClure did several years ago for his uncle, a retired schoolteacher from Chicago. The uncle and his fishing cronies made annual pilgrimages to northern Wisconsin and Canada. Health problems prohibited them from traveling to the North Woods, so McClure arranged a week-long guided fishing tour of southern Iowa farm ponds.

"I got out my little black book," he says. "I have each pond listed by who owns it, their address and phone number, how deep it is, what species are in it, directions on how to get to the pond, and all the rules for each pond. I also keep a record of what size and kind of fish I catch, along with the usual weather and tackle information.

"I put together a list of ponds I could take these guys to and called all the pond owners a couple weeks in advance. I asked if they'd mind if I brought in a small group of retired schoolteachers from Chicago to fish in their ponds. I emphasized that these guys were from out of state and wouldn't come back on their own, and every owner said it would be fine. The

Selective harvest is critical for maintaining the health of pond catfish populations. Keep a few fish for the table where fish are abundant, but release all the cats you catch where they aren't.

guys came out and had the time of their lives catching bass, crappies, bluegills, and catfish. They said it was one of the best fishing trips they'd ever had."

POND TIPS & TRICKS

"The best ponds are 3 to 6 acres in size and can be found on county maps or aerial photos, but can't be seen from any road," McClure says. "The real prizes are hidden ponds that the farmer doesn't use to water his cattle. Cattle tromp down the edges, make ponds muddy and shallow around the edges, and the nutrients from their manure tend to make those ponds weedy during the hot months. I try to fish "cattle" ponds early in the year, before the water warms up and weeds and algae blooms become a problem."

For all the effort McClure puts into identifying, locating, and getting permission to fish his pool of ponds, his catfishing techniques are starkly simple.

"If I'm after catfish in a pond, I use the same bait and tackle spring, summer, and fall," he declares. "My system never lets me down, and I've never felt a need to experiment with other baits or techniques.

The best ponds are 3 to 6 acres in size and can be found on county maps or aerial photos, but can't be seen from any road.

"We were having a family outing at one of my ponds a couple years ago with some friends and their families, and the owner had told me there were a lot of nice catfish in that pond," he recalls. "We'd fished all day for crappies, bass, and bluegills, but at night, while everybody was cooking hot dogs and marshmallows around the campfire, I decided to take some nightcrawlers and try for a catfish.

"All I got was bullhead after bullhead on nightcrawlers, then I remembered reading an article that said hot dogs are good catfish bait. I went up to the campfire and stole a raw hot dog, broke it into thirds and threaded a chunk onto my hook. Within a minute I was trying to land an 8-pound channel cat.

"All the whooping and hollering brought everybody down from the campfire. I didn't even get that cat unhooked before they'd robbed all the hotdogs out of the coolers and were casting out their lines. We caught (and released) 5- to 10-pound catfish all night. I've never seen any reason to bait for cats with anything but hot dogs since then."

McClure emphasizes that 95 percent of his farm pond fishing is catch and release. Many pond owners require it, and McClure recommends it.

"I'll negotiate with owners about keeping bluegills and crappies, but I'm pretty much pure catch and release for bass and catfish," he says. "Bass and cats are the predators that keep ponds in balance. You don't have to take too many big bass or cats out of a pond before the panfish take over. And some of the pond owners are protective of their fish. I've got one pond where there's an 8-pound bass they call 'Big Sally.' Big Sally *has* to go back if you catch her. And I have other ponds where the owners have nicknamed big cats they've hooked and lost while fishing for crappies or bluegills."

Maintaining an adequate predator base isn't difficult. Pond bass populations are self-sustaining, but their numbers and top-end size are limited by the availability of forage fish. Catfish can reproduce in farm ponds and have the potential to overpopulate in rare situations.

"Catfish don't need running water to spawn," says Marion Conover, Chief of Fisheries for the Iowa Department of Natural Resources. "We rear all the catfish we use to stock lakes in our hatchery ponds and get great reproduction. But they do need holes and crevices. Cats are cavity spawners, and if a pond is a smooth–bottomed bowl, they're going to have a tough time finding suitable places to lay their eggs.

"But if there's a bunch of old tree roots, or somebody anchored a pile of old tires on the bottom, or there's any sort of holey-habitat, there's a good chance channel cats will be able to reproduce in a pond," Conover continues. "The trick is to get those catfish fry to catchable size. Anybody who has seen a school of little catfish or bullheads in shallow water knows that they tend to school in a dense cloud. All it takes is about two passes for a big largemouth bass to wipe out those schools.

"To keep a viable population of catfish in a pond, you'll probably have to stock them on a regular basis. We recommend an initial stocking of 100 channel catfish per acre in the fall, followed by a maintenance

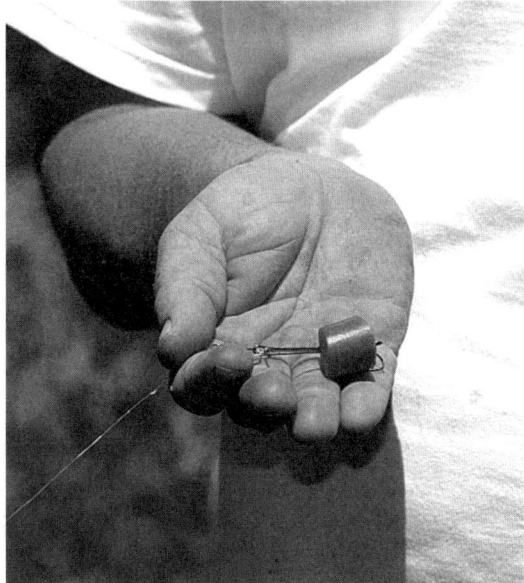

Simple rigs and grocery store baits usually work fine for pond cats, since they receive little angling pressure.

stocking for ponds of about 20 eight-inch or bigger fingerlings per acre per year. But don't overstock. More than 100 pounds of catfish per acre is hard on the bluegill population in a pond or small lake. That's why you need at least some bass to stay ahead of the cats."

Conover notes that anglers who want to catch and transfer "wild" catfish from rivers will notice no difference in size or growth rates compared to catfish purchased from commercial hatcheries. He says that anglers who want to spice up their farm pond's potential might consider adding a few flathead catfish to the mix.

"Flatheads are real predators, and as they grow they'll be in competition with anglers for the bluegills and crappies," Conover says. "Big flatheads think 9- and 10-inch crappies are snacks. I wouldn't stock more than 3 or 4 flatheads per surface acre."

McClure hasn't tangled with any flatheads in his string of farm ponds yet, and doesn't expect to. "To my knowledge, none of the ponds I fish have any flatheads, and don't really need them. The channel catfishing already is dynamite."

And that brings us back to the possibility of McClure sharing his fishing bonanza with other anglers. He's toyed with the idea of starting a guide service that would provide clients with species-specific, one-day, multi-day, or week long tours of ponds in southern Iowa.

"I guided in the Boundary Waters, and know what it takes to give clients their money's worth," he says. "I just have to be careful about giving away the locations of all my ponds and having guys start fishing them without me, or without permission from the owners. I'd like to do it, and would do it for a fair price, but it would take special arrangements."

PAY LAKES PAY

Where can a bank fisherman with limited fishery access, and even more limited time and budget go to (a) catch enough eatin'-size catfish for a tasty meal, (b) introduce a child to the thrill of catching fish, (c) spend a relaxing day in the sun swapping tales with friendly folk, or (d) tangle with a 30-, 40-, or even 50-pound cat? One easy answer–a pay lake.

HOW PAY LAKES WORK

Ardath and Jerry Moorman own Moor-Aker Lakes, a popular fishing park in Jeffersonville, Ohio. "We're open 24 hours a day, 7 days a week from April 15 through September 30," Ardath says. "We average 250 fishermen per night on a weekend, 40 per day during the week. Many customers arrive Friday evening and fish all weekend." Rates usually are based on 12 hours of fishing, with discounts for seniors and handicapped anglers–practices typical of most pay lakes.

The 45-acre Moorman property includes three lakes: a half-acre kid's pond, a small lake full of small and midsize cats, and a 15-acre lake stocked with trophy-class cats. "We stock channels, flatheads, and blues, plus bass and bluegills," Moorman says. "We stock catfish at the rate of 3,000 pounds per week until July 4, then 3,000 pounds every other week until we close. We get our catfish from commercial fishermen at Barkley and Kentucky lakes and are licensed to transport them in our tank truck."

Some lakes pay a bounty of 50 to 75 cents per pound on cats over 10 pounds, or offer a free admission pass

Big catfish are a major drawing card at Moor-Aker Lakes. "The two biggest cats caught so far were a 72-pound blue and a 57-pound flathead. But we know of a 100-pound-class flathead in one of the lakes, because divers have seen it." The 15-acre lake, dug in 1960, is 37 feet deep, spring-fed, and contains prime catfish cover, including several trees, a sunken johnboat, and telephone poles.

"A pay lake is a way to enjoy catfishing without investing a lot of time or money," Moorman says. "It provides fishing on several levels. You have an excellent shot at a trophy-size cat. If you want to teach your kids to fish, they'll get plenty of bites here. And a community of regulars provides a social outlet. We have picnic tables, a playground, and a 24-hour bait shop. All our lakes are handicapped-accessible, and the shorelines are well maintained."

Middletown, Ohio catman Doug Hensley frequents several pay lakes in southern Ohio and northern Kentucky. "These ponds are ideal for the angler who doesn't own a boat," he says. "I grew up near Georgetown, Kentucky, where my father used to take me to Parrish Lakes at nearby Stamping Ground, which still are in operation today. The owners tagged big fish when they released them so they could keep track of them. In 1995, a friend fishing one of the Parrish lakes caught a 40-pound blue cat with a tag in its dorsal fin dating back to the late 1970s. According to the tag, this fish weighed 10 pounds when first stocked. How catfish live so long in a lake with such heavy fishing pressure remains a mystery."

But Hensley warns that not all pay lakes are created equal. "Each lake has its own character," he says. "Some are extremely deep, others shallow. They may be oval, L-shaped, U-shaped, or long and narrow. They're often stocked according to catfish size—some with 'pond splashers' for folks who want to catch some small cats for supper, others with trophy-size cats."

Anglers who land a big catfish at a pay lake often are enticed to return it to the water and collect a bounty. "Some lakes pay a bounty of 50 to 75 cents per pound on cats over 10 pounds, or offer a free admission pass," Hensley says. "They want you to bring the fish to the weigh station in a landing net and return it to the lake quickly in good condition so it can be caught again."

Most pay lakes in Hensley's region are regularly stocked with flatheads, channels, and blues; some also receive stockings of carp, drum, crappie, bass, and even paddlefish. "Cross Keys Lake in Shelbyville, Kentucky, is rumored to hold a blue cat weighing over 100 pounds," Hensley says. "A $500 reward is posted for anyone who lands that fish on a rod and reel. Darrell's in Clay City, Kentucky, also produced a 52- and a 50-pound flathead last season. No question, these are big-cat spots."

Contests and prizes are a main attraction at many pay lakes. At some lakes, you can enter a big fish pot simply by dropping a dollar in a jar. Cash or merchandise prizes frequently are offered for the biggest blue, flathead, and channel of the day, weekend, month, or season. Some pay venues also hold fishing contests for kids and seniors. One operation in Ohio reportedly offers a $10,000 jackpot to the lucky angler who catches a specially tagged fish.

Legal And Ethical Concerns About Pay Lakes

Pay lakes offer plenty of positive attributes. But concerns are being raised about where and how the fish used to stock them are obtained. A pay lake receiving heavy traffic must be routinely stocked in order to provide excellent fishing opportunities, some at the rate of more than 12,000 pounds of catfish per month. So where do all these cats come from?

"In my opinion, pay lakes operate at the expense of the fishery as a whole," catfish guide Frank Van Winkle says. "How these lakes are stocked raises legal and ethical questions."

According to Van Winkle, the majority of catfish used to stock pay lakes in his region come from public waters in Ohio, Kentucky, and Tennessee. "Many of the public waters I fish have been hit hard by commercial fishermen who sell their catch to pay lakes," he claims. "I cringe when I pull up to the launch ramp and see a flatbed truck with big tanks parked there. I know that commercial fishermen are hauling 600 to 1,000 pounds of live catfish a day out of public waters and selling them to pay-lake proprietors. If I were from Tennessee, Kentucky, or South Carolina, I'd be upset about these big cats being shipped off to pay lakes in other states.

"Ohio has stringent commercial fishing regulations, many of which are ignored by pay-lake owners and those who supply them with fish," Van Winkle says. "It's illegal here to run a net within 500 feet of a tributary mouth, yet I see the same people violating this statute again and again. Also, selling live catfish is illegal in Ohio without a propagator's license, which most commercial fishermen doing business in my area don't have. Some of them have been fined repeatedly by wildlife officials, but they view the fine as a cost of doing business. If I poached a deer and got caught, I'd be fined and I'd lose my hunting license. But these guys just smile, pay their fine, and keep setting their nets. The pay-lake market is far too lucrative to quit.

"Fish stocked in pay lakes often languish," Van Winkle adds. "I see pictures of guys holding up pay-lake cats weighing 20 pounds with a 45-pounder's head. They're nothing but skin and bones. The available forage in these lakes can't support such large numbers of fish, and most owners don't feed them. I think catfishermen should ask about the source of the stocked fish before supporting a pay lake."

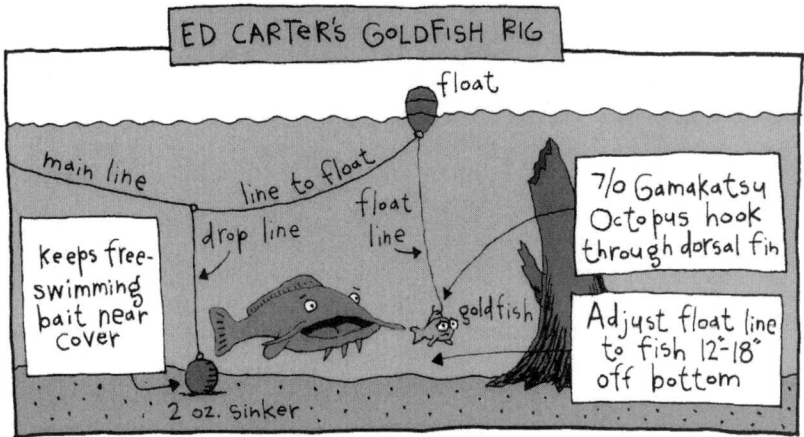

ED CARTER'S GOLDFISH RIG

float

main line

line to float

drop line

float line

Keeps free-swimming bait near cover

7/o Gamakatsu Octopus hook through dorsal fin

goldfish

Adjust float line to fish 12"-18" off bottom

2 oz. sinker

PAY LAKE SAVVY

Many fishermen frequenting pay lakes simply plunk down the entrance fee, head for an empty spot on the bank, and start fishing. But if you're after bigger fish, the right location, bait, and presentation are as important in these private ponds as on any lake or river system. Columbus, Ohio, angler Ed Carter, a pay-lake regular who uses a big-water approach to catch heavy cats from these mini-fisheries, offers these tips:

"First, you need to know what's stocked in each of the lakes so you can optimize your fishing time," Carter says. "If you're after a trophy, ask the proprietor which of his lakes will provide your best shot at a big fish. The owners, wanting you to have a successful outing so you'll come back often, willingly share information with you."

Many pay lakes are shallow. Carter says he usually forgoes these and targets deep water. "My favorite pay lake has some 40-foot water, plus plenty of structure and cover—the kind of things big catfish relate to wherever they live," Carter says. "I concentrate on areas with deep wood or rock cover and adjacent shallower flats and ledges. In summer, I key on 6-foot flats near deep water. Some pay lakes are loaded with cover—rockpiles, standing and fallen trees, stumps, even old cars—while others are relatively barren. Ask the proprietor where to find the deepest water and the most cover. I guarantee the biggest cats won't be far from it."

Carter chooses his baits and rigging methods with big fish in mind. "My favorite bait, a live goldfish about 4 inches long, is active on the hook and hardy, even in hot weather. They're especially good for flatheads, but they work for big channels and blues as well. I hook the goldfish through the dorsal fin on a 7/0 Gamakatsu Octopus hook and fish it close to cover with a combination sinker and float rig. This allows the bait plenty of movement but keeps it close to the cover or structural edge you want to fish. Some pay lake customers use goldfish up to 14 inches long, but I prefer smaller baits. On occasion, I also use shiners and chubs. Our local bait shops sell soft craws, which also are effective. I don't use crawlers or stinkbaits, because pay lakes have so many small fish that constantly clean these baits off your hook."

Carter fishes clear-water pay lakes mainly at night. "I usually show up at 6 p.m. and fish until 2 a.m. or so," he says. "Big cats move up shallow after dark and bite more readily, plus fewer fishermen usually are competing with you once the sun sets."

Carter's biggest pay-lake cat to date is a 53-pound blue. "I've also caught several 20s and 30s—all from shore, while fishing maybe once a week during summer," Carter concludes. "You'd have to fish for years from a boat in a big lake or river to contact that many big cats, and even then, maybe never a 50-pounder."

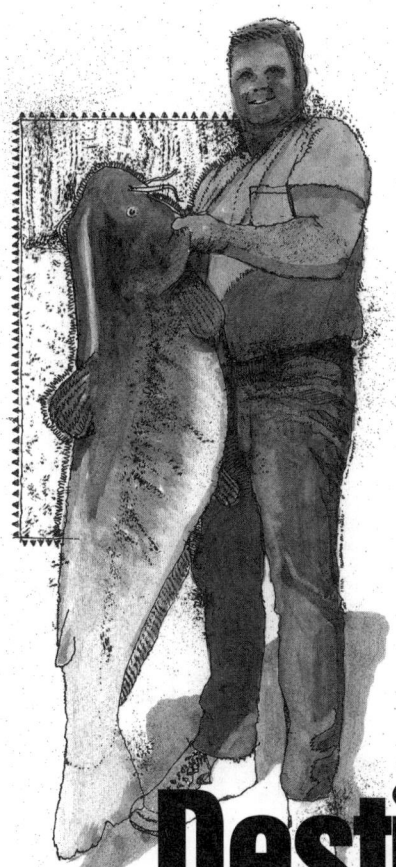

John Collins' former California record, "looked like a seal!" when it surfaced. This 82.1-pounder, an omen of big things to come from California, is no great shakes measured against fish swimming in the Carolinas, Tennessee, Kansas, and other waters in the heart of the blue cat's range.

Trophy Catfish Destinations

WHERE FOR TROPHY CATFISH

From California to the Carolinas, blue cats have made a comeback from the days during the '40s, '50s, and '60s, when dams changed much of their traditional habitat. Like their ancestors, the fish today are of monstrous proportions and, seemingly, getting even larger. Now too, perhaps more than at any other time in history, we are learning how to catch them.

Anyone reading this who wants to catch a blue cat of gargantuan proportions has a good chance to do so. In at least a dozen states from California to Virginia and the Carolinas, the colder water of fall and throughout winter and early spring seems to move these monsters into areas where they're easier to catch. The resulting opportunities for tangling with fish of legendary size remain unknown to most of the fishing world. We ride here the edge of fishing history.

The dimensions of some of the blue cats swimming in these waters—big lakes, rivers, and reservoirs—will remain hard for folks riding the "main stream" of the fishing world to fathom. Most anglers, after all, are these days used to thinking in terms of bass. Or walleyes. So it is that the largemouth and the walleye and certainly the muskie have come to be considered our freshwater monsters. Pshaww. Bass are big at 10, that's big for walleyes too, and muskies rarely reach 30. Blue cats, on the other hand, well . . .

In California, John Collins, an accomplished bass angler, is working a crawfish along the bottom in Lower Otay Reservoir. He and his partner have already boated a 10-pound bass this April morning, when . . . "I thought it might have been a big bass for a moment," Collins says. "But then it stripped 75 yards of line." Fifteen minutes later, as the fish surfaced, Collins could only exclaim, "It looks like a seal!"

Big blues really do assume grotesque proportions. Collins' fish measures a mere 51 inches but has a robust 35½-inch girth. Spread your arms 4 feet. Now

make a big circle with your arms, as in pretend you're reaching around Rosanne's waistline. That's Collins' fish. "People just aren't used to seeing fish made like that," Collins says. "Really, it's almost impossible to imagine how big a fish like this is." At 82.1 pounds, the fish established a new California record, surpassing the old record by nearly 20 pounds.

Meanwhile, suppose you were in the boat one fine day with Clarksville, Tennessee, catfish guide Jim Moyer. Moyer, you might remember, was the primary source to help us break the news about how mega blues can be caught during Coldwater Periods. He annually catches a dozen blues over 50 pounds and hundreds over 30 pounds. This day he is fishing a big river in Alabama. "People just aren't prepared to deal with these creatures," he is saying, shaking his head, and then adding, "and add me to that list when it comes to the most monstrous of them, even after all the big fish I've handled.

Virgil Agee poses matter-of-factly beside another mega blue. "Sometime soon, someone will land a blue that will make the present record seem like small change," he offers.

"It was just one of those days when you park perfectly on a hole that has monsters—and they're hungry," he continues. "The first fish we hook, well, he just spools me—250 yards of 30-pound test. Gone, like that. Spools me without so much as my turning the fish or even slowing it down. So another 30 minutes pass, and I hook another one. I can tell you I don't have a net that will handle a world record, for this old boy wouldn't go in no net.

"Can't tell you exactly how long this fish is. Girth? Well, hey, I'm a big guy and I don't think I could reach around it. We get a weight, though, before releasing the fish. The hog scale in the boat registers 87 pounds, but I think the fish has to be bigger. The fish has to be some 56 inches, maybe 40 inches around. These fish are something from another world. Consider this, though—I've been spooled four times the past year. How big are some of these fish?"

Virgil Agee is certain some of those fish are kicking near the 150 mark. Agee, a seasoned catman from Jefferson City, Missouri, these days pursues monster blues almost exclusively. "That fish two Octobers ago," he says, referring to one of the largest blues he's landed, "had me all over the Osage River." Then, as in the case with Moyer's struggle with the near 90, Agee had to wrestle the fish to string it alongside the boat. "It was a monster," he says. "But I'd seen bigger, so I decided to continue fishing instead of heading right in to weigh it."

Agee's 101-pound fish, however, is the present Catch-and-Release World Record, which made his 121 the unconfirmed Catch-and-Release World Record.

Eight hours later the fish weighed 101 pounds 7 ounces. Shortly thereafter a fishery biologist suggested the fish might have weighed near 114 when it was caught. The Missouri record is 103. Virgil just shrugs. "I'm interested in records, but not overwhelmed by them," he says. "I do wish I would have weighed the fish sooner—just out of curiosity." Like Collins' California fish, this fish measures 51 inches, but is 3½ inches more rotund, with a 40-inch girth.

Two months later Agee lands another monster blue, a fish he hasn't told many folks about. "This fish weighs—well, we'll never know for sure—but the scale says 121 on the nose," he says. "But, we learn after the fish is released, the certification sticker on the scale is out of date. So the fish could never be confirmed—kind of an unconfirmed world record at the time." Agee's 101-pound fish, however, is the present catch-and-release world record, which made his 121 the unconfirmed catch-and-release world record.

But the stories get even bigger, for Agee believes he'll get another shot at a fish he lost during a stretch of fall and winter fishing several years ago. "I had him boatside," he says. "I don't tell many folks the story because they can't believe such a fish exists. But I've caught 70s and 80s, and the 101 and 121. I know what those fish look like. This fish, though . . . well, this fish was just in another class—150 easy. I couldn't get him on board—no gaff, no way to land the fish other than kill it. And I don't kill big fish. So I reached for a channel lock pliers, thinking I can get a grip on the fish and run a rope through his gills. But as I reach, the fish surges—I have my drag tightened down at the end of the battle in order to control the fish. My line breaks before I can loosen the drag."

Agee and Moyer lend a lean and persistent perspective to what we have been telling you right along for the past few years. The big blues, apparently first adversely affected by the dams of the '50s and 60s are back in a big way—in such a big way that the fish may actually be getting as large or larger than in times past. Mega fish are there, in perhaps some 12 states, and only a few folks presently understand how to catch them. Few folks also realize the mystique that is bound to quickly envelop the continuing quest for these new-age monsters. This story should become one of the most compelling stories in fishing as it begins to gain publicity.

Agee: "A fish will be caught sometime soon that will make the present record look like medium change. At least, my 101 and 121 are back in the river. Those fish could weigh 150 now. And who knows what that 150 weighs?"

Mega fish are there, in perhaps some 12 states, and only a few folks presently understand how to catch them.

Collins' fish, also released back into Lower Otay, could also approach 100 pounds by now. And in many other waters across North America, fish of such mammoth proportions probably reside. Certainly, the lower Missouri River and portions of the middle and lower Mississippi, in the heart of the original blue-cat range, remain prime water for a world record.

The Missouri 103, the world record for a short time and the present Missouri record, was taken from the Missouri River below Omaha several years ago. Lake Texoma, on the Oklahoma-Texas border, produced the current 121-pound world record. Arkansas has monster fish, too. And we haven't even attempted (and won't here) to chronicle the catches from Santee-Cooper, South Carolina, one of the best waters in the country for mega blues.

That blue cats today can grow big quickly in some waters is supported by Larry Bottroff, the fishery biologist who witnessed Collins' California record. According to Bottroff, fin clips identified the Collins cat as belonging to a batch of 1-pound blues planted in Lower Otay and San Vicente reservoirs in 1985. Collins' fish had grown at least 81 pounds in 11 years.

That the nature of a fish species can change as those fish age and grow is well documented, and so it appears to be with blue cats. Our friend Zacker, that old commercial cat man from a generation of catmen familiar with the record blue cats of the 1950s and 1960s, used to say simply that "little fish aren't big fish—different as night and day. Little blues," he'd say, "fish to about 8 to 25 pounds—are pesky varmints. Fun to catch and good to eat, but they're everywhere, doing everything at the same time."

His point was that some small blues might just as soon be grubbing on the bottom as nitpicking stuff off the surface. Then, too, some blues will likely be running shad in open water, while others are snacking on snails and clams from deep river or reservoir flats. "But big cats are big cats wherever they swim," he'd say. And by Zacker's standards, that meant fish with a yearning for big water, deeper and cooler water, and a monster food source.

Most of Agee's fish come from some of the deepest holes in the Osage, itself a pretty good piece of water that runs into that mega-blue-cat sanctuary, the Missouri River. Much of his best fishing has been in October, November, and December. But he admits that he wants to spend more time exploring the fishing during midwinter, so long as current is present and the water doesn't freeze. It's during this period, Agee now knows, that Moyer catches many of his fish.

Moyer's fish, though, mostly run channel banks in main current in big rivers, territory from which Agee rarely catches big cats. Most of the huge cats Agee catches hold in deep holes near but not in heavy current. In each case, though, current remains a key factor. In rivers, monster blues rarely feed

---

during periods of reduced water generation. Meanwhile, in reservoirs like Marion and Moltrie (Santee-Cooper), current is only indirectly a factor. Most Santee-Cooper guides contend, though, that big blues rarely range onto shallow flats. Most of the monsters run the deep water in old channel beds, often many miles from shoreline flats.

Moyer favors depths from 20 on the shallow end, into 40 or 50 feet of water. It's the bank or drop-off, though, in conjunction with current, that keys good fishing. Only occasionally do blues roam the shallow flat next to the drop-off, preferring instead to run the drop-off from about 20 or so down into 35 feet or more. Often the fish are at the base of the channel drop-off, in current that might be running 7 miles per hour. Of course, these fish are on the bottom, probably holding in depressions or behind bottom debris where the current's minimized.

As Zacker always contended, monster fish need a monster food source, not necessarily large baits or baitfish so much as lots of them. In many waters, blue cats range over mussel beds, chowing down on shell and all, then digesting the soft body of the clam before eliminating the shell. Some of the fish in Santee-Cooper actually rattle when you shake them, they're so full of clams. Some of these fish also have anal pores the size of a 50 cent piece, from eliminating the clam shells.

We believe it's doubtful that monster blues run baitfish in open water; built as they are like small freight trains, they likely don't function well there. But we don't know for sure. Certainly, in reservoirs, the big boys drift suspended during certain periods. But the bigger fish seemingly feed most often along the bottom, keying on banquet sources of dead shad, which often are most abundant during winter. Indeed, it may be the combination of mega food sources in conjunction with colder water, which reduces metabolism, that combines to fuel mega growth and a measure of increased longevity.

Moyer's Approach—Most of Moyer's best fishing is in the upper 1/2 to 1/3 of the riverlike portions of river-run reservoirs. He rarely finds big fish in tailwater areas because the tailwater areas available to him offer only shallow water. Thus, shad flushed through the roller dams are washed along through relatively shallow water until they tumble into deeper channel areas downriver. Big blues apparently push upriver until they reach areas that naturally gather the most drifting shad.

Only occasionally can the best areas be identified by looking at eddies and other typical river structural elements with the naked eye. "The bank eddies are channel cat territory," Moyer offers. "It's the portion of the channel bank as it drops into

Jim Moyer hefts a mega blue.

the deepest part of the channel that keys where the blues hold. If, say, a huge eddy formed by a bank projection coincides with a drop-off into the channel, it might hold fish. But I don't think the eddy is the key."

Moyer has spent time anchored along almost every edge of channel in the 50-mile section of river that forms the upper portion of the river-reservoir below Cheatam dam. "Some areas almost always hold fish," he says. "The combination of old stumps and bottom or bank depressions and other nooks helps. And often these things just can't be seen, even with electronics. You just have to fish to determine if fish are using an area. But once I catch fish in an area, it almost always continues to produce."

A former all-tackle record: Bill McKinley's 55-inch long, 41½-inch girth, 111-pound fish from Wheeler Reservoir, on the Tennessee River in Alabama.

But not every day for days in a row. "A number of fish seem to move into an area and hold there. Pull up and anchor and toss baits out and you'll get a shot at those fish in short order if they're feeding," he offers. "No use staying more than 20 minutes if you're not getting bit. And if you catch two or three fish, it might take four or five days for new fish to move in and hold in the area. Don't camp on areas. Keep moving from spot to spot."

When Moyer is searching in what has proven to be a productive area, or in a new area that he believes should be productive, he anchors for 20 minutes, then moves downriver or upriver 150 to 200 yards and anchors again.

"Fresh bait's absolutely critical," he emphasizes. "I use 1-inch portions of skipjack herring fillet, some of the oiliest baits, threaded on a 6/0 or 7/0 hook. But I constantly change my bait. I mean, I put new bait on almost every cast. That's how to call cats in from where they're holding in each anchor area. You don't always land a bait right in front of their nose, but current carries the bait-fish oils downriver, and the cats sense something good is in the area and move to find it.

"Most fishermen think that just because they still have bait on, the bait's working for them. The bait needs to be oozing. As soon as the water removes the blood and oils and turns the meat firm, I switch bait. From what I've seen, all other things being equal, this is the one thing that keys consistent catches."

Moyer anchors right on the channel edge so he can place baits up and down the drop-off. Perfect placement in a new anchor position would be one bait each at the top of the drop-off and the base of the drop-off, and two more baits somewhere on the drop-off. He holds anchor position in the swift current by dropping a 35-pound portion of railroad track on a 100-foot rope, using whatever length of rope necessary to hold nose-first in the current. We've held almost as well using a 28-pound navy-style anchor, although a navy anchor is more prone to snag.

He then favors making about a 50-yard cast behind the boat to place each bait instead of fishing the bait almost vertically below the boat. "Wouldn't seem to make any difference," he offers, "but it does. It must have something to do with the combination of how the current plays on the length of line that allows the bait to work more effectively on a longer line."

"Fresh bait's absolutely critical," Moyer emphasizes.

To hold the rig down, Moyer uses a 2- or 3-ounce egg sinker above a swivel connected to about a 30-inch section of leader. From what we've seen, though, leader length is open to experimentation and probably depends on the situation. It's hard to argue with Moyer's success in rivers, but particularly in a reservoir with little current, we prefer a leader no longer than a foot. The rest of his tackle consists of 7½-foot medium-heavy-power rods, and 30-pound-test Berkley Big Game line on Garcia 7000 reels.

"My favorite hook has always been the Mustad #37160 Kahle-style design or a similar hook from Eagle Claw—6/0 or 7/0," Moyer says. "It's a deadly hooker that lies well in current when it's threaded full of cutbait. But these day' I'm a little concerned that a Kahle hook might not hold a huge fish, so I've been experimenting with an 8/0 octopus-style hook."

Agee's Approach—Baitwise, Agee prefers to fish with a lively 7- to 11-inch redspot chub, which he rigs on a 4/0 octopus-style hook. Skipjack herring aren't available in the Osage, so Agee has experimented with cut gizzard shad. "It's great for lots of action," he says, "but the biggest fish to date have always gone for a live chub."

Agee rigs with tackle he feels fits the situation. Occasionally, he uses saltwater tackle and heavy line. Often, though, his tackle is scaled down compared to Moyer's rigging. His 101 was taken with 12-pound line, a 7-foot Daiwa rod, and an old Garcia 5000D reel.

"Big cats will only spool you if you try to land a big boy from anchored position in current," Agee insists. "When you hook a big one, pull anchor and follow the fish—stay over him. Not being able to control a fish if it gets near a snag is possible. But in the areas I'm fishing, I haven't had much of a problem."

Agee: "One of my favorite spots is a classic big-fish hole just off main current. A shallow riffle runs about 2 feet deep across the river then drops sharply onto several 25- to 35-foot shelves and finally into a 50- to 60-foot hole. I motor slowly around this big hole, watching my electronics. When I see fish activity near bottom, I anchor just up from those fish.

They're not all going to be mega fish, of course, but we won't be even slightly surprised if someone rolls a world record soon.

"Nothing fancy about the terminal rigging—just a standard slipsinker rig; that is an egg sinker, as light as I can get away with, sliding on my main line, connected to a swivel, then a leader several feet long, and a 4/0 hook. I usually run the hook through the tail of the bait just back from the dorsal fin. Sometimes I cast a bait onto one of the shelves and another bait into the base of the hole—just depends where the fish seem to be. And when I can't see fish on electronics, I set up the same way.

"I don't want fish to be gut hooked, so once the rod's in a rod holder, I switch on the clicker mechanism and don't wait long to strike once a fish has turned the clicker over a time or two. I just pick up the rod, follow the fish by dropping the rod tip as it moves off, then I set. Really, once a fish takes like that, it's rare to miss the fish."

As we've so often said in *In-Fisherman* magazine and *Catfish In-Sider Guide*, blue cats are creatures of big rivers and impoundments. They like a lot more current than either channel cats or flatheads. And as we've further explored, we believe that wherever blue cats and river-run impoundments coincide, blue cats can be caught during winter. Just as they can be caught from reservoir systems like Santee-Cooper and a yet undefined number of other southern, midsouthern, and western reservoirs.

Certainly, though, somewhere along a still ill-defined northern boundary of blue cat territory, the bite will shut down. Iced-up water appears to shut fishing down, at least until warmer weather gets the bite going again. South Carolina's prime. So are Tennessee and California. And we'd be surprised if numerous waters in Oklahoma, Arkansas, Kansas, southern Missouri, Kentucky, Virginia, and parts farther south don't also offer prime fishing for monster blues. They're not all going to be mega fish, of course, but we won't be even slightly surprised if someone rolls a world record soon.

You're not likely to have much competition either. But someday soon, as the word spreads about this phenomenon—fishing for these fish of legendary size—well, for his part, Agee likes to wear a hat that says, "Bass fishermen are just catfishermen in transition." Most catmen hope not. Most bass anglers should be so lucky.

THE SEARCH FOR JUMBO CHANNEL CATS

"My biggest channel cat weighed just over 30 pounds," says Doug Stange, In-Fisherman editor in chief. "But if you don't include the Red River of the North, my biggest was closer to 20." Doug, of course, has been hunting cats of all sizes throughout most of the country for over 30 years.

Al Lindner's personal best was an amazing mid-30-pounder from the Red. But he hasn't caught a channel cat over 10 anywhere else. Steve Quinn tallies a Red River 25-pounder, but never touched a 20 in years of fishing cats in Georgia and Alabama. Meanwhile, Steve Hoffman has taken a 30-pound Red River fish and also nabbed a fine 17-pounder from Iowa's Cedar River.

All this is to say that big channel cats are rare fish. In most fine rivers throughout the central United States, a 10-pounder is special.

All this is to say that big channel cats are rare fish. In most fine rivers throughout the central United States, a 10-pounder is special. In tributaries of those rivers, a 6 rates congratulations.

We therefore ponder the world-record channel cat with amazement. If there were any way to raise doubts concerning the legitimacy of that 58 pounds, we would. After all, the venerable records for muskie, smallmouth bass, and walleye have fallen not to larger fish but to discredit, as the record fish were proven not so large as claimed. But the old shots of Mr. W. B. Whaley hefting his catfish on a rope and displaying it in a parking lot pictures an amazingly large channel catfish.

Mike Leech, Vice Chairman of the International Game Fish Association reports that Whaley's application in 1964 to the *Field & Stream* annual contest is well documented. It includes a signed and notarized affidavit from Whaley; a report on the certification of the scale used to weigh the fish, which was checked by the South Carolina Department of Agriculture; a form signed by Dr. Reeve Bailey,

Curator of the University of Michigan Museum of Fishes that verified the fish's identity; and even a line sample.

Now, of course, Lake Marion is full of blue and flathead catfish, and many exceed 58 pounds. Those two species were introduced in the mid-1960s, and the channel cat population hasn't been the same since. What probably spurred the outlandish growth of that fish and other giant channels reported from San-

tee-Cooper at the same time was the flooding of that incredibly productive river delta system with waters from farmlands, ponds, and forests.

Catfish fed on a booming population of natural shad forage plus anadromous herring that continue to fuel the food chain at Santee. After the Pinopolis Dam flooded the system, white catfish also exploded in numbers and size. The introduced predatory cats severely reduced their numbers, however.

As we've said before in the pages of *In-Fisherman* and our annual *Catfish In-Sider Guide*, the Red River of the North stands alone for producing big cats, fish that average a solid 18 to 20 pounds. And incredibly, after fishing the Red for more than a decade, Stange notes that the average size actually seems to be increasing. "Until 1989, I never saw a 30," he says. "Now fish of that size are reported with some regularity, though they're far from common. This increase in size has come in the face of steadily increasing fishing pressure by catfish fans visiting the 'Mecca.' Yet the Manitoba record stands at 44½ pounds, a monster, but far from the world record."

The second biggest channel catfish on record was the South Dakota 55-pounder pulled from the James River in 1949, which almost certainly was a blue cat. The James also is a far different river today, suffering from excess siltation as a result of poor farming practices throughout the watershed. Twenty-pounders now are unusual in the "Jim."

The third-ranked cat is a recent addition to the record charts, a California grown, if not raised, fish taken from a pay pond in 1993. The "Santa Ana Lakes" are small, excavated ponds regularly stocked with adult catfish obtained from private producers. Although blue cats sometimes are included in shipments, a biologist with the California Department of Fish and Game verified the record fish's identity as a channel. Heavy feeding presumably helped this big cat grow huge. Whatever the case, it's an unusual situation with unusual circumstances that could rarely occur.

FACTORS FOR GIANT CHANNEL CATS

Like other fish species, channel catfish seem to have a built-in growth potential and limit. When discussing giant fish, observers often wonder why, despite apparently good habitat and abundant food, fish don't grow bigger. Anglers consider large size an attribute, but fish don't. A catfish as big as a tuna could not succeed despite its obvious ability to eat nearly anything it wanted and its immunity to predation. Dinosaurs are extinct and whales are endangered while mosquitoes march on.

Prime natural habitat for channel catfish is in small to medium-size rivers that provide a diverse selection of invertebrate and vertebrate prey. Water levels fluctuate dramatically with wet and dry seasons, which are linked to cycles of prey abundance. Water clarity also varies.

A middle-size omnivorous fish with keen senses can best survive, grow, and reproduce in this sort of environment. And that's what channel cats are. A 20-pounder simply would run out of food and space when stream levels fall in late summer, reducing available habitat to the deepest pools. And such a cat likely couldn't find a big enough crevice in a small stream to lay a clutch of eggs and guard the brood. No, a 3- or 4-pound fish is much more efficient. In larger streams, channel cats seem to grow larger, but a governor on growth is imposed by the nature of the fish.

In bigger waters, channel cats don't grow as fast or as large as blues or flatheads, and often they can't compete with the larger species. Channel cats choose habitats within a big river that are more like stream environments, leaving the big water to their larger cousins.

Annual discharge of the Red River of the North averages around 3,000 cubic feet per second, while flows in the middle and lower sections of the Missouri and Mississippi are many times higher. This great force of water may push channel cats into limited areas, where they must compete for food. Compared to flathead and blue catfish, channel cats often are abundant, and competition within the species limits growth rate and ultimate size. The exception occurs when prey is provided in unlimited quantities, as in intensively managed ponds.

Prime natural habitat for channel catfish is in small to medium-size rivers that provide a diverse selection of invertebrate and vertebrate prey.

Some individual fish grow faster, live longer, and reach greater ultimate size than average members of the population. It's these special fish that can reach record size in favorable environments. And all things being equal, male channel cats grow bigger than females, unlike many other gamefish species.

Ultimate size of catfish also depends on an abundance of prime preyfish. Biologists theorize that one factor in the excellent growth and condition of channel cats in the Red River of the North is the abundance of many potential preyfish, particularly goldeye. Threadfin and gizzard shad, plus anadromous herring and American shad also are prime prey, if they're available in appropriate sizes at appropriate times.

Water temperature also seems to play a role in the growth of channel catfish. Some researchers say that cats grow best in water warmer than 72°F. Yet the Red River fish, which winter in ice-covered Lake Winnipeg for six months of the year, grow faster than most southern populations. And record fish from Manitoba, Minnesota, Iowa, and the Dakotas are similar in size to fish from the Southeast where water temperatures exceed 70°F for five months of the year.

Perhaps excessively warm water, say over 80°F, limits catfish growth by over-stimulating the metabolism or by causing cats to seek cooler spots where prey may be scarcer. No scientific data backs up or refutes this theory. Catfish feed fast and grow well in southern ponds with no thermal refuge, but again, fish over 20 pounds are uncommon.

Waters that provide diverse habitats seem to foster big cats. In Santee-Cooper's early days, the combination of tailrace areas, canals, and diverse reservoir features along with abundant forage and a warm climate may have given cats a growth boost. The Red River of the North's connection to Lake Winnipeg provides areas for catfish to feed and spawn in lake, river, tributary, and marsh habitat.

In Wyoming, a surprisingly fast-growing population of channel cats inhabits the Powder River and a tributary, Crazy Woman Creek. Despite an annual growing season of just 120 days, cats live past 20 years and commonly reach 15 pounds. They move back and forth between the river and the creek, to spawn, feed, and over-winter. The giant catfish from the James River in South Dakota likely spent time in the vast Missouri, using the James for spawning and feeding in early summer.

Another factor for big cats, not often heeded by management agencies, is limiting harvest through regulations. Age-growth studies show that channel cats typically grow slowly even in productive environments like the Red River or Santee-Cooper Reservoir. Big fish either are extremely old or unusual specimens with capability for growth far greater than the average cat. In either case, high harvest cuts the odds of big cats growing huge.

Opportunities exist where regulations are strict, such as the Red River of the North, where only one catfish over 24 inches may be harvested per day in Minnesota and North Dakota, and harvest of cats over 24 inches is banned in Manitoba. Opportunities also exist in waters with little fishing pressure or where harvest is banned due to contaminant problems. Where forage and habitat are prime, cats can attain their genetically set maximum size.

WHERE FOR BIG CHANNEL CATS?

To satisfy the lunker-hunting hunger that lurks in so many of us, we've scoured record books and biological studies and talked to catmen from Ontario to Louisiana, to find the best waters for big channel catfish. Again, your own definition of big and thus your expectations must be realistic for the waters you fish.

We also recognize that many catfish anglers could care less about unusually large fish. Fun and fillets are the name of the game. We in no way want to insinuate that this isn't the best catfishing has to offer. If you read our list and find your favorite hot spot ignored, be glad, for you won't have to share it with the visiting catmen who read this book. And if you let us know of spots we've missed, we might be tempted to pay a visit ourselves.

Far West

Channel cats have become abundant following stocking in southern and central California reservoirs, from San Diego north to Clear Lake. In Castaic and Casitas, bass anglers often tangle with cats in the low 20-pound range. Spawning seems limited, due perhaps to substantial water level fluctuations around spawning time. Moderate levels of stocking keep fish numbers fair, which should increase growth rates if preyfish are plentiful. We don't know if the Santa Ana River Lakes contain any more giants.

Cats introduced into the Columbia and Snake river systems have established stable populations, with Brownlee on the Snake River in Idaho one of the most noteworthy. The perpetual cool temperature of these waters may cut growth rates, though winter temperatures don't reach the extreme lows of the Midwest. Channel cats rarely exceed 20 pounds, maxing at around 30.

Cowboy Country

OK, so the Dallas Cowboys no longer are America's Team, but we still call channel cats America's Fish. The land of lunker bass and home of some of the biggest blues and flatheads can't make similar boasts for channel catfish. The Texas record of 36½ pounds from the Pedernales River has stood for more than 30 years without being challenged, and 20-pounders are unusual in public waters.

The natural habitat of channel catfish has been altered by reservoir construction. While flathead and blue catfish, largemouth bass, crappies, and other species have benefited from the increased biomass of shad and diverse habitat of impoundments, channel cats haven't capitalized. And following reservoir construction, long stretches of free-flowing river, prime habitat for channel cats, have become scarce.

This story is repeated in Oklahoma where a 23-year-old record stands, a 30-pounder from the Washita River. In both states, channel cats are abundant but rarely reach trophy size.

Farther west in Utah, New Mexico, and Arizona, the story repeats, though unlike Texas and Oklahoma, stocking is required in some rivers and reservoirs to sustain populations. In the desert southwest, the chronic lack of forage that afflicts western waters probably limits production of giant cats. While Utah Lake produced the record fish (32½ pounds) in 1978 and ranks as the state's top water, growth studies document cats reaching only about 20 inches at age 10, with only minute increments in growth thereafter. The record fish was a most unusual specimen, a genetic anomaly that occasionally occurs in fish populations.

Northcentral

We've already highlighted the top water for big channel cats in the Midwest, the Red River of the North, which runs north along the Minnesota-North Dakota border and flows to Lake Winnipeg in Manitoba. Average size of channel cats increases as we proceed north, as the size of the river increases. The tailrace of the dam at Lockport, Manitoba, has become the Mecca for big cat fans. A study found the average size of fish caught in that section at 19.6 pounds. Ninety-two percent of cats there were over 30 inches long.

Tagging studies show these fish reside south to Halstad, Minnesota, with many 20- to 30-pound resident fish present from there north to the Manitoba border. Other cold rivers of the upper Midwest also produce surprisingly large channel cats.

In Ontario, channel cats from Lake Erie ascend the Grand River and stack below the dam at Dunnville. In 1994, a fishway big enough to accommodate sturgeon was constructed at Dunnville, in hopes that the rare fish would return to spawn. Sturgeon so far have ignored the invitation, but big cats pass through, and 20-pounders are common between Dunnville and Brantford. Officials with the Grand River Conservation Authority speculate that other major Lake Erie tributaries offer similar potential.

Waters connected to the St. Lawrence River in Quebec produce cats into the 20-pound range that receive little fishing pressure. Lac des Deux Montagnes and its tributary, the Des Outaouais River, are top spots. The Ottawa River is another fine fishery.

In Minnesota, the Minnesota River produces channel cats in the teens up to 20 pounds, particularly from Granite Falls to Jordan. The St. Croix River on the Wisconsin border offers a smaller population but occasional fish to 20 pounds. The Wisconsin River, another tributary of the Mississippi, also produces large channel cats, in lower reaches, below the Prairie du Sac Dam.

In-Fisherman's Master Angler program also reveals Wisconsin's Yahara River, just north of Madison, as a big-cat hot spot. Cats apparently move up the Yahara from Lake Mendota in June. Iowa's Cedar, Des Moines, Raccoon, and Skunk rivers produce cats in the teens to low 20s. The 36½-pound record came from the Raccoon in 1993.

Farther south in Nebraska, angler surveys indicate channel cats as the favorite fish, but the state's top trophy fishery receives little fishing pressure. Since Merritt Reservoir yielded the record 41-pounder in 1985, it has produced hundreds of channel cats that qualify for Nebraska's Master Angler program, most caught by anglers targeting walleyes. Many of Kansas' midsize and large impoundments produce occasional big cats. The Kansas River still produces the odd giant, even into the 30-pound range.

Houghton Lake in northcentral Michigan produced two 40-pound records in the early 1960s, but only a small population reportedly remains. The state's best spots are major tributaries of Lake Michigan, including the Menominee, Saginaw, and Muskegon rivers and connected waters like Lake St. Clair and Saginaw Bay. Twenties are possible. Baldwin Lake in Illinois, producer of the 45-pound 4-ounce record, continues to offer trophy potential.

Many Indiana and Ohio waters support stable catfish populations capable of producing 20- to 30-pound fish. The Ohio River population is strong, with 20s appearing in most pools. Inland, Ohio's Buckeye Lake and LaDue Reservoir, producer of the record cat (37 pounds 10 ounces) in 1992, are trophy territory.

Southcentral

Channel cats are widely distributed throughout Mississippi, with the best chance for a giant fish at little Lake Tom Bailey, a 234-acre state-owned impoundment east of Meridian. This water produced the last four state records, the current one, 48 pounds 7 ounces taken in March, 1995. Could be the best shot going for a 50, but we suspect these fish actually are blue cats.

Next door in Louisiana, channel cats have long been considered a commercial species, with records kept only since 1994. The category is open, so here's your best chance for a record cat. In many waters, though, the extreme density of channel cats limits their growth rates.

In Arkansas, the top cat, a 38-pounder, came from Lake Ouachita in 1989. Major reservoirs like Ouachita, Bull Shoals, Beaver, and Norfork with their abundant forage, limited catfish populations, and low fishing pressure are top choices for giant fish. Biologists with the Missouri Department of Conservation rate Smithville Reservoir, Indian Creek Lake, Thomas Hill Lake, and Lake Jacomo as top impoundments for channel cats, with the Black and Platte rated the best rivers. Jacomo produced the 34-pound 10-ounce record in 1976.

Southeast

Although creel surveys on Santee-Cooper Reservoir, South Carolina, in the late 1950s reported channel cats over 70 pounds, this potential has been lost due to reservoir changes and competition from blues and flatheads. Channels from 10 to 15 pounds still are abundant, though. Channel cats in the Altamaha

Big channel cats are rare fish, and selective harvest is necessary to sustain fine fishing.

River, Georgia's best water for big fish, also have suffered competition from introduced flatheads.

Channel cat populations in the Cape Fear River in North Carolina, the Rappahannock and James rivers in Virginia, and the Potomac also have declined with increases in non-native blues. Blue cat populations may eventually reach an equilibrium with channel cats. But it's likely that the big bossy blues will push channel cats into habitats suited to smaller fish, which will limit their growth and ultimate size.

While pond-dwelling cats in Georgia and Alabama occasionally surpass 20 pounds, fish from public waters rarely approach this size. And while small state-owned impoundments have the potential to grow huge cats, management emphasizes numbers over size by stocking high numbers of fish. Reports indicate that the possibilities for unusually big channel cats include the tailwaters of Barkley Lake on the Cumberland River and Lake Eufaula on the Alabama-Georgia border.

Northeast

Folks in this region will have to plan a trip if jumbo channel cats are their passion. The Connecticut River holds New England's only stable river population. And fish over 10 pounds are scarce, although this productive river offers a relatively mild climate, abundant forage, and diverse habitat.

Lake Erie tributaries offer untapped opportunities in Ohio, Pennsylvania, and New York. In New England, Lake Champlain, home to more fish species than any North American lake, supports the best population of big cats, including the Vermont mark of 32 pounds 4 ounces. Fish from 10 to 15 pounds are fairly common for the few anglers who target them. In Pennsylvania, the Allegheny River seems the likeliest water to produce a 20.

Wherever you live, big cats are available. Just depends on your definition of big. Look for waters that run free, with riffles, holes, and runs, waters with rock, gravel, sand, and snags. Look for waters that lack flathead and blue cats, unless they coexist naturally. In impoundments, catfish species tend to segregate according to their different needs, though channel cats always get the short end of the turf war.

When you catch that big cat, examine its silky sensitive skin and barbels, watchful eyes, and muscular body. Then release it to grow even larger.

IN SEARCH OF GIANT FLATHEADS

"Had my johnboat on the river one morning when I hooked a monster," relates the old fisherman." I was fishing 75-pound test on a saltwater rod, but as soon as I set the hook, he swam to the bottom of a deep hole. I tried to raise him, but as soon as I'd get him 2 feet off bottom, down he went. I motored upstream to get a better angle on him, but that didn't do any good. After almost four hours, the line broke. Now I use 100-pound test."

In our travels around the country, we've heard versions of this story from fishermen on dozens of rivers. Since catfishermen are known never to exaggerate, awesome beasts must reside in our rivers. And, you probably believe the one about the divers inspecting the dam, too.

Fodder here for your own tales—information about the best waters for big flatheads, with a caution that catfishermen aren't always eager to reveal their secret holes. Many of the waters where the big guys reside haven't been thoroughly studied by biologists. The native range of flathead catfish includes the larger rivers of the Mississippi, Missouri, Ohio, and Rio Grande river basins from the Great Lakes south into Mexico. During the past 30 years, introductions and subsequent movements have increased the flathead's range. Populations occur from the Atlantic to Pacific coasts and from the Canadian to Mexican borders.

Flatheads thrive in rivers that range from tributaries 30 yards wide to the lower reaches of our biggest rivers. Although rightly considered a warmwater fish, flatheads can survive and grow large in cool waters as well. In August 1978, the first flathead ever caught in Canada was taken in a commercial trap-net in Ontario waters of Lake Erie.

A few years ago, a 43¼-pound flathead from Muskegon Lake, Michigan, was entered in our Master Angler program. This lake is connected to Lake Michigan, where water temperatures rarely exceed 70°F. Minnesota's state record is a most respectable 70 pounds, taken from the St. Croix River in 1970.

The slower, warmer waters of the central and southern regions seem most conducive to growing big flatheads. Until 1992, the International Game Fish Association and National Fresh Water Fishing Hall of Fame recognized a 98-pounder caught in 1986 at Lewisville Reservoir, Texas, as the all-tackle rod-and-reel record. They disqualified this fish, however, because it was accidentally snagged.

A 123-pound flathead taken from the Elk City Reservoir, Kansas, stands as the current record. Kentucky lists a 97-pounder, caught in the Green River in 1956, as their state record. Texas lists a 122-pounder from the North Fork of Buffalo Creek as the trotline record.

Most of the rivers in the flathead's original range have been dammed, creating large reservoirs that provide good habitat. Gizzard and threadfin shad typically are abundant and provide forage for all sizes of cats. Flooded creeks that haven't silted in provide spawning areas.

Catfish also move up rivers to find natural spawning sites in undercut banks and rocky ledges. Hollow sunken logs and root wads also provide a nest cavity that cats need to deposit and defend eggs. As a result, flatheads are abundant and large in many reservoirs, but often are fished little, except where trotlining is popular.

We're surprised that a 100-pounder hasn't turned up in Oklahoma or Arkansas. We believe one will, however, as more anglers use sophisticated catfishing techniques on these waters, and as more catfish specialists release nearly all their biggest fish.

Texas lists a 122-pounder from the North Fork of Buffalo Creek as the trotline record. This creature measured an inch less than 6 feet and is one of the largest flatheads ever documented.

Eastern States

Flatheads didn't occur in Atlantic coast rivers until 1966, when biologists with the North Carolina Wildlife Resources Commission released 11 adults weighing a total of 236 pounds into the Cape Fear River near Fayetteville. Ten years later, biologists collected young fish, documenting that the population had become established.

Flatheads now are the most common catfish species in the river and the dominant predator in the 125-mile stretch from Lillington to the mouth of the Black River. It's an excellent fishery with many fish in the 30- to 40-pound range. The section from Fayetteville upstream to Buckhorn Dam is particularly productive.

Flatheads are native in the western parts of North Carolina, in the New and Tennessee river systems. The Yadkin River below Idles Dam at Clemmons is particularly productive for big fish; it produced a former 62-pound 7-ounce state record in 1987.

New England is devoid of flatheads, and among the mid-Atlantic states, only Pennsylvania contains flatheads—in the Allegheny and Ohio drainages in the western region. A few flathead specialists have discovered this fishery and concentrate on the section of the Allegheny from Pittsburgh upstream into Clarion County. Many fish run in the 20-pound range, and the state record (43 pounds 9 ounces) was caught there in 1985.

This eastern boundary of the native range extends south through the western ends of West Virginia, Virginia, North Carolina, and into the northwest tip of Georgia. In West Virginia, the Ohio, New, and Kanawha rivers and their larger tributaries offer good fishing. And Bluestone Reservoir on the New River in Summers County produces large numbers of fish and has trophy potential.

In Virginia, the New and Clinch rivers and Kerr Reservoir (Buggs Island) on the North Carolina border and Claytor Lake near Radford have strong flathead fisheries. In 1965, 12 flatheads were stocked in Occoquan Reservoir near Washington D.C. The small stocking was successful there as well, producing a string of state records, including the current 66-pound 4-ounce record.

South Carolina's flathead populations haven't been studied, but giants are known to occur in that greatest of all catfish reservoirs, Santee-Cooper. This pair of impoundments produced the former world-record blue cat, the current channel cat record, and a 77-pound state-record flathead. Connecting rivers, the Cooper, Santee, and Wateree, also have many large fish.

In Georgia, flatheads native to the Tennessee River drainage have thrived in the north Georgia impoundments of Carter's Reservoir, Blue Ridge Reservoir, and High Falls Lake. Populations aren't large, but trophy fish turn up, including a former 53-pound state record caught in High Falls in 1987.

Introduced populations in the southern part of Georgia offer the most consistent fishing. Commercial catfishermen reportedly liberated a few adults in the upper Flint River in the 1950s, hoping that they'd prosper and provide a greater harvest than the native channel cats. As in other areas, they survived, multiplied, and spread.

The Flint River and its impoundments, Lake Blackshear and Lake Worth, offer excellent flathead fishing, although giant fish haven't yet been taken. Flatheads moved through the Woodruff Dam at Lake Seminole and entered the Apalachicola River in Florida. The population is expanding, and a state record 43.5-pounder, was caught in 1997. Flatheads also occur in Florida's Escambia River in the Mobile Bay drainage, but the status of the population is unknown.

An introduced population of flatheads that has expanded fast in the Altamaha River in southeastern Georgia offers excellent fishing for fish to 70 pounds. The species has entered the Oconee and Ocmulgee rivers and likely will thrive there as well.

Southcentral States

The flathead catfish distribution map shows 12 states fully shaded, indicating species presence. It's possible that Alabama should be almost fully shaded since flatheads have entered the Chattahoochee River via Lake Seminole and may have moved upstream at least as far as the Walter F. George Dam. Alabama's prime waters include Millers Ferry and Claiborne reservoirs on the lower Alabama River and Demopolis Reservoir on the Warrior River. Two lesser-known but excellent fisheries are the Tallapoosa and Cahaba rivers. An 80-pound state record was caught in Millers Ferry, but rivers across the state are capable of producing 50s.

Mississippi is a catfish wonderland with big flatheads present throughout its river systems. They're the second most popular fish statewide, and stream fishing is popular. Yet with so many good waters, overfishing doesn't seem to be a problem. Studies of exploitation, including the noodling catch, are underway.

Top spots are the Yazoo River system, the Big Black River, Leaf River, Noxubee River and much of the TennTom Waterway. Also check the tailraces of major impoundments; their deep holes and abundant baitfish provide prime habitat for giant flatheads.

Louisiana also has excellent flathead populations, from the Atchafalaya River basin in the south to the Red and Ouachita river systems on the northern border. And don't overlook Toledo Bend Reservoir on the Texas border, where bass, crappies, and stripers dominate the sport fishery but magnum cats eat them for lunch.

Other top spots for big cats are the Bogue Chitto and Tchefuncta rivers, where catching a 40-pounder is easier than pronouncing the name of the river. Lac Des Allemands west of New Orleans is another trophy water. According to biologists, a 50-pounder is possible almost anywhere in the state.

Due north, Arkansas offers more great catfishing waters. Biologist Thomas Bly says it's easier to name the waters that don't contain giant flatheads than those that do. Still, the Arkansas and White rivers and their associated impoundments—large Corps of Engineer reservoirs such as Greers Ferry, Ouachita, Bull Shoals, Norfork, Millwood, and Beaver—offer the best shot for huge fish.

Flathead Catfish Distribution

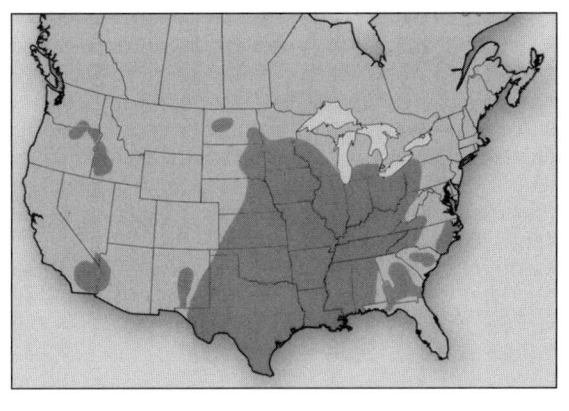

A state record 80-pounder came out of the Arkansas in 1989, but users of trotlines, jug, and limblines have taken many over 100 pounds. Smaller state-owned impoundments, including Conway, Overcup, Hams-Brake, Atkins, and Upper and Lower White Oak, consistently produce 40- to 50-pounders.

Missouri shares Arkansas' northern impoundments on the White River (Beaver, Bull Shoals, and Norfork) and the cats don't stop at the state line. Lake of the Ozarks produced a former 66-pound state record in 1987, but the population in Truman and its tailwaters appears to be peaking. As in Arkansas, many of the biggest fish are caught by methods other than angling. But anglers can share the big-fish bounty by fishing high-percentage areas with heavy tackle and prime bait.

Kentucky and Tennessee share the Cumberland and Tennessee rivers, which produce big flatheads throughout their reaches. Lake Barkley and its tailwaters are prime trophy waters.

Rivers and reservoirs throughout Kansas contain excellent populations. Flatheads are among the most underutilized resources in the state, according to biologist Jim Stephen of Kansas Parks and Wildlife. Eastern Kansas contains the best waters. The Neosho may be the best of all, with fish over 60 pounds taken annually. An 86-pound 3-ounce former state record was taken there in 1966.

Flathead catfish are abundant and large throughout Oklahoma, where many large low-gradient rivers provide excellent habitat. Prime waters are Lake Eufaula and its tailwaters; Lake Oolagah and its tailwaters; and the Arkansas River system.

Fishing pressure for this species likely is higher in Oklahoma than in any other state, and cats may be taken by many means. A bag limit and minimum length limit of 20 inches were recently imposed, and other conservation measures are being considered.

Flatheads thrive throughout Texas and outgrow the Lake Lewisville record in some waters. The Texas Parks and Wildlife Department has granted lake-record status to 100-plus-pound flatheads from Madisonville, McQueeney, the North Fork of Buffalo Creek, and lakes Livingston and Tawakoni. All were taken on trotlines. In western Texas, other top spots include the Medina and Rio Grande rivers and lakes O.C. Fisher, Kirby, and Calaveras.

Northcentral States

Eastern Nebraska has excellent populations of flatheads, but the species apparently doesn't exist much west of the Republican River. This drainage produces good catches, but the prime spot is the Loup Power Canal from Genoa to Lincoln. The Missouri River contains flatheads, but commercial overharvest has reduced their abundance and size. A moratorium on commercial fishing has improved angling, though.

Iowa's former state record was caught in the Skunk River; it's possible that even larger fish swim there. The Missouri and Mississippi rivers provide good flathead fishing, though the smaller interior rivers, including the Des Moines, Iowa, Cedar, and Raccoon produce larger fish.

The DNR has stocked flatheads into Prairie Rose Lake in Shelby County and Little Wall Lake in Hamilton County to reduce overabundant bullheads. They may grow quickly in these impoundments.

In the Dakotas, the Missouri River offers the only major fishing opportunity for flatheads. In South Dakota, Lake Francis Case and the section from Sioux City to the Fort Randall Dam are best.

Flatheads are limited to three rivers in Minnesota–the Minnesota, Mississippi, and St. Croix–all in the southern third of the state. Although a 70-pound state record was caught in the St. Croix in 1970, the Minnesota is the most consistent producer of big fish. The stretch from Granite Falls to Mankato is most productive, but the stretch from Mankato to the Twin Cities probably holds the largest fish.

Following the successful stocking of flathead catfish into Richardson Lake to control bullheads, crappie, and carp, the Minnesota DNR has stocked this predator into several lakes in the Waterville area. Good fishing should occur over the next decade, though reproduction is unlikely.

The St. Croix and Mississippi rivers in western Wisconsin produce big flatheads. The Wisconsin River from Sauk City to the mouth of the Mississippi is another good stretch. The Fox River near Lake Winnebago has a strong population with lunker fish, including a 65-pound former state record, caught in 1987.

In Michigan, flatheads are limited to the southern half of the Lower Peninsula. The Grand River near Grand Rapids is the state's best known fishery. A tributary, the Maple River, produced a 47½-pound state record in 1974. A 43¼-pounder has been caught in Muskegon Lake. The Muskegon and White rivers may contain record flatheads that have been overlooked for years.

In Ohio, Indiana, and Illinois, flatheads are present in all major rivers and their impounded waters. They're more abundant in the southern halves of these states. In Illinois, top waters include 54 miles of the Illinois River in Tazewell and Peoria counties, the Rock River in Lee and Whiteside counties, and lakes Springfield and Carlyle.

The Muskingum River is Ohio's premier flathead fishery. Cats are abundant throughout 90 miles of river that run through the southeastern part of the state, and plenty of 35-pounders are available. Tailraces of the 10 lock-and-dam structures are prime spots. Clendening Lake in eastern Ohio is a prime trophy fishery and producer of a 76-pound 8-ounce state record. Numbers of 60s and 70s are taken there each year.

Piedmont Lake has fewer fish, but held a former state record and continues to produce giants. The population in Seneca Lake is increasing, with 30s and 40s fairly common. Fishing pressure is light.

In Indiana, try the East and West Forks of the White River and the Ohio and Wabash rivers. Populations are self-sustaining.

Out West

New Mexico's largest flathead catfish population is in the Gila River, downstream of the confluence of the east and west forks, according to Mike Hatch of the Department of Game and Fish. Sections of the Rio Grande produce the largest specimens, however, including a 78-pound state record caught in Elephant Butte in 1979.

Other good sections of the Rio Grande include Cochiti Reservoir and the deep gorges around Pilar, both north of Albuquerque, and the stretch around Abeytas, south of Albuquerque. Tales of giant specimens suggest flatheads may grow as large there as anywhere.

Flatheads aren't native west of the Rio Grande, but the species has adapted well to Arizona waters, particularly the Colorado, Gila, Salt, and Verde rivers. The best areas are the Gila River from San Carlos Lake upstream to the New Mexico border; the Salt River from Roosevelt Lake upstream; the Verde from Bartlett Lake upstream to the Verde Valley, and the Lower Colorado from below Lake Havasu to the Mexico border. According to biologist Bill Silvey of the Game and Fish Department, any of those areas could produce state-record flathead.

"Flatheads aren't native west of the Rio Grande, but the species has adapted well to Arizona waters . . ."

Flatheads entered California via the lower Colorado River and moved into the vast canal system of the Imperial Valley. The extent of their range isn't well documented, but a state record 55-pounder was caught in Imperial Reservoir in 1980. The long growing season and fertile waters of this area could produce giant fish.

The 65-mile stretch of the Snake River between Idaho and Oregon, from Brownlee Reservoir south to Swan Falls Dam, contains one of the few other flathead populations in the West. The best fishery is in the lower section between the mouths of the Boise and Weiser rivers.

Glossary

Anal fin: The fin located on the ventral (under) side of a fish between its urogenital pore and its tail fin.

Backwater: A shallow area of water off the main channel of a river.

Baitfish: A small fish often eaten by predators.

Bar: A long ridge in a body of water, usually composed of sand or gravel.

Barbel: A sensory organ in all catfish species used to detect food.

Break: A distinct variation in an otherwise constant stretch of cover, structure, or bottom type.

Breakline: An area of abrupt change in depth, bottom type, or water quality.

Channel: The bed of a stream or a river.

Channelize: To straighten, line, levee, or otherwise simplify the channel of a river or stream.

Chumming: Attracting fish by placing foods attractive to them into the water near a fishing site.

Cline: A vertical or horizontal stratum of water in which water characteristics differ markedly from those adjoining them.

Coldwater Period: Periods in spring and fall preceding, respectively, Prespawn and Winter periods. Often good periods for catfishing.

Cover: Natural or manmade objects in the bottom of lakes, rivers, or impoundments, especially those that affect fishes' behavior.

Crankbait: A lipped diving lure.

Current: Water moving in a single direction.

Dam: A manmade barrier to control flow or raise water level.

Dipbait: A cheese-based bait used to attract catfish.

Dissolved oxygen: Usually expressed in parts per million (ppm); the amount of oxygen molecules that are dispersed in a given amount of water.

Dorsal fin: The fin at the center of a fish's back.

Drop-off: An area where the bank or bottom of a body of water suddenly increases in depth.

Edge effect: The increased concentration of animals that sometimes appears where two habitats meet.

Eutrophic: Old, fertile body of water characterized by warm, shallow basins.

Fall Turnover Period: Bodies of water that stratify into three distinct clines in summer experience a mixing of warmer bottom water and colder surface water in fall; usually a time of poor fishing.

Fecundity: The number of eggs produced by a female fish in one season.

Feeder creek: A tributary to a larger stream, lake, or reservoir.

Fishery: The populations of fish in a body of water.

Flat: An area of lake, reservoir, or river that changes little in depth.

Floodplain: The area adjoining a river that becomes flooded during high water.

Gamefish: A fish species sought by anglers.

Habitat: The environment in which an organism usually lives.

Harvest: To remove fish from a body of water.

Hole: A deep section of stream or river in which fish sometimes hold.

Hybrid: The offspring of two different species or subspecies.

Impoundment: A body of water formed by damming a running river.

Jugline: A setline attached to a floating jug and set unattended in a body of water.

Lateral line: An electroreceptive sensory system in a fish that detects low-frequency vibrations through water.

Levee: An earthen ridge or dike designed to channelize a river and to prevent flooding of the river's floodplain.

Management: Manipulation of biological systems by fishery biologists to produce a positive goal.

Mesotrophic: Middle-aged body of water lying between eutrophic and oligotrophic in fertility.

Nares: The nostrils of fish and other aquatic vertebrates.

Native: A species or organism that evolved and is naturally present in an area.

Noodling: A traditional method of catching catfish by passing the hand through the fish's mouth and gills.

Olfaction: The sense of smell.

Oligotrophic: A geologically young, infertile body of water characterized by deep, cool, clear, oxygenated waters and rocky basins.

pH: A measurement of hydrogen in a liquid.

Pheromone: A hormone secreted by catfish; may be used to maintain social hierarchies.

Photoperiod: The interval during a single day when daylight is present.

Poikotherm: A cold-blooded vertebrate animal such as a fish.

Postspawn Period: The period immediately after spawning; the In-Fisherman calendar period between Spawn and Presummer.

Postsummer Period: Cooler weather leads to lower water temperatures and migration to wintering areas; it often spurs feeding.

Predator: A fish that preys on other fish.

Prespawn Period: The period prior to spawning; the In-Fisherman calendar period between Winter and Spawn.

Presummer Period: The transition period during which fish search for summer habitat and establish their summer patterns.

Prey: A species often sought by other fish species.

Range: An area throughout which a fish species is distributed.

Ray: The bony segment supporting a fish's fin.

Revetment: A stone or concrete facing that reinforces a natural bank or levee.

Riffle-hole-run: The classic structural sequence of streams.

Riprap: Large rocks placed along a bank to reinforce it.

Selective harvest: Applying the criteria of species, size, and relative abundance in deciding whether or not to release or harvest a fish.

Sensory organ: A part of the biological system that registers sight, hearing, taste, smell, touch, or lateral line electroreception.

Sharptooth: A large species of catfish found in southern Africa.

Silt: The fine sediment found on the bottom of a body of water.

Snag: (n) Brush or trees in a stream or river. (v) To catch fish by dragging hooks through the water.

Spawn: Reproduction among fish; the In-Fisherman calendar period associated with spawning.

Species: A group of organisms capable of interbreeding.

Spine: A stiff, sharp segment of fin.

Sportfish: A fish species pursued by anglers.

Stock: (v) To place fish in a body of water. (n) A population of animals.

Structure: Changes in the shape of a lake, river, or impoundment bottom, especially those that influence fish behavior.

Structure theory: The theory that fish location and behavior are affected by physical changes in bottom and habitat.

Substrate: The type of bottom in a body of water.

Summer Peak Period: The period in which fish establish their summer habitat; competitive feeding usually leads to good fishing.

Summer Period: The long period when fish remain in their chosen habitat; fish activity and location are predictable during this time.

Suspended fish: Fish in open water that hold above bottom.

Swim bladder: An organ in most bony fish that holds a volume of gas that makes the fish neutrally buoyant at different depths.

Thermocline: A layer of water with a markedly different temperature than that below or above it; for example, the layer between the warm surface layer (epilimnion) and the cold bottom layer (hypolimnion).

Tributary: A stream that flows into a larger river or reservoir.

Trophic: Referring to the fertility of a body of water (eutrophic, mesotrophic).

Trotline: A setline to which a number of hooks are attached.

Turbid: Water made murky by suspended sediment.

Watershed: The area that run-off drains into a body of water.

Weberian ossicles: Bony structures connecting the catfish's swim bladder to its inner ear.

Wing dam: A manmade earth or rock ridge that deflects river current. Also referred to as a rock dike.

Winter Period: Frozen water in the North; river catfish hold in deep holes away from heavy current.

CATCH IT ON VIDEO!

In-Fisherman has an extensive library of the finest catfish-catching videos in the world. Each video brings you detailed information from the catfish experts at In-Fisherman that is guaranteed to help you catch more catfish. Plus, there's plenty of big cat action. Here are just a few of the titles you can see at in-fisherman.com or at your local tackle retailer:

EXTREME CATFISH

In-Fisherman takes cat fishing to extremes in our most unique and exciting cat video to date. Learn how and where to catch early season blues, how to rig for big flatheads and draw them to you, overlooked lures for more cats, and cat-catching through the ice that should not be missed. *49 min.* **#201004....$12.95 VHS**

CLASSIC CATFISH

Welcome to the real world of catfishing. Tips and techniques from the In-Fisherman experts for more bread and butter fish every time out. Rods, rigs, small river cats and more! *65 min.* **#201006....$12.95 VHS**

BIG CATFISH CONNECTION

Find big cats fast— spring, summer or fall. The best snags, eddy areas, and wintering holes. Rigging right, presentations, hot spots. Big Cat Action! *44 min.* **#201001....$12.95 VHS**

CATFISH: PREDATOR ON THE PROWL

Catfish didn't get to be the third biggest fish in fresh water by lying on the bottom-they're hunters! Now, In-Fisherman shows you what it takes to be a hunter of the hunters with bait, equipment, and location secrets. *67min* **#201007....$12.95 VHS**

CATFISH FEVER

Breakthrough tactics for catfish in rivers. Location and presentation secrets. The basis for modern catfishing. *62 min.* **#201000....$12.95 VHS**

BIG WATER CATFISH

Learn what it takes to tangle with a big cat. Seasonal locations and presentations and the country's top cat waters. The most cat-catching action ever captured on video. *56 min.* **#201003....$12.95 VHS**

BIG CAT SAFARI

For really big cats you have to go hunting, you have to go on a safari. In Big Cat Safari, the cat catching experts from In-Fisherman guide you to the best times, locations, and equipment to catch big Blues, Flatheads, and Channels. *68 min.* **#201005....$12.95 VHS**

CATFISH LOCATION SECRETS

Be an expert at locating catfish in any season— Pre-Spawn, Post-Spawn, Early Season, Cold Water. Top rigging and bait options are revealed! 61 min.
#201009....$12.95 VHS
#201009D....$14.95 DVD

BIG CATFISH CONNECTION II

Focus on presentation. Catfish tackle for every situation...Rods, Reels, Hooks, Sinkers, Floats. Top techniques for big cats. *57 min.*
#201002....$12.95 VHS

DAY ON THE RIVER

Catfishing legends Doug Stange and Steve Hoffman demonstrate their game plan for locating and catching flatheads. Identifying hotspots, using maps, looking below the surface, and more. *65 min*
#201008...$12.95 VHS

Catch More Catfish
GUARANTEED!

Every issue of In-Fisherman magazine features articles loaded with exclusive catfish-catching information from the In-Fisherman staff. No wonder it's subscribed to by the top catfish fishing pros in the country.

START CATCHING MORE CATFISH. *SUBSCRIBE NOW!*

Call 1-800-441-1740 or subscribe on line at www.in-fisherman.com

---